THE GYPSIES

OF EASTERN EUROPE

EDITED BY DAVID CROWE AND JOHN KOLSTI
WITH AN INTRODUCTION BY IAN HANCOCK

M. E. Sharpe, Inc.
ARMONK, NEW YORK
LONDON, ENGLAND

Available in the United Kingdom and Europe from M. E. Sharpe, Publishers,
3 Henrietta Street, London WC2E 8LU.

Library of Congress Cataloging-in-Publication Data

The Gypsies of Eastern Europe / edited by David M. Crowe and John Kolsti.
    p.   cm.
    Includes bibliographical references and index.
    ISBN 0-87332-671-7
    1. Gypsies—Europe, Eastern. 2. Europe, Eastern—Ethnic relations. I. Crowe,
  David M. II. Kolsti, John.
DX145.G95   1991
305.891′497—dc20
                                          90-46710
                                                  CIP

Printed in the United States of America

TS   10   9   8   7   6   5   4   3   2   1

Contents

Preface and Acknowledgments

The recent upheavals and sociopolitical transformations taking place in Eastern Europe have once again brought to the fore some deep ethnic divisions that have traditionally colored the history and culture of that part of the continent. The essays in this volume are an effort to explore the story of one of the most fascinating yet misunderstood groups in that region—the Romani or Gypsies. The seed for this study came from a variety of scholarly origins. Several of the papers on the *Pořajmos*, or Gypsy Holocaust, were delivered at a 1988 meeting of the Western Social Science Association in Denver, Colorado, while others were presented at an American Association for the Advancement of Slavic Studies convention in Honolulu later that year. It was at this gathering that several of the authors met to discuss this project. Each of the editors represents one of the two different avenues of interest that led to this volume.

What has emerged from this effort is an attempt to look, in as much chronological depth as possible, at the origins of the Romani in Eastern Europe and at their historical, social, and cultural experiences after their arrival there in the Middle Ages. Since several of the authors have been able to maintain direct contact with observers in the region, some of the material included in a few chapters is quite current. Although we have tried to make this study as complete as possible, there are some gaps that we hope future studies will cover. Poland has traditionally had a significant Romani population which suffered tremendously during the *Pořajmos*. Unfortunately, only sparse coverage of that group is found in this volume. Other countries in Eastern Europe that are not touched here are Bulgaria, which has a large Gypsy community, and certain parts of Yugoslavia. We hope that this collection will stimulate others working in the field, particularly in those areas not discussed here, to share their work in similar volumes.

The editors would like to acknowledge a number of individuals for their role in helping to put this manuscript together. We would like to thank Heidi DePreiter, a student assistant in the History Department at Elon College, for retyping the manuscripts received from each author; Brenda Cooper, the secretary of the Department of History at Elon College, who coordinated this typing and did some of the work herself; and Teresa LePors, reference and public service librarian at the McEwen Library at Elon College, who has provided invaluable bibliographical and research help throughout this project. A special thanks goes to R. Craig Plumlee, a graduate assistant in the Department of Slavic Languages at the University of Texas at Austin, who compiled and typed the bibliography from each author's references.

And finally, we are most grateful to our ''silent editor,'' Kathryn Moore Crowe, reference librarian and Coordinator of Instruction at Jackson Library at the University of North Carolina at Greensboro. Early in our work, she agreed to take over complete computer preparation of the final manuscript. Without her tireless efforts, the editors would not have been able to complete the book in a timely manner.

THE GYPSIES

OF EASTERN EUROPE

1

Introduction

IAN HANCOCK

The most easily accessible publications dealing with the Roma ("Gypsies") invariably present them as a mysterious, marginal people steeped in occult lore and guarding secrets forbidden to the uninitiated. This notion of mystery is perhaps anomalous, since the identity of the Romani people and their language has been known to Western scholars for over two centuries, and books devoted to the Roma number in the thousands.

By far the largest proportion of those books, however, are works of romantic fiction which simply perpetuate such an otherworldly image (e.g., the novels by Crane, Foldes, Kramer, Lawrence, Somers, von Stroheim, or Weyrich listed in the bibliography). A much smaller number consists of overviews of the Romani people, the contents of which have usually been culled from the earlier works of other writers and which are of varying quality (e.g., Clébert, Ficowski, Simson, Vaux de Foletier, Vossen). Titles even less in evidence are those which deal with linguistic or anthropological aspects of the Romani populations, while those addressing social issues such as schooling, racism, housing, health care, and so on may be counted on the fingers of one hand (e.g., Acton, Liégeois). Most of the work done in these areas is confined to articles in specialist journals, not easily accessible to the average reader. Thus the appearance of this book marks a welcome departure from this pattern.

Because most works dealing with Gypsies fall into the category of romantic fiction, it is easy to see why the popular image should persist; it is an image that is reinforced even in standard works of reference: the 1911 edition of the *Encyclopaedia Britannica*, for example, describes Gypsies as "gaudy, ostentatious, boastful, arrogant and superstitious," and in its 1958 edition states that "Gypsies have the mental image of a child of ten," that they "have never accomplished anything," and that they are "quarrelsome, quick to anger or laughter, unthinkingly cruel," "love bright colors," and "have little idea of time." The *Oxford English Dictionary* lists a Gypsy as "a cunning rogue . . . deceitful . . . fickle." The *American International Encyclopedia*'s 1953 edition told its readers that Gypsies have "no idea of education," that "their children grow up in idleness and the habits of stealing and cheating." In the 1952 edition of the Grolier Society's *Book of Knowledge* it is stated that "gipsies are fast dying out in America," that they "are a mysterious people," and that "the average gipsy is a swarthy, olive-skinned man or woman, with clear, brilliant black eyes, shining black hair and pearly teeth . . . they are off and away down the roads at the first signs of spring . . . they are highly superstitious, all nature is alive to them." In print, the word is still frequently spelled without a proper noun's initial capital letter, as though the identity were an acquired and not an inherited one, an editorial policy that unconsciously reinforces the rift between the real Gypsy and the gypsy of popular tradition. Children looking for information about Gypsies in their school libraries invariably come away with very mixed impressions: a population that is both romanticized and feared, both real and mythological.

The reasons for the persistence of this strange dual identity are not difficult to identify: anti-Gypsyism dates back to the time of the Roma's very first arrival in Europe in the thirteenth century, when they were confused with the Islamic invaders encroaching upon Europe from the South and the East.[1] Names still borne by Roma today reflect this: *Saracens, Tatars, Egyptians* (hence "*Gypsy*"), *Heathens*, and so on. Dark-skinned foreigners in every country, without a territory of their own, the Roma had nowhere to retreat to. Establishing the Romani state of Romanestan, Rotaru's "refuge in the event of persecution," is a recurrent theme among some contemporary nationalists.[2] Perceived as Muslims, the Roma were therefore regarded as a threat to the Christian establishment and were dealt with accordingly. After seven centuries, anti-Gypsyism has become very deeply ingrained in the Western tradition, as folktales, proverbs, and folk beliefs attest.

The Roma were kept on the move by legislation; even in this country, current laws forbid Romani Americans to remain in some states, while in modern Britain Gypsies may only stop legally on government reservations, and in modern France they are obliged to carry passes that must be stamped by the police in each parish. Although Gypsies are required to keep moving by law, the establishment reinterprets this as evidence of their romantic and free spirit. Forbidden to do business with shopkeepers, the Roma have had to rely upon subsistence theft to feed their families; and thus stealing has become a part of the stereotype. Forbidden to use town pumps or wells, denied water by fearful householders, uncleanliness becomes a part of the stereotype. Using fortune telling as a means of livelihood suitable to life on the move, and sometimes as a means of protective control, sorcery becomes a part of the stereotype as well.

The romantic literary image can be traced to the period of industrialization in Western Europe during the last century, when machines replaced people and created increasing numbers of poor and homeless. Soot-blackened factories sprang up in the cities, in bleak contrast to the preindustrial days idealized in the literature of the period. The Gypsies lived with all of this, continuing to exist according to their own traditions, forever on the outskirts of non-Gypsy society, and never wishing to be a part of it. It is little wonder that they came to epitomize an idyllic, lost rural life. George Borrow, more than anyone else in the English-language tradition, was responsible for idealizing the Gypsy, and his books are still a principle source for journalists and novelists seeking material for their own endeavors. His representations of the Romani language, often incorrect and sometimes of his own creation, turn up in subsequent works by other writers with monotonous regularity—the same is true of the proverbs scattered throughout the works of Jan Yoors, which have been shamelessly co-opted by many authors since. The nineteenth-century literary image of the Gypsy in Britain has been dealt with in detail by Mayall, and in France by Brown.[3]

In addition to these external factors that have distanced the Gypsy, the Romani society itself has contributed to the situation. Together with the language, the Roma have inherited certain cultural behavior from India as well, the most pervasive of which is the concept of ritual purity. The Gypsy way of life, called *romanipen* or *romañija*, involves, among other things, the observation of rules governing one's state of personal cleanliness. Details of this can be found, for example, in Sutherland or Miller (1968), and include restrictions upon contact with other people or animals, the preparation of food, the washing of the body, crockery, or clothing, and so on. *Gadže*, or non-Gypsies, are regarded as unclean since they do not observe these restrictions, and as a result they are seen as being able to defile by contact; for this reason, and because non-Gypsies have never presented themselves favorably to Gypsies but instead have always meant trouble, they are kept at arm's length. Unable to become too intimate with Gypsies, non-Gypsy investigators have sometimes embellished their work with assumptions of their own; Gypsies may freely provide false or misleading information about themselves, too, and even prefer the idea that non-Gypsies believe the literary image, since it serves to shield the real population. On the other hand, unlike other minority peoples, until recently the Roma have not been able to organize protest against media defamation through lobbying or boycotting, so that relatively frequent racist wording continues to appear in the media, helping to sustain the popular image of the Gypsy. The point has been made by Cohn, Kephart, Sibley, and others that the Gypsy image also exists because there is an actual *need* for it in the larger society, either to provide a scapegoat or as a yardstick by which to measure its own boundaries. It might also be noted that it is simply easier, and certainly more attractive, to believe the myth rather than the reality; and if the Gypsies aren't perceived to be "real," then generating sympathy for their plight is not easily achieved.

Whatever accounts for it, it is necessary to understand the full significance of this dual identity, because it stands as the single most problematic obstacle in the path of the Romani effort to be recognized as a real people with a real history and real problems. In lectures I give around the country on Gypsy slavery, for instance, or the *Poŕajmos* (the Romani Holocaust), the questions from the audience that follow are usually not concerned so much with the details of the presentation, but instead with what a Gypsy *is*: Where do Gypsies live and what do they wear and eat, is it true that they have spiritual gifts, and why are they never in evidence if over a million of them live in the United States? Thus, in bringing the details of the Romani experience before the public, *two* stories have to be told: the public has first to be educated away from its preconceptions and reintroduced to the real Roma; only then will the true impact of Romani history be properly understood.

The chapters in this book deal with the real Roma. The picture they paint is not a cheerful one; the Roma in Eastern Europe are still, fifty years later, suffering the consequences of the Nazi genocide—the second attempt to exterminate them since their arrival in the Balkans. Whether the rapidly changing political scene in that part of the world will improve their lot is doubtful; attitudes must change at the folk level as well, and in "free" societies Gypsies fare just as badly. A British Gypsy remarked that changing the word "Gypsies" to "Romanies" on a sign that said "No Gypsies served here" provided very little comfort. Gypsies are still trying to attract the attention of human rights organizations to help them fight for equality. In this country, Gypsies still have not been successful in obtaining fair representation on the U.S. Holocaust Memorial Council, despite losing a higher percentage of their overall numbers than any other targeted population in Nazi Germany,[4] as well as being "the first ethnic group selected by Nazi leadership for genocide."[5] Yet the council has only one Romani representative among its sixty-five members, appointed seven years after it was founded. Gypsies in this country are still trying to have the legislation against them rescinded as unconstitutional and discriminatory, and to have those of their number who have come here illegally to escape repressive East European regimes treated as political refugees rather than as targets of specially created police squads. Gypsies are still trying to obtain war crimes reparations, and to stop the deportations or sterilizations that are going on in Poland, Czechoslovakia, and Germany. Gypsies have yet to receive adequate health care to bring an end to an infant mortality rate that is fifteen times higher than the national average in Britain,[6] and a life expectancy rate that is fifteen years shorter than the national average in Hungary[7] and that is between the ages of forty-eight and fifty-five for American Roma.[8]

In this last decade of the twentieth century, there are already indications of a restlessness among ethnic minorities and a polarization with the establishment; it is not difficult to predict that there will be a "return to the sixties" in terms of dissatisfaction and civil disobedience during the 1990s. For African Americans, for example, life expectancy has decreased over the past thirty years, while the rate of unemployment for that population has risen steadily. Fewer and fewer are graduating and entering our universities, and murder is now the leading cause of death in the Black community. Asian and Mexican Americans are facing increasing discrimination in housing and employment, while Native Americans continue to remain at the bottom of the social heap. Diseases and drugs are destroying more and more lives in ethnic America, and no proposed solution so far shows any sign of being effective. The number of Romani American families on welfare is increasing, and Romani youth are also beginning to succumb to the social ills that affect other minority populations.

Unlike other ethnic minorities who are pressing for integration into the mainstream society, Romani Americans have dealt with the situation by treating the establishment as the enemy, to be held at bay and exploited. This has been a necessary position to take throughout our entire history in Europe, any alternative leading to extermination. Two of the United Nations criteria for genocide, namely the permanent removal of children from their families, and sterilization, are in effect against Roma in Europe today.[9] Most of Franklin Littell's fifteen ''early warning signs'' for impending genocidal action by a state against a people clearly apply in the case of the contemporary Romani population,[10] as the most recent entries in the ''Chronology'' (chapter 2 in this volume) testify.

While the Romani struggle to retain their identity has been one of keeping the barrier between *Rom* and *Gadžo* firm, the increasingly complex structure of society makes such tactics less and less possible, or indeed desirable. Some Roma are beginning to recognize the fact that integration need not mean assimilation, and that acquiring mainstream skills and putting them to use within the Romani community need in no way jeopardize their integrity, but instead would allow them to deal with the mainstream more equably and to profit by doing so. But if Romani efforts to be recognized as a distinct population with a legitimate, albeit painful history are to succeed, *gadže* must in turn disabuse themselves of their prejudgmental notions about the Romani people and turn to sources such as the present volume for their information.

Notes

1. Ian Hancock, *The Pariah Syndrome: An Account of Gypsy Slavery and Persecution.*

2. See ''The East European Roots of Romani Nationalism,'' in this volume.

3. The political motives for maintaining the literary Romani image have been dealt with by Katie Trumpener, in her ''Peoples without History and the Narratives of Nationalism,'' a study dealing, in particular, with the situation in Germany.

4. Jim Miller, ''Mačwaya Gypsy Marime,'' p. 66.

5. Walter O. Weyrauch, ''Gestapo Informants: Facts and Theory of Undercover Operations,'' p. 584.

6. According to the 1983 Report of the Save the Children Fund.

7. According to the *World Press Review* for October 1983.

8. According to a medical survey conducted at Harvard University, summarized in James D. Thomas et al., ''Disease, Lifestyle and Consanguinity in Fifty-eight American Gypsies.''

9. Ian F. Hancock, ''Uniqueness of the Victims: Gypsies, Jews and the Holocaust,'' p. 49.

10. Franklin H. Littell, ''Early Warning,'' pp. 2128–29.

2

Gypsy History in Germany and Neighboring Lands
A Chronology Leading to the Holocaust and Beyond

IAN HANCOCK

1407 First appearance of Gypsies in Germany, in Hildesheim.[1]
1414 Second possible appearance of Gypsies in Germany, in Hesse.[2]
1416 First anti-Gypsy law issued in Germany. Forty-eight such laws are passed between this date and 1774.[3]
1417 First detailed description of arrival and appearance of Gypsies in Germany.[4]
1418 Arrival documented in Hamburg.[5]
1419 Arrival documented in Augsburg.[6]
1428 Arrival documented in Switzerland.[7]
1449 Gypsies driven out of Frankfurt-am-Main.[8]
1496 Gypsies accused of being foreign spies, carriers of the plague, and traitors to Christendom at the Reichstag meetings during this year, and in 1497 and 1498 in Freiburg and Landau.[9] These charges are repeated frequently over the following centuries.
1498 New anti-Gypsy laws issued by the Freiburg Diet.[10]
1500 Maximilian I orders all Gypsies to be out of Germany by Easter, 1501. Cases on record of Germans who killed Gypsies being protected by this law, which states that ''taking the life of a Gypsy . . .

is not an act against the policy of the state.''[11] A general order is issued at Augsburg stating that Gypsy men may be shot and their women raped if found in Germany.[12]

1514 Switzerland encourages ''Gypsy hunts'' among its citizens as a means of urging Gypsies to leave the country.[13]

1531 The Augsburg Reichstag forbids Gypsies the use of travel documents in order to make reentry impossible once banished.[14] This method is being used in modern-day Poland.[15]

1566 Ferdinand I maintains expulsion and extermination orders; two Gypsies are drowned in the Elbe for violating this order in Dresden.[16]

1568 Pope Pius V banishes all Gypsies from the realm of the Holy Roman Church.[17]

1579 Augustus, Elector of Saxony, confiscates Gypsies' travel permits and banishes them from the state.[18]

1580 Governments encourage Gypsy hunts in Switzerland, The Netherlands, and Germany.[19]

1652 Townspeople in Bautzen are fined by the local magistrate for doing business with Gypsies.[20]

1659 Mass murder of Gypsies in Neudorf, near Dresden.[21]

1661 Elector Johann Georg II of Saxony imposes death penalty on Gypsies found in his territory. ''Gypsy hunts'' instigated as means of exterminating Gypsy population.[22]

1709 Gypsies apprehended for any reason, whether criminal or not, are to be sent to the galleys or deported, according to a law in the district of Ober-Rhein.[23]

1710 Frederick I of Prussia condemns all male Gypsies to forced labor, women to be whipped and branded, and their children permanently placed with white families.[24]

1714 An order is issued in Mainz sending all male Gypsies apprehended to the gallows, and requiring the branding and whipping of women and children. Frederick Augustus, Elector of Saxony, orders the murder of any Gypsy resisting arrest.[25]

1721 Emperor Charles VI orders extermination of Gypsies.[26]

1722 In Frankfurt-am-Main Gypsy parents are branded and deported while their children are taken from them and placed permanently with non-Gypsy families. During this period, Frederick William makes it a hanging offense in Prussia merely to be born a Gypsy for all those over the age of eighteen.[27] A thousand armed Gypsies confront German soldiery in an organized fight for their freedom.[28] Nineteen Gypsies arrested at Kaswasser are tortured to death: four broken on the wheel, three beheaded, and the rest shot or stabbed to death.[29]

1725 An edict from King Frederick William I of Prussia condemns all Gypsies throughout the land, eighteen years or older, to be hanged.[30]

1726 Johann Weissenbruch[31] describes wholesale murder on November 14 and 15 of a community of Gypsies in Germany: five are organized nationwide in order to expel them from the land.[32] German monarch Charles VI passes a law that any male Gypsy found in the country is to be killed instantly, while Gypsy women and children are to have their ears cut off and be shipped to the nearest foreign border.[33]

1736 Document relating the punishment of a runaway Gypsy slave in Siebenburgen. He has his feet burned in lye, and his lip cut off, which he is forced to roast and eat in front of his owners.[34]

1740 All Gypsies entering Bohemia are to be hung by decree.[35]

1782 Two hundred Gypsies are arrested and tortured until they confess to charges of cannibalism in Esabrag, Frauenmark, and Kamesa in Hungary.[36]

1783 Heinrich Grellmann publishes the first treatise establishing the Indian origin of the Romani people, but claims in it that in doing his research among them, he felt a "clear repugnancy, like a biologist dissecting some nauseating, crawling thing in the interests of science."[37]

1793 Establishment attitudes are further expressed by the minister Martinus Zippel, who writes that "Gypsies in a well-ordered state in the present day are like vermin on an animal's body."[38]

1830 Using the method introduced by Maria Theresa in the Austro-Hungarian Empire during the previous century, authorities in Nordhausen attempt to bring about the eventual extinction of the Romani population by forcibly and permanently removing children from their families for placement with non-Gypsies.[39]

1835 November 11, record of a "Gypsy hunt" for sport in Jutland, which includes over 260 in the list of kills. A Rheinish landowner enters "a Gypsy women and her suckling baby" in his record of the hunt.[40]

1890 (exact date not known; early 1890s). The Swabian parliament organizes a conference on the "Gypsy Scum" (*Das Zigeunergeschmeiss*), and suggests means by which the presence of Gypsies could be signalled by ringing church bells.[41] The military is also empowered to apprehend and move Gypsies on.

1899 In March, under the directorship of Alfred Dillman in Munich, Bavarian police create a special Gypsy Affairs unit, later to be named The Central Office for Fighting the Gypsy Nuisance, to regulate the lives of Gypsies. Available historical documents relating to Gypsies begin to be collected, particularly those pertaining to legislation and "criminality."[42]

1904 Prussian Landtag unanimously adopts proposition to regulate Gypsy movement and means of livelihood.[43]

1905 A census of all Gypsies in Bavaria is taken, in which they are described as "a pest against which society must unflaggingly defend itself." Citizens are urged to report all Gypsy activity to the Gypsy Affairs Office in Munich.[44]

1906 February 17, the Prussian minister issues special instructions to the police to "combat the Gypsy nuisance." A special register is started to keep a record of Gypsy activities.[45]

1907 Increasing anti-Gypsy terrorism in Germany leads to influx of Gypsies from that country into western Europe, including Britain.[46]

1909 Recommendations coming from a policy conference on "the Gypsy question" in Hungary include the confiscation of their animals and carts, and permanent branding for the purposes of identification.[47]

1920 In Germany, psychiatrist Karl Binding and magistrate Alfred Hoche argue for the killing of those who were *Ballastexistenzen*, i.e., whose lives were seen to be simply a dead weight within humanity. This includes Gypsies. The concept of "worthless life" becomes crucial to Nazi racist policy after 1933.[48]

1922 In Baden, requirements are introduced that all Gypsies be photographed and fingerprinted, and have documents completed on them.[49]

1926 The Bavarian parliament brings a new law "to combat Gypsy nomads and idlers" into effect, and the Provincial Criminal Commission endorses a law dated July 16 aimed at controlling the "Gypsy Plague."[50] In Switzerland, "proto-Nazi ideas of racial hygiene" are used to justify a program of forced permanent removal of Gypsy children from their families for placement in foster homes. This remains in effect until the mid-1980s.[51]

1927 Legislation requiring the photographing and fingerprinting of Gypsies is instituted in Prussia, where eight thousand Gypsies are processed in this way. Bavaria institutes laws forbidding Gypsies to travel in family groups, or to own firearms. Those over sixteen are liable for incarceration in work camps, while those without proof of Bavarian birth start being expelled from Germany.[52] A group of Gypsies in Slovakia is tried for cannibalism, which Friedman interprets as part of the growing campaign against the Romani population.[53]

1928 After April 12, Gypsies in Germany are to be placed under permanent police surveillance. The law is reaffirmed in May 1928.[54] These acts are in direct violation of the Weimar Constitution, which guaranteed equal rights for all citizens.[55] In the same year, Professor Hans F. Günther writes that "it was the Gypsies who introduced foreign blood into Europe."[56]

1929 April 16 and 17, the Munich Bureau's National Center jointly establishes a Division of Gypsy Affairs with the International Criminology Bureau (Interpol) in Vienna. Working closely together, they enforce restrictions on travel for Gypsies without documents, and impose up to two years' detention in "rehabilitation camps" upon numbers of Gypsies sixteen years of age or older.[57]

1930 Recommendation is made by a Norwegian journalist that all Gypsies be sterilized.[58]

1933 On January 20, officials in Burgenland call for the withdrawal of all civil rights for Gypsies, and the introduction of clubbing as a punishment.[59] On May 26, Nazis introduce a law to legalize eugenic sterilization. On July 14, Hitler's cabinet passes a law against the propagation of "lives not worthy of life" (*Lebensunwertesleben*) called "the law for the prevention of hereditarily diseased offspring." It orders sterilization for certain categories of people, "specifically Gypsies and most of the Germans of black color" (i.e., those resulting from the contact between German women and the Senegalese troops deployed by the French during the First World War to patrol the Ruhr Valley, as well as residents in Europe from ex–German colonies in Africa).[60] The Oberwarth District Prefect submits a petition demanding that the League of Nations investigate the possibility of establishing a colony for the resettlement of European Gypsies in the Polynesian islands.[61] In September the Reichsminister for the Interior and Propaganda initiates a roundup of "vagrants," including large numbers of Gypsies.

1934 From January onward, Gypsies are being selected for transfer to camps for processing, which includes sterilization by injection or castration. These camps will be established at Dachau, Dieselstrauss,

Sachsenhausen, Marzahn, and Vennhausen during the next three years. Two laws issued in Nuremberg in July forbid Germans from marrying "Jews, Negroes, and Gypsies."[62]

1935 Starting on September 15, Gypsies become subject to the restrictions of the Nuremberg Law for the Protection of Blood and Honor, which forbids intermarriage or sexual relationships between Aryan and non-Aryan peoples. A policy statement issued by the Nazi party reads "In Europe generally, only Jews and Gypsies come under consideration as members of an alien people."[63]

1936 In June and July, several hundred Gypsies are transported to Dachau by order of the Minister of the Interior for the Third Reich, who serves on the panel on racial laws and declares that "In Europe, only Jews and Gypsies are of foreign blood,"[64] and race-hygienist Dr. Robert Körber writes in his book *Volk und Staat* that "The Jews and the Gypsies are today remote from us because of their Asiatic ancestry, just as ours is Nordic." This sentiment is reiterated by Dr. E. Brandis, who wrote that "only the Gypsies are to be considered as an alien people in Europe (besides the Jews)."[65] German anti-Gypsyism becomes transnational in Europe when Interpol in Vienna establishes the International Center for Combatting the Gypsy Menace, which has grown from the earlier Bureau of Gypsy Affairs.[66] Martin Block publishes his general study of Gypsies in Leipzig, and justifies Nazi racist attitudes by speaking of the "nauseating Gypsy smell," and the "involuntary feeling of mistrust or repulsion one feels in their presence."[67] The main Nazi institution to deal with Gypsies, the Racial Hygiene and Population Biology and Research Unit of the Ministry of Health, is established under the directorship of Dr. Robert Ritter at Berlin-Dahlem; its expressed purpose is to determine whether the Romani people are Aryans or subhumans (*Untermenschen*).[68] By early 1942, Ritter has documented the genealogy of almost the entire German Gypsy population. In Berlin Gypsies are cleared off the streets, away from public view, because of the upcoming Olympic Games.[69]

1937 An order released on December 14 states that persons can be incarcerated on the grounds of their being inherently, as well as habitually, prone to criminal activity whether they actually commit it or not, depending upon "genetic makeup" and potential threat to Aryan security.[70] By the end of this year, large-scale roundups of Gypsies begin. At Buchenwald, a special camp for "pure" Gypsies is set up, and there are Gypsies incarcerated in camps in Nazi-controlled territories throughout Europe. Four hundred are sent to Taucha; others end up in Mauthausen, Gusen, Dautmergen, Natzweiler, Stutthoff, Flossenberg, Salzwed, Ravensbrück, Düsseldorf, Lackenbach, Westerbork, Malines, and elsewhere.[71] An SS study group recommends the mass drowning of Gypsies in boats to be towed out to sea and sunk, though it is not implemented.

1938 Himmler's decree of May 16 orders that the Bureau of Gypsy Affairs be moved from Munich to Berlin. Between June 12 and June 18, *Zigeuneraufräumungswoche* (clean-up week) is in effect, and hundreds of Gypsies throughout Germany and Austria are rounded up.[72] In Mannworth in Austria, three hundred Romani farmers and vineyard owners are arrested in a single night. A decree dated September 4 forbids Gypsy children from attending school.[73] After November, the same year, Jewish children may attend only Jewish, and not state, schools.[74] On December 8, Himmler signs a new order[75] based upon the findings of the Office of Racial Hygiene, which had determined that Gypsy blood was "very dangerous" to Aryan purity. Dr. Tobias Portschy, Area Commander in Styria, writes in a memorandum to Hitler's Chancellery that "Gypsies place the purity of the blood of German peasantry in peril," and recommends mass sterilization as a solution. The Gypsy problem is identified "categorically as a matter of race,"[76] a statement supported in this same year by race hygienist Adolph Wurth, whose report contains the statement that "the Gypsy question that we face today is above all a racial question,"[77] and Dr. Kurt Ammon, who states that Nazi policy "views the Gypsy problem as being foremost a racial one." Himmler thereafter puts groups of Gypsies at the disposal of a team of doctors for experiments on sterilization techniques.[78] Ironically, the more Romani ancestry an individual has, the less threatening he is seen to be. Himmler's suggestion that a number of "pure" Gypsies be exempt and subject to the "law for the protection of historic monuments" for future anthropologists to study is mocked and never implemented.[79] Gypsies are categorized by percentage of Romani ancestry; if two of an individual's eight great-grandparents are even part-Gypsy, this individual later has too much "Gypsy blood" to be allowed to live.[80] If the criteria for determining Jewishness had been applied to Gypsies, some 18,000 (nine-tenths of the total number of Gypsies in Germany at that time) would have escaped death.[81] Romani women married to non-Gypsies, and children over the age of thirteen, are sent to Düsseldorf-Lierenfeld to be sterilized.[82]

1939 In March, instructions for carrying out the order to register and categorize Gypsies are issued, which state "The aim of the measures taken by the state must be the racial separation, once and for all, of the Gypsy race from the German nation, then the prevention of racial mixing." Every police headquarters is to set up a unit to monitor Gypsy matters, and one or more persons are to be permanently responsible for Gypsies.[83] According to the minutes of a meeting organized by Heydrich on September 27, Hitler instructed that German Gypsies and Jews are to be moved by rail into Poland.[84] Following Himmler's order of the previous December, Hitler issues a new decree dated 17 November 1939 in preparation for these transportations, forbidding all "Gypsies and part-Gypsies" not already in camps from moving out of their areas.[85] Trains are reported moving east "packed with Gypsies" from the fall of 1939 on.[86] Dr. Johannes Behrendt of the Office of Racial Hygiene issues the statement that "All Gypsies should be treated as hereditarily sick; the only solution is elimination. The aim should therefore be the elimination without hesitation of this defective element in the population." In that report, he estimates that, based on Nazi research, the total world Gypsy population is two million, of which eighteen thousand live in Germany.[87]

1940 In January or February, 250 Gypsy children from Brno in the concentration camp at Buchenwald are used as guinea pigs for testing the gas Zyklon B, which is later used for mass killings at Auschwitz-Birkenau. This is the first mass genocidal action of the Holocaust.[88] Nazis in Alsace comply with an order to round up "criminals, asocials, the sick, French nationalists, and, of course, the Jews and the Gypsies."[89] In this year, Nazi statisticians Wetzel and Hecht estimate that "one hundred thousand Gypsies and others" are scheduled for deportation to Poland,[90] and are shipped between May 15 and 18. A law passed on August 14 forbids official employment of any kind to Gypsies. Five thousand German Gypsies are concentrated a Łódź.[91]

1941 An ordinance dated February 11 forbids Gypsies and "part-Gypsies" from serving in the German army "on the grounds of racial policy."[92] This is repeated on July 10 the following year. On July 31, Heydrich, who had been entrusted with the details of the "Final Solution," includes Gypsies together with Jews: "The Einsatzkommandos received the order to kill all Jews, Gypsies and mental patients."[93] On October 10, Heydrich proposes that the German Gypsies be sent to Riga with the Jews instead of being sent to Auschwitz and Chelmno in Poland. At the same meeting, the motion that Lodz be chosen as the "final destination" for non-German-born Gypsies is approved,[94] and between November 9 and 11 five trainloads, transporting a thousand Gypsies each, leave for that camp, where they are joined by a transport of 20,000 Jews.[95] Of the 5,000 Gypsies deported, nearly two-thirds are children; some die from typhus, others are brutalized to death by the guards.[96] On the night of December 24, eight hundred Romani men, women, and children are shot to death at Simferopol in the Crimea by the Einsatzgruppen.[97]

1942 Shipments of Gypsies to Chelmno in groups of two or three hundred begin in January, followed shortly thereafter by mass shipments of Jews to the same camp.[98] In the spring, Gypsies are selected for experimentation at Dachau and Buchenwald by Dr. Adolf Pokorny to see how long they can survive on sea water, claiming that they "must not only be conquered, but exterminated also."[99] At Sachsenhausen, race scientist Ludwig Fischer attempts to show that Romani blood is different from that of Germans, starting his medical experiments on forty Gypsies. "At Himmler's request, he promised to widen his research by exploring Jewish blood also."[100] That same spring, one thousand Gypsies are shot and buried alive in a single action on a collective farm near Smolensk.[101] Nazi death squads enter Greece in June, murdering hundreds of Gypsies.[102] In Serbia, Military Governor Harald Turner is able to announce that "Serbia is the only country in which the Jewish Question and the Gypsy Question have been resolved." In the same statement he warns that "one must not forget that the Jews and the Gypsies generally constitute a threat to security and as such, pose a threat to peace and public order; it is the Jewish nature which is responsible for this war and, as for the Gypsy, by his nature he can never be a useful member of international society."[103] For each German soldier killed in the war, a hundred Gypsies and Jews are murdered in retribution; in Greece, fifty Gypsies are murdered for each German casualty.[104] Most Gypsies in Yugoslavia are killed by the *Ustaša* or Croatian Fascists; figures on the numbers dispatched in this way are not complete. On July 31 the Ministry of the Eastern Occupied Territories reaffirms to the Wehrmacht that Gypsies are to be treated in the same way as Jews.[105] Gypsies are being exterminated at Treblinka, Majdanek, Belsec, Sanok, Sobibor, and Chelmno.[106] In Bucharest, the policy statement that "For Romania, the Gypsy question is as important as the Jewish" is published.[107] In the minutes of a September 14 meeting Justice Minister Otto Thierack proposes that "Jews and Gypsies should be unconditionally exterminated."[108] Nazis begin compiling data on Gypsy populations in Britain and elsewhere in anticipation of eventual takeover of those countries.[109]

1943 In February, a roundup of the remaining Gypsies throughout Germany takes place;[110] in March, Dutch Gypsies are transported to Auschwitz.[111]

1944 Eva Justin's book dealing with Gypsy children is published. In it she expresses the hope that it will serve as a basis for future race hygiene laws regulating such "unworthy primitive elements." SS Reichsphysician Ernst Grawitz rejects Pokorny's use of Gypsies as subjects for sea-water experiments "for racial reasons."[112] In the early morning hours of August 1, four thousand Gypsies at Auschwitz-Birkenau are killed and cremated in one mass action referred to as *Zigeunernacht*.[113]

1945 War ends on September 2 with the surrender of Japan. Nuremberg Trials begin in October, though not one Gypsy is called to testify. Current estimates now indicate that between one and one and a half million Gypsies died during the period 1933–1945.[114] If this estimate and Behrendt's (probably rather low) official Nazi estimate for the world total are correct, between 50 and 75 percent of the entire Romani population perished at the hands of the Nazis, victims of racist genocidal policy. This may be compared with the estimated 5.7–6 million Jewish deaths,[115] out of a then total world population of eighteen million,[116] or roughly 33 percent.

1947 At the Nuremberg Military Tribunals in September, former SS General Otto Ohlendorf tells Presiding Judge Michael A. Musmanno that in the killing campaigns: "There was no difference between Gypsies and Jews."[117] As late as this date, Romani survivors from the camps are afraid to show themselves publicly because pre-Nazi laws are still in effect that would put them back into detention centers if they were unable to show documentation of German birth.[118]

1950 The Württemburg Ministry of the Interior issues a statement that judges, hearing restitution claims, should bear in mind that "Gypsies were persecuted under the National Socialistic regime *not* for any racial reason, but because of an asocial and criminal record."[119] Members of the shattered postwar remnants of the surviving Romani population lack the wherewithal legally to challenge this preposterous statement, and no outside agency comes forward to take up the Gypsy case. Commenting on this at the time, medical genealogist Professor Montandon in Paris observes that "everyone despises Gypsies, so why exercise restraint? Who will avenge them?

Who will complain? Who will bear witness?''[120]

1968 In Birmingham, England, in a political debate broadcast in March, a speaker maintains that ''there are some of these Gypsies you can do nothing with, and you must exterminate the impossibles; we are dealing with people whom members of this council would not look upon as human beings in the normal sense.''[121] A similar call for ''extermination'' is made again in Britain in 1984.[122] In the same country in October, the *Sundon Park Tenants' Association Report* includes the statement that ''there is no solution to the Gypsy problem short of mass murder.''[123]

1971 Although war crime victims are to be compensated under the terms of the Bonn Convention, the Bonn government frees itself from its responsibility to Gypsies by claiming that their disposition was strictly on the grounds of security.[124]

1973 In November a villager in Pfaffenhofen opens fire upon a Gypsy family that has come to his farm to buy produce, killing three. The sympathies of the police are with the farmer.[125]

1980 West German government spokesman Gerold Tandler calls Romani demands for war crimes reparations ''unreasonable'' and ''slander[ous].''[126] The U.S. Holocaust Memorial Council is established in Washington and sixty-five members are appointed, though no Gypsies are invited to be a part of the representation. In Poland, groups of Gypsies are forcibly deported by boat after having documents allowing their return confiscated.[127]

1983 In evidence of a new wave of anti-Gypsy racism in Hungary, a song calling for their extermination by flame-thrower for a ''Gypsy-free land'' becomes popular, and the slogan ''Kill the Gypsies'' is found decorating public walls.[128]

1984 Chairman of the U.S. Holocaust Memorial Council tells the *Washington Post* in July that Gypsy demands for representation are ''cockamamie,'' and questions whether Gypsies really constitute a distinct ethnic people.[129] Council liaison officers tell the press that Gypsy activists are ''cranks'' and ''eccentrics.''[130]

1985 In Germany, Werner Nachmann, president of the Jewish Central Council, repeatedly refuses to allow Romani participation in a ceremony commemorating the liberation of Bergen-Belsen.[131] At the same time, Darmstadt city mayor Günther Metzger tells the German Council of Sinti and Roma that it had ''insulted the honor'' of the memory of the Holocaust by wishing to be associated with it.[132] Apartheid laws are introduced in Bradford, England, making it illegal for Gypsies to come within city limits without a permit.[133] In Kumla, Sweden, "police watched from a patrol car as fifty youths attacked a Gypsy family with stones and a firebomb."[134] Authorities in Yugoslavia arrest a gang of kidnappers, which has been abducting children from defenseless Gypsy families for sale abroad to Italians and Americans, and to be trained as thieves in Rome and Paris.[135]

1986 A report is issued by the German Ministry of Finance, which concludes that "all those victimized by Nazism have been adequately compensated . . . the circle of those deserving compensation need not be extended any further."[136] The Romani Union is informed by the Office of Presidential Appointments that none of its eight candidates for membership in the U.S. Holocaust Memorial Council was successful. "Proto-Nazi ideas of race hygiene" in Switzerland come to public attention in June, when it is learned that since 1926 a state-run foundation has been forcibly and permanently removing Gypsy children from their families for placement in non-Gypsy homes, the intention being to destroy the Romani way of life.[137] In October, the U.S. Congressional Caucus on Human Rights sends a petition to the government of Czechoslovakia protesting its policy of coercive sterilization of Gypsy women and the forcible permanent removal of Gypsy children from their families.[138] The response from the Czech government is that "[it] was the Gypsies' fault for refusing to let their children be civilized."[139]

1987 In February the U.S. Holocaust Memorial Council holds an international conference on "Other Victims" of Nazism, which includes a panel on the Romani situation, though no Gypsies are invited to participate in its organization or are included in the program. The first Romani representative to the council is appointed in May by President Reagan. Despite this, Gypsies continue consistently to be excluded from participation in the Annual Days of Remembrance ceremonies every year, and are still being excluded in 1990.

1988 In February the East German government announces its resolution to pay $100 million in war crimes reparations to Jewish survivors, but refuses to pay anything to Romani survivors.[140] First West German money set aside to compensate Gypsy victims is stolen by a committee member and never paid.[141] An Irish councillor calls for the incineration of Gypsies in a garbage dump.[142] In Hungary, street gangs are beating up Gypsies, although "police are giving the violence against Gypsies low priority."[143] The California State Board of Education votes not to include information on Gypsies in the

Holocaust in its *Model Curriculum for Human Rights and Genocide* published this year for use throughout the school system.[144] The Capitol Children's Museum in Washington, D.C., established as "a tribute to the victims of the Nazis,"[145] adamantly refuses to include Gypsies. In October the Munich city council announces plans forcibly to relocate Gypsies to a containment center on the site of an earlier Nazi deportation and slave-labor camp. The area is a toxic waste dump, is surrounded by barbed wire, and will have guards and guard dogs posted.[146] In Austria, on the anniversary of the Anschluss, Gypsy survivors tell a *London Times* reporter that they are still haunted by fears of recurrent Nazi persecutions.[147]

1989 As West Germany welcomes incoming refugees from East Germany, officials are moving to deport several thousand Gypsies from their country, some of whom have lived there for thirty years. The Gypsies are obliged to seek refuge in an abandoned concentration camp at Neuengamme, near Hamburg, to avoid deportation, where they have no food or sanitation, and where they are attacked and evicted by riot police and dogs. Numbers of Gypsies, including mothers with their babies, are wounded. This prompts a letter of protest from the U.S. House of Representatives to Chancellor Helmut Kohl, who replies that "the federal government does not deem it necessary or expedient to introduce special rules for this category of persons, 'whose situation cannot be compared' with that of the German refugees."[148] Chairman of the U.S. Holocaust Memorial Council Harvey Meyerhoff refuses to sign a petition protesting this, drawn up by the one Romani member of the council, who is told by Mr. Meyerhoff that he is not there to represent Gypsies. Several other members do sign the petition. For the first time ever, the national press, in *Newsweek*, acknowledges the extent of Romani losses in the Holocaust: "Germany had exterminated roughly 70 percent of Europe's Jews and an even higher percentage of its Gypsies."[149] In Spain, reports come of "extreme racism in some towns in Andalusia, where people wanting to expel Gypsies are lynching some in the towns of Pegalajar and Torrendonjimeno in Saens County."[150] In Romania, fifty Gypsies are shot and killed by border guards after having fled from that country only to be turned back by Hungarian officials. Others were wounded in separate incidents involving Yugoslavian border officials.[151]

1990 In February East German Prime Minister Hans Modrow announces that his government will "provide material support to Jewish victims of the Holocaust,'' forty years after West Germany made the same pledge.[152] On April 12, the East German government releases a statement apologizing for the ''immeasurable sorrow'' the National Socialist regime inflicted upon its victims, including Roma and Sinti.[153] Yet, ''while the world celebrates the changes in Eastern Europe, the traditional Gypsy role of scapegoat is already being resurrected in countries like Romania and Hungary,''[154] and ''Collective rights for minorities such as . . . Gypsies remain as elusive as ever.''[155] One account from Romania, whose Romani minority is officially reported as 2.3 million but is unofficially estimated to be closer to ''six million, more than a quarter of the population,''[156] tells of treatment at the hands of Ceauşescu's militia, by which Gypsies were first starved then brutalized: ''We were stripped naked, our legs and hands were tied, and we were made to lean on a table. Then they beat our backs using a rubber hose with iron nuts which they had taken from a tractor.'' The purpose was to force the Gypsies to surrender their personal savings to the government.[157] Reports since Ceauşescu's disposition confirm that brutality against the Roma has increased sharply in Romania, where in the city of Reghin pogroms directed at Gypsies have led to their homes being burnt to the ground and men, women, and children have been dragged to the local cemetery and brutally beaten. In Czechoslovakia and Hungary, street gangs are terrorizing and killing Gypsies;[158] in the latter country Gypsies are being denied entrance into stores, and bus drivers now alert their passengers over the public address system whenever Gypsies board their vehicles.[159] At a governmental session on May 5 in Bremerhaven, Democratic Peoples' Union representative Wilhelm Schmidt, commenting upon the murder of Gypsies in the Third Reich, announces for the record that ''it is a pity that only so few were killed.'' In Recklinghausen a ''Citizens' Patrol'' is organized by State Parliament member Marr Müller, to keep Gypsies out of the town.[160] On March 19, British Conservative Councillor Tookey states in a public address that she wants to see ''the filthy, dirty Gypsies recycled and dumped in the sea,'' following a similar public statement by the Mayor of Dartford in Kent that Gypsies be ''pushed over the White Cliffs of Dover.''[161] A campaign announcement appearing in a British Conservative party periodical reads ''Gypsies: Filth: Crime: One day after the election, we promise to move them OUT.''[162] In June, Gypsy crime specialist Detective Dennis Marlock tells American viewers on the nationally broadcast ''Geraldo Rivera

Show'' that Gypsies had not evolved as a people to the point where they could distinguish between right and wrong "like the rest of us," and that those who became "professors, musicians, and other professionals" were no longer Gypsies, a point reaffirmed by Gypsy specialist Professor John Dowling of Marquette University on the same program.[163] It is revealed that between 75 percent and 80 percent of the children suffering in the Romanian orphanages, where they are dying of AIDS and hepatitis, are Gypsy children, although no attention is drawn to this in the American media.[164] The long-awaited *Encyclopedia of the Holocaust* is published, but devotes just three and a half of its 2,000 pages (a quarter of a percent of its total) to the Romani Holocaust, and provides the figure of Romani losses as 200,000.[165] Yehuda Bauer interprets current "anti-Gypsy sentiment" in Europe as being "in competition" with "radical anti-Semitism" there.[166]

Notes

1. Jean-Pierre Liégeois, *Gypsies: An Illustrated History*, p. 90.

2. Jean Paul Clébert, *The Gypsies*, p. 31.

3. Liégeois, *Illustrated History*, p. 90.

4. Krautz, p. 2, in Sebastian Münster, *Cosmographiae Universalis*, p. 5.

5. Clébert, *Gypsies*, p. 31; François de Vaux de Foletier, *Mille ans d'histoire des Tsiganes*, p. 55.

6. Ibid.

7. Ibid.

8. H. Mode and S. Wolffling, *Zigeuner: Der Weg eines Volkes in Deutschland*, n.p.

9. Liégeois, *Illustrated History*, p. 90.

10. Ibid.

11. Donald Kenrick and Grattan Puxon, *The Destiny of Europe's Gypsies*, p. 44.

12. Vaux de Foletier, *Mille ans*, pp. 61–62.

13. Kenrick and Puxon, *Destiny*, p. 46.

14. Martin Block, *Zigeuner: Ihre Leben und Ihre Seele*, p. 54.

15. Bogumila Michalewicz, "Another Sour Note From Poland," p. 7.

16. Liégeois, *Illustrated History*, p. 90.

17. Kenrick and Puxon, *Destiny*, p. 28.

18. Liégeois, *Illustrated History*, p. 90.

19. Ibid., p. 89.

20. Ibid., p. 90.

21. Ibid., p. 92.

22. Ibid.

23. Kenrick and Puxon, *Destiny*, p. 43.

24. Liégeois, *Illustrated History*, pp. 89, 92.

25. Clébert, *Gypsies*, p. 76.

26. Liégeois, *Illustrated History*, p. 92.

27. Ibid.

28. Elsie M. Hall, "Gentile Cruelty to Gypsies," p. 56.

29. *The Manchester Guardian*, 1969, n.p.

30. Block, *Zigeuner*, p. 62; Liégeois, *Illustrated History*, p. 92; Miriam Novitch, *Le génocide des Tziganes sous le régime nazi*, p. 1.

31. Johann B. Weissenbruch, *Ausfürliche Relation von der famosen Zigeuner-Diebs- Mord- und Räuberbände*, n.p.

32. O. Van Kappen, *Geschiedenis der Zigeuners in Nederland*, n.p.

33. Ian Hancock, "Uniqueness of the Victims: Gypsies, Jews and the Holocaust," p. 58; Liégeois, *Illustrated History*, p. 86.

34. Anon., "Gypsy Punishment in 18th Century Germany," p. 45.

35. Liégeois, *Illustrated History*, p. 89.

36. Kenrick and Puxon, *Destiny*, p. 33.

37. Heinrich Grellmann, *Die Zigeuner*, p. 7.

38. Johann E. Biester, "Über die Zigeuner: besonders im Königreich Preussen," n.p.

39. Kenrick and Puxon, *Destiny*, pp. 50–51; A. Thesleff, "Report on the Gypsy Situation," pp. 91–92.

40. Kenrick and Puxon, *Destiny*, p. 46.

41. Ibid.; also *Journal of the Gypsy Lore Society*, 8:159.

42. Kenrick and Puxon, *Destiny*, p. 60; Liégeois, *Illustrated History*, p. 92; Novitch, *Génocide*, p. 4; Gabrielle Tyrnauer, *The Fate of the Gypsies during the Holocaust*, p. 17.

43. Streck, in G.A. Rakelmann, *Loseblattsammlung für Unterricht und Bildungsarbeit*, p. 70.

44. Liégeois, *Illustrated History*, p. 92.

45. Streck, in Rakelmann, *Loseblattsammlung*, p. 72.

46. Ibid., p. 73; Colin Holmes, "The German-Gypsy Question in Britain, 1904–1906," in Kenneth Lunn, *Hosts, Immigrants and Minorities*, pp. 134–59.

47. Kenrick and Puxon, *Destiny*, p. 56.

48. Karl Binding and Alfred Hoche, *Die Freigabe der Vernichtung Lebensunwertes Lebens*, n.p.; Gisela Bock, "Racism and Sexism in Nazi Germany," p. 401.

49. Binding and Hoche, *Lebensunwertes Leben*, n.p.; Bock, "Racism and Sexism," p. 401.

50. Streck, in Rakelmann, *Loseblattsammlung*, p. 73.

51. Frances Williams, "Swiss Shame over Stolen Children" p. 10.

52. Jeremy Noakes, "Life in the Third Reich," p. 18.

53. Philip Friedman, "How the Gypsies Were Persecuted"; Kenrick and Puxon, *Destiny*, p. 33.

54. Liégeois, *Illustrated History*, p. 92; Novitch, *Génocide*, p. 5.

55. Art. CIX, para. 3, 1918.

56. H. Günther, *Rassenkunde des Deutschen Volkes*, n.p.; Novitch, *Génocide*, p. 5.

57. Novitch, *Génocide*, p. 5

58. J. Scharfenberg, "Omstreiferondet."

59. *Vienna Times* 1 January 1933; *Le Temps* 20 January 1933, p. 33.

60. Bock, "Racism and Sexism," p. 408.

61. Henry W. Shoemaker, "Banishment to Polynesia," pp. 158–60.

62. The laws are numbered RGB-1934/1:531 and BAK-NSD-50/626:10 See also Bock, "Racism and Sexism," p. 409 and Kenrick and Puxon, *Destiny*, p. 71.

63. Emil Brandis, *Ehegesetze von 1935 erläutet*, n.p.; Hans-Joachim Döring, *Die Zigeuner im Nationalsozialistischen Staat*, p. 37; Kenrick and Puxon, *Destiny*, p. 59.

64. J.S. Hohmann, *Geschichte der Zigeunerverfolgung in Deutschland*, p. 102; Kenrick and Puxon, *Destiny*, p. 59.

65. Brandis, *Ehegesetze*, n.p.

66. Grattan Puxon, "The Forgotten Victims," p. 4; Kenrick and Puxon, *Destiny*, p. 70.

67. Block, *Zigeuner*, p. 16.

68. Kenrick and Puxon, *Destiny*, p. 61; Tyrnauer, *Fate of the Gypsies*, p. 20.

69. Kenrick and Puxon, *Destiny*, p. 71.

70. Ibid., p. 72; Novitch, *Génocide*, p. 6.

71. Novitch, *Génocide*, p. 6.

72. Ibid., p. 7.

73. Tobias Portschy, "Kein Schulbesuch für Zigeuner," p. 1.

74. Raul Hilberg, *The Destruction of the European Jews*, p. 48.

75. No. 5557-VIII/38-2026-6.

76. Kenrick and Puxon, *Destiny*, p. 73.

77. Hohmann, *Geschichte der Zigeunerverfolgung*, p. 201.

78. Hilberg, *Destruction of the European Jews*, p. 608.

79. Tyrnauer, *Fate of the Gypsies*, pp. 23–24; Joseph B. Schechtman, "The Gypsy Problem," p. 54.

80. Robert Ritter, *Die Bestandsaufnahme der Zigeuner*, n.p.

81. Kenrick and Puxon, *Destiny*, p. 68.

82. Novitch, *Génocide*, pp. 8–9.

83. Kenrick and Puxon, *Destiny*, p. 74.

84. Novitch, *Génocide*, p. 9.

85. Ibid.

86. J. Tenenbaum, *Race and Reich*, n.p.

87. Johannes Behrendt, "Die Wahrheit über die Zigeuner," p. iii.

88. F. Proester, "Vraždění čs. Cikánů v Buchenwaldu."

89. Novitch, *Génocide*, p. 11; Hilberg, *Destruction of the European Jews*, p. 392.

90. Novitch, *Génocide*, p. 11; Hilberg, *Destruction of the European Jews*, p. 392; Richard Plant, *The Pink Triangle: The Nazi War against the Homosexuals*, p. 218.

91. Novitch, *Génocide*, p. 9.

92. Kenrick and Puxon, *Destiny*, p. 82.

93. Benno Müller-Hill, *Murderous Science: Elimination by Scientific Selection of Jews, Gypsies and Others, Germany 1933–1945*, p. 56.

94. Plant, *The Pink Triangle*, p. 219.

95. Novitch, *Génocide*, p. 11.

96. Ibid., p. 12.

97. Kenrick and Puxon, *Destiny*, pp. 145–46.

98. W. Bednarz, *Obóz stracen w Chełmnię* p. 96; Novitch, *Génocide*, p. 12.

99. Memo from Grawitz to Hitler, No. NO-179; Hilberg, *Destruction of the European Jews*, pp. 602, 1275.

100. Hilberg, *Destruction of the European Jews*, p. 608.

101. Kenrick and Puxon, *Destiny*, p. 86.

102. Yoannis Vrissakis, "Nazis and the Greek Roma: A Personal Testimonial," p. 16.

103. Hilberg, *Destruction of the Jews*, p. 438; Novitch, *Génocide*, p. 13.

104. Vrissakis, "Nazis and the Greek Roma," p. 17.

105. Nuremburg Document No. 1113.

106. Kenrick and Puxon, *Destiny*, p. 86.

107. *Eroica* (Bucharest), October 1942.

108. Nuremburg Document No. PS-682

109. Kenrick and Puxon, *Destiny*, p. 146; Nuremburg Document No. 110.

110. Jerzy Fickowski, *The Gypsies in Poland*, p. 110; Plant, *The Pink Triangle*, p. 220.

111. Plant, *The Pink Triangle*, p. 220.

112. Hilberg, *Destruction of the European Jews*, p. 612.

113. P. Broad, "Zigeuner in Auschwitz," pp. 41–42; Rudolf Franz Höss, *Kommandant in Auschwitz*, pp. 105–6.

114. Various estimates, with sources, are discussed in Hancock, "Uniqueness of the Victims," pp. 54–57.

115. Gerald Reitlinger, *The Final Solution: The Attempt to Exterminate the Jews of Europe, 1939–1945*, p. 489

116. Yehuda Bauer, "Jews, Gypsies and Slavs: Policies of the Third Reich," p. 75.

117. Glenn Infield, *Secrets of the SS*, p. 61.

118. Liégeois, *Illustrated History*, p. 93.

119. Puxon, "Forgotten Victims," p. 24.

120. Christian Bernadac, *L'Holocauste Oublié: Le Massacre des Tsiganes*, p. 34.

121. W.F. Kerswell, "Gipsy Sites," p. 6.

122. Dennis Binns, "The Most Persecuted Minority," p. 4.

123. *Essex Post*, 24 November 1969, p. 3.

124. *Christian Century*, 1971, p. 519.

125. Henriette David, "Novelles de l'étranger: Allemagne," p. 75.

126. Elizabeth Pond, "Romanies: Hitler's Other Victims," p. 17.

127. Bogumila Michalewicz, "Another Sour Note from Poland," p. 7.

128. Lloyd Grove, "Lament of the Gypsies: 40 Years after Auschwitz, Still Petitioning for a Place," p. C4.

129. Reporter Leslie Doolittle of the *Dallas Times Herald*, August 1984, in personal communication.

130. In the Budapest newspapers *Magyar Hirlap* and *Kritika,* spring 1984. See also János Kenedi, "Why Is the Gypsy the Scapegoat and Not the Jew?" p. 14.

131. Simon Wiesenthal, *Justice n' est pas vengeance: Une autobiographie*, p. 237.

132. Simon Wiesenthal, "Tragedy of the Gypsies," p. 6.

133. *Leeds Other Paper*, p. 6.

134. *London Times*, 21 August 1985, n.p.

135. Hans P. Rullmann, "Child Slave-Trade in Yugoslavia: Gypsies' (Romas) Oppression"; see also the *Daily Colonist* (Victoria, B.C.), 1 December 1985, p. 5.

136. Anna Tomforde, "Holocaust Victims Seek Payments: Denial of Further Compensation by West Germany Revives Debate," n.p.

137. Williams, "Swiss Shame," p. 10.

138. Vereniging Lau Mazirel Special Report, Amsterdam, August 1988; letter from CHRC to Czechoslovak government dated 7 October 1986.

139. Mort Rosenblum, "The Gypsy Problem Grows: East Europeans Can't Control Gypsies," p. C1.

140. Robert J. McCartney, "East Berlin Said to Agree to Holocaust Payments," p. A25; Don Oberdorfer, "East Germany Agrees on Reparations for Nazi's Jewish Victims," n.p.

141. Schechtman, "The Gypsy Problem," pp. 52–60; Serge Schmemann, "Case of the Missing Millions," p. A5.

142. Belfast, " 'Burn Gypsies' Belfast Councillor to Visit Glasgow."

143. *Insight Magazine*, 29 August 1988, p. 37.

144. Letter from CSBE President Francis Laufenberg dated 25 April 1988.

145. Bruce Weber, "A Hard Lesson," n.p.

146. *Die Tageszeichnung*, 26 October 1988, n.p.

147. Robert Fisk, "Fear of Nazis Reigns among Vienna Gypsies 50 Years On," p. 2.

148. *Frankfurter Rundschau*, 29 August 1989; *Die Zeit*, 15 September 1989, p. 19; *Tageszeitung*, 23 September 1989, p. 5; letter from Congressman Tom Lantos to Dr. Helmut Kohl dated 18 September 1989; reply from Chancellor Kohl via the West German Embassy in Washington dated 8 November 1989.

149. Jim Miller, "A War to Remember," p. 66

150. Antonio Martinez Amador, "Technical Racism and Transformation in Spanish Gypsy Society," p. 140.

151. Andrew Graham-Yooll, "In Search of Saint George," p. 75.

152. Bob Twigg, "East Germany to Aid Holocaust Victims," p. 4A.

153. Joint Statement from the Second Session of the People's Chamber of the German Democratic Republic, dated 12 April 1990.

154. Fred Goodman, "The Conquering Kings," p. 23.

155. Mary McGrory, "Romania Feeling Free to Hate Again." p. 8A.

156. Victoria Clark, "Gypsies Caught in Spell of Hate," p. 2

157. Oliver Gillie, "The Gypsy King Tortured under Ceauşescu Returns to the Fold," and "Ceauşescu Is Dead, The Gypsy King Lives!"

158. Information bulletin distributed by Phralipe, a Budapest-based Romani organization, dated 3 May 1990.

159. Scott Smedley and Christopher Stephen, "Gypsies in Fear as Democracy Unleashes Hate," p. A23.

160. Pressestelle of the Rom and Cinti Union, Hamburg, dated 13 May 1990.

161. Acton, "The Social Construction and Consequences of Accusations of False Claims to Ethnicity and Cultural Rights," p. 13.

162. *Fight Back*, Spring 1990, no. 23, p. 1.

163. "Gypsies: Fortune Tellers or Fortune Takers?" "The Geraldo Rivera Show," NBC Television, Thursday, 3 June 1990.

164. James Nachtwey, "Romania's Lost Children," p. 31. Also "20/20" Report on the Romanian orphans, ABC Television, Friday, 5 October 1990.

165. Yehuda Bauer, "Gypsies," in Israel Gutman, ed., p. 637.

166. Yehuda Bauer, "Continuing Ferment in Eastern Europe," p. 1.

3

The Romani Pořajmos
The Nazi Genocide of Gypsies in Germany and Eastern Europe

HENRY R. HUTTENBACH

The Nazi assault on Gypsies as an undesirable group was launched in the first months of the Third Reich. By the end of 1933, the outlines of a policy of total removal and, if possible, extinction, were in place. In addition, Gypsies had also been numbered among those destined for mass sterilization. The goal of preventing their propagation had been pronounced on 14 July 1933, when the new cabinet issued a statement that proclaimed the concept of *Lebensunwertesleben* (lives unworthy of life), a category of person that, at the time, specifically and indiscriminately included and embraced all Gypsies.[1] Shortly thereafter, exploratory contacts were made with the League of Nations to assess the practicability of allocating one or two Polynesian islands to which Gypsies could be deported.[2] By September 1933, the Ministry of Interior announced a more realizable preliminary plan to arrest persons with no fixed and permanent addresses (i.e., primarily Gypsies) and to place them in special detention camps to take them out of the mainstream of society.[3] There the Gypsies would be rendered criminally harmless and biologically "futureless" (*Zukunftslos*) through mass sterilization.

In retrospect, the central ingredients for a formula of genocide, for the complete extermination of the Gypsies, had been created: an ideology that deprived them of the basic right to life; a process of law by edict that subjected them to totalitarian rule; a hypothetical plan to deport them abroad, and a more concrete one to isolate them from the citizenry, through imprisonment and a technology of physical mutilation, that would deny them progeny and a link with a biological future. Thus, by the end of 1933, a skeletal blueprint for the genocide of Gypsies by the racial architects of the Nazi regime had been drawn up on the eve of the first Nazi roundup of Gypsies in January 1934.

It is a familiar story, except that it has largely been told and retold in conjunction with the Jews' experience. The National Socialist vision of a racially purified Europe, however, extended far beyond their self-proclaimed and obsessive anti-Semitism. Though the war against Jews remained at the core of their racial thinking and actions, the National Socialist dream of an Aryan-German dominated empire from the Atlantic Ocean to the Ural Mountains encompassed a revolutionary rearrangement of Europe's demographic composition. According to their racial scheme, Europe's populations consisted of a descending hierarchy of peoples ranging from the racially superior Aryans, of whom the Germans were the highest embodiment, to those racially inferior, all the way to the Jews who were perceived as an anti-race, a people outside the pale of humanity, whose extermination became a sacred cause of the party and the state through which it exercised its demonic power.

Between the Germans, at the zenith of the pyramid of human races, and the Jews, at the nadir of racial existence, lay the sundry nations of Europe whom the Nazis classified either as essentially "redeemable" (*Lebenswertesleben*), such as the Scandinavians, or as fundamentally "expendable" (*Lebensunwertesleben*), such as the Slavs. The latter were categorized as *Untermenschen* (subhumans) and were, as such, candidates for eventual annihilation. Existentially, the Slavs were particularly vulnerable because they inhabited the strategic territories east of Germany, from the Elbe to the Volga. German rulers had long coveted these territories as part of their quest for a global, geopolitical advantage and as an area of *Lebensraum* (living space) that the German people could colonize and thus become a *Weltvolk* (world nation) that rivaled that of the English-speaking Anglo-Saxons.

In the initial classification by the Third Reich's racial specialists,

Gypsies ranked between Slavs, who were considered subhumans, and Jews, who were antihumans. While policy toward Slavs remained moot until the invasion of Poland in September 1939, actions against Gypsies intensified during the prewar years. Though they made up less than 0.1 percent of the German population (between 20,000 and 30,000), Gypsies, like Jews, received disproportionate attention from the authorities as the various agencies of the state sought to transform Germany into a racially pure society. Between 1934 and the outbreak of World War II, a series of laws and regulations created a web of restrictions that set Gypsies apart and severely restricted their ability, individually and collectively, to survive. In July 1934, a decree forbade intermarriage between Germans and Gypsies.[4] The same year, the law permitting the deportation of aliens was extended to foreign Gypsies.[5] In September 1935, the Nuremberg Laws declared the Gypsies "an alien People"[6] and restricted all sexual contact between Aryans and non-Aryans.[7] During the summer Olympics of 1936, hundreds of Gypsy men in Bavaria were arrested by the police under Gestapo supervision and shipped off to the Dachau concentration camp outside Munich where they were sterilized.[8]

In order to buttress the Gypsy classification as "an alien people," the government and its pseudo-intellectual racists shored up its anti-Gypsy ideology in 1937. The Ministry of Interior's Dr. Hans Globke introduced the general theory of "foreign" blood running exclusively through Gypsy and Jewish veins,[9] while Dr. Robert Körber linked Gypsies and Jews to their foreign, Asiatic roots.[10] According to Dr. Emil Brandis, this made them an "alien" element in the midst of a Nordic (Aryan) population.[11] With this ideological foundation, Nazi anti-Gypsy thought linked up historic prejudices toward Gypsies that saw them as unclean and antisocial.

These policies were based on age-old discriminatory practices and attitudes that predated the Nazi assumption of power in January 1933. Soon after the Gypsies arrived on German territory in the fifteenth century, they were met by violent, negative reactions.[12] Over the next 100 years, both Protestants and Catholics expressed their disapproval of the continued Gypsy presence, and felt that the Gypsies threatened the spiritual values of Christian society, were a security threat to the various German states, and affected the physical health of the general population. Increasingly, Gypsies were characterized and caricatured as non-Christians, as foreign spies, as bearers of fatal diseases, and accused of uncivilized practices such as cannibalism. As a result, intensive steps were taken to prevent their immigration or to expedite their departure. In some cases, it was legal to kill and rape Gypsies; in other instances, they were banished, or were terrorized to force them to leave. Similar policies were adopted elsewhere in Europe, from the Papal States to the Lowlands, from the Rhine to the Vistula.[13] Throughout the seventeenth and eighteenth centuries, Gypsy communities suffered from trumped-up charges punishable by execution, lynch mobs, pogroms, corporal punishment, and torture that included compulsory branding. In Prussia in 1722, it became a capital offense just to be a Gypsy.[14]

Early scholarly studies of Gypsies, inspired by the inquisitive spirit of the Enlightenment, merely aggravated the general climate. Most of the "findings" betrayed the prejudices of the investigators, who found Gypsies to be an "unwholesome" subject of inquiry. Again and again, Gypsies were depicted as "nauseating" and as "vermin."[15] In Prussia, Bavaria, and Swabia, the police, the military, the church, census takers, educators, and other government officials were recruited to "combat the Gypsy nuisance."[16]

After World War I, the climate of intolerance and racism toward Gypsies intensified, despite the more liberal intentions of the architects of Weimar Germany. As early as 1920, the German language was "enriched" by the ominous term *Ballastexistenz* (deadweight) in connection with Gypsies[17]—a forerunner of the potentially lethal Nazi label, *Lebensunwertesleben*. Some ideologues supported the execution of Gypsies to rid society of these *Ballastexistenzen*. Meanwhile, Weimar's federal states passed special Gypsy legislation that included the prohibition of group travel and forced work in labor camps for those who were not gainfully employed, a status that was determined by government agencies.[18] By 1933, almost all Gypsies had been fingerprinted, especially in Baden and Bavaria.[19]

Within four years, the mainly traditional twin character of Nazi anti-Gypsy policy, segregation and removal, began to metamorphose into a recognizable system that evolved from one that focused on elimination by means of mass deportation beyond the borders of the state to one that generated its own still unexpressed "means" of ridding itself of an unwanted population within its own borders. The recently established *Rassenhygienische und bevölkerungsbiologische Forschungsstelle* (Department of Racial Hygiene and Population Biology or RHPB), a research branch of the Ministry of Health, set about to determine the precise racial classification for Gypsies as *Un-*

termenschen and to find workable criteria to determine Gypsy identity so that they could be accurately classified as such. Spurred on by its director, Dr. Robert Ritter,[20] the Berlin-based organization set up a network of regional and local bureaus whose staffs were to prepare a data bank of non-Aryans according to specific racial rubrics, among them the Gypsy race. Gypsies, like Jews, were considered a race because they had "alien" (*artfremdes*) blood.[21]

According to the RHPB, Gypsy genealogical and racial identity stemmed from one's immediate ancestors. Upon the recommendations of Ritter,[22] RHPB investigators went back four generations, to eight great-grandparents, which was in contrast to the more "lenient" Jewish guidelines, which required a search of four grandparents. Depending on the number of Gypsy ancestors, individuals investigated by the RHPB were classified according to five categories ranging from "Z" (*Vollzigeuner* = Full Gypsy) to "NZ" (*Nicht-Zigeuner* = Non-Gypsy); in between were three grades of "M" (*Mischling* = Mixed Blood): (a) "ZM+" (five or more Gypsy great-grandparents, (b) "ZM–" (four Gypsy great-grandparents), and (c) "ZM" (three or fewer Gypsy great-grandparents). Nazi racial guidelines dictated that as few as two Gypsy great-grandparents were enough to "condemn" a person as a member of what had been defined by the RHPB as a "parasitical" race. At the same time, Nazi racial propaganda was widely disseminated throughout the Reich to persuade the public to support state policy.[23]

On order by Reichsführer-SS Heinrich Himmler, head of the Gestapo and the Waffen-SS, Gypsies were further classified by tribes: Lalleri, Sinti, and Romani, who, Ritter recommended, should be isolated and put on reservations. According to Himmler and his advisers, the Lalleri, German Gypsies because of their long residency in the country, and the racially "pure" Sinti, who made up about 10 percent of all Gypsies in the Reich, were to be declared Aryans. The Romani were considered racially "stained" for having intermarried over the centuries before coming to Germany and for bringing racial impurities with them. Himmler created considerable confusion at the RHPB with these guidelines because they fundamentally contradicted prevailing racial policy. If Gypsies were "parasites" and "asocials," then 100 percent pure Gypsies should be the most "dangerous" and the most *Lebensunwertesleben*. But if Gypsies were considered Aryans that originated in India, then "full-blooded" Gypsies ought to be ranked alongside German Aryans! The discrepancy was never resolved, and, as will be shown, did not significantly alter their final fate, regardless of their tribal status. More operable were the policies of the security police, the SS and SD, who arrested anyone declared a Gypsy. For the next four years, the RHPB compiled a comprehensive racial file for every Gypsy in the Third Reich and its annexed territories in Eastern Europe. By the time of the Wannsee Conference of 20 January 1942 that officially decided to implement the "Final Solution" of racial undesirables, Berlin was ready to launch a Gypsy extermination program.[24]

Domestically, these policies were buffeted by a series of mass arrests of Gypsies on a variety of "charges." Beginning in April 1938, German Gypsies were arrested for begging and sent to Buchenwald. In order to locate Gypsies not yet classified and registered, the authorities used the records of the *Wohlfahrtsamt* (Welfare Bureau). Gypsies were also rounded up during drives by district criminal police to meet their quota of able-bodied men for highway construction.[25] But beneath the surface of these practices developed a groundswell of far more radical thinking. It is best exemplified by a memorandum sent on 9 January 1938 by Gauleiter Portschy of Steiermark to Reichsminister Dr. Heinz Lammers. In it, Portschy argued that since Gypsies were a concern of public health, "a parasite on the body of our people," the logical solution should be mass sterilization and extermination through slave labor.[26] In late 1939, the government passed a decree on nomads and arrested 400 Gypsies, who were sent to Dachau. By 1941, large numbers of Gypsies were confined in major concentration camps.[27] These actions were motivated by the Nazi conviction that Gypsies were an inherent "danger" by virtue of their "alien blood," a view formalized by Himmler, who was now in charge of the implementation of most Nazi non-Aryan racial policies.[28] Thanks to the work of the "scientists" in RHPB, the theory that the "Gypsy Question" was largely a matter of race had been given significant support and affected all future government decisions on this matter.

In Germany proper, more and more Gypsies from the pre-1938 Reich had been subject to incarceration and deportation. Those selected for deportation, taken from lists compiled since 1937, were usually shipped by train from one of several assembly points, such as Berlin, Prague, Vienna, Magdeburg, Munich, and Neubrandenburg. Those not deported were kept in Mauthausen and its satellite camps, which had the largest Gypsy death toll of any single concentration camp. Most that died were killed or worked to death as part of the Extermination-through-Work policy *Vernichtung durch Arbeit*.[29]

There was some delay in the deportations from the pre-1938 Reich because of Himmler's idiosyncratic desire to spare the few "pure" Lalleri and Sinti; the vast majority of Romani were shipped out bit by bit from the various camps where they had been incarcerated since 1937. The last of the Lalleri and Sinti were finally expelled after strong urgings by Martin Bormann, head of the Chancellery, on 3 December 1942.[30] Till then, there had been hesitation to deport all Gypsies because some felt that they were to be spared for some officially condoned work.[31] It is possible that Bormann had been influenced by the discussions between Otto Thierack, the Minister of Justice, and Joseph Goebbels, the Minister of Propaganda, in August 1942, about the extermination of asocials.[32] A month later, both had spoken of the *annihilation* of all asocials with Goebbels stressing that "Jews and Gypsies should be exterminated unconditionally."[33] Thierack won Himmler over to this policy on 18 September while Himmler was in the Ukraine,[34] though the latter still wanted to make an exception of the "German" Gypsies. On 13 October, Thierack called on Bormann to "free" Germany of *all* Jews, Poles, Russians, *and Gypsies*.[35] A week later, the former ordered all asocials, including Gypsies, currently held in jails and psychiatric wards, to be turned over to the SS.[36] He then persuaded Bormann to have all Gypsies, regardless of their tribal/clan nomenclature, removed from German soil. Himmler followed this up with a memo on 16 December that ordered all remaining Gypsies to be sent to Auschwitz,[37] though many ended up in Mauthausen.[38]

In general, Gypsies were deported along with other groups, though, sometimes, they were placed in separate railroad cars that were attached to Jewish transport trains. They never knew their destination, received no drink or food, and lived in unheated cars where they were indiscriminately beaten and shot by their guards. Those who were not deported from Germany remained in concentration camps at Buchenwald, Dachau, Mauthausen, Ravensbrück, and elsewhere. During the war, they were subjected to two consecutive genocidal policies: *Vernichtung durch Arbeit* and *Sonderbehandlung* (special handling, i.e., direct execution). The former used Gypsies as exploitable labor, where excessive work was combined with extremely cruel treatment and workers were deprived of all basic needs. The latter involved those too ill or weak to work who were put to death.[39]

One of the most infamous camps was Ravensbrück, the special concentration camp for women, which had inmates from all over Nazi occupied Europe. The Gypsies there were categorized as "asocials," confined in separate "blocs," and forced to wear a black triangle. Shortly after their arrival in Ravensbrück, all Gypsy women were sterilized, a policy not uniformly extended to other groups.[40]

On 2 March 1944, the authorities began to dismantle Ravensbrück and shipped Gypsies and others in closed cattle cars to Mauthausen, a killing center for asocials, on 29 June. Over the next two months, 440 Gypsy women and children were transferred from Ravensbrück to Mauthausen. During this period, all Gypsy children under fourteen years old were killed according to a blanket order that affected all concentration and labor camps. Toward the end of August, Johann Schwarzhuber, the former commandant of the men's camp at Auschwitz II, who oversaw the *Zigeunernacht* of 1 August 1944, became commander of Mauthausen. Shortly after his arrival, he ordered almost 800 Gypsies to be gassed, in keeping with a new policy to allow only able-bodied adults to live. By the beginning of 1945, there were still 550 Gypsies in Ravensbrück. They were sent to Auschwitz for immediate extermination since that facility was scheduled to cease operations soon because of the rapid advance of the Red Army.[41]

Throughout the rest of Europe, the state machinery designed to deal with Gypsies went into high gear after war broke out in the fall of 1939. German officials were determined to empty the Third Reich of this "asocial" element, and by 1 December 1939, had shipped 18,000 Gypsies to the General Gouvernement in Poland, which was becoming a dumping ground for all unwanted races.[42] According to Dr. Johannes Behrendt of the RHPB, Gypsies ought to be subject to physical extermination because they were, without exception, a congenitally sick people that had to be stamped out like any fatally contagious disease. On 30 January 1940, a special conference was held, which decided to deport 30,000 more European Gypsies to Poland. Berlin, Prague, and Vienna were chosen as coordination sites for the transports, and most were sent to Jewish ghettos such as Łódź and Warsaw.[43]

In the ghettos of the General Gouvernement, Gypsies suffered the same fate as the Jewish majority. In response to an order issued by Adolph Eichmann, head of the Gestapo's section IV B4 for Evacuations and Jews, in July 1941, 5,000 Reich Gypsies were deported to the Łódź Ghetto between 16 October and 4 November 1941.[44] It was decided to halt further transportation of the remaining 25,000 because Łódź was to be annexed to the Reich in November, which meant the inhabitants of the ghetto would have to be removed.[45]

The Gypsies in Łódź were kept physically apart from others and were placed in houses on 70–100 Brzezińska Street, which was separated from the rest of the ghetto by a deep ditch and a high barbed-wire fence. According to the German officials, Gypsies were suspected to be arsonists, and Himmler suggested that if a fire took place anywhere in the ghetto, ten Gypsies would be shot for each incident.[46] In the first two weeks, they were subjected to barbaric treatment by the Germans. Repeatedly, drunk Germans would attack the Gypsy sector at night, and beat and rape the helpless prisoners. They also suffered from complete deprivation. Unlike the Jews, they were not allowed to work and had no way even to get scraps of food. Without nutrition, or adequate sanitary and medical facilities, the Gypsies quickly fell victim to the ravages of spotted typhus. Within two weeks after their arrival, 5,000 Gypsies were ill with this disease, though it had one "positive" effect: it kept the Germans away. Instead, they ordered Jewish doctors into the Gypsy quarter to "treat" the sick without medicine. All of the Jewish physicians contracted the deadly fever and died.[47]

To help administer the Gypsy quarter, the Germans appointed a *Zigeunerrat* (Gypsy Council) of nine men from the "favored" Lalleri and Sinti tribes.[48] In January and February 1942, they were ordered to draw up lists of names for those to be "resettled."[49] In March and April, all of the quarter's Gypsies were shipped to Chelmno (Kulmhof), where they were immediately killed in new gas vans.[50]

In April 1942 the Nazis resumed the deportations of Gypsies from the Greater Third Reich, and began to send them to the Warsaw Ghetto. Upon arrival there, the Gypsies were first locked in its prison, deloused, issued an armband with a "Z," and then released into the ghetto.[51] On 17 June 1942, approximately 250 Reich Gypsy families were given housing on Pokorna Street.[52] According to Emmanuel Ringelblum, the chronicler of the Warsaw Ghetto, the arrival of the Gypsies was an ominous signal of the impending doom awaiting the Jews. Recognizing the Gypsies as a people specifically designated by the Nazis for extermination, Ringelblum concluded that this was also to be the fate for the Jews.[53]

When the order came to dissolve the entire ghetto system, Gypsies and Jews faced mass destruction. As a part of Operation Reinhard, which was designed to rid the General Gouvernement of all Jews and Gypsies, they were shipped by train to Belsec, Sobibor, and Treblinka, the three locations expressly set up for one purpose only—mass killing in gas chambers. Approximately 2,000 Gypsies perished in Treblinka from the summer of 1942[54] through February 1943.[55] Most were gassed, though a few were shot. An unknown number of Gypsies are also believed to have been killed in Sobibor.[56] For the most part, though, the majority of Gypsies in ghettos in the General Gouvernement were shot on the spot. Another 1,000 were executed by firing squads in the counties of Jaslo, Rzeszow, and Sanok. In 1943 another 100 perished in the same manner in Radomsk. The same year, several hundred Gypsy families were shot in the region of Ostrow-Mazowiecka and Siedke counties.[57] The same pattern of systematic extermination must have taken place throughout the General Gouvernement, though there is no data to confirm this assumption.

Auschwitz-Birkenau, a huge forced-labor camp and mass extermination center, had the largest concentration of Gypsies. Initially, 16,000 Gypsy men, women, and children were deported to Auschwitz from all over Europe,[58] including virtually all of Slovakia's Gypsies, who had been deported on a trumped-up charge of cannibalism.[59] Though categorized formally as ''asocials,'' and identified with a black triangle, the Auschwitz Gypsies were confined to a special Gypsy quarter, the so-called ''Family Camp.''[60] Though Auschwitz Commander Rudolf Höss claimed the Gypsies were his ''favorite'' prisoners, they suffered as much as the Jews from lack of adequate food, horrid sanitary facilities, and improper medical attention.[61]

Initially, Himmler had intended to ''spare'' some of the Gypsies, but changed his mind during his inspection tour of the camp on 17–18 July 1942. After seeing their terrible, hopeless conditions, he ordered the sick and those unable to work killed on ''humanitarian'' grounds.[62] He was not ready, however, to issue a blanket order totally to exterminate all Gypsies, since he needed those still able to work. On 31 July–1 August, the bulk of the Auschwitz Gypsies were gassed under the supervision of Johann Schwarzhuber during what is now remembered as the *Zigeunernacht* (the Night of the Gypsies);[63] only 1,500 were spared.[64] However, with new arrivals, and the constant weeding out of ''useless'' Gypsies, the number at Auschwitz finally stabilized at around 4,000–5,000. Some came from Belgium and France, where they had been rounded up by the Vichy government and by the Gestapo in northern France.[65]

On 14 September 1942, Dr. Gerig Thierack of the Justice Ministry told Propaganda Minister Joseph Goebbels that "Gypsies should be exterminated unconditionally." Four days later, he proposed to Himmler that he be able to turn over all present and future Gypsy criminals under his jurisdiction directly to the SS for *Sonderbehandlung* (execution). On 20 October Thierack ordered his ministry to send all jailed Gypsies to concentration camps, though Himmler hesitated to send them on to death camps. Instead, Martin Bormann issued a blanket order (*Erlass*) to have all Gypsies deported to Auschwitz on 29 January 1943. The next month, Eichmann began to deport all Gypsies remaining in the dozens of concentration camps scattered throughout the Greater Reich to Auschwitz.

Once there, Gypsies, especially from Slovakia and Galicia, were subjected not only to the "usual" inhumane conditions and treatment but also to medical experimentation.[66] Though Dr. Josef Mengele was in charge of the actual experiments, he had to obtain permission to work on his "subjects." Gypsies were under the jurisdiction of the RSHA (*Reichssicherheitshauptamt*, Reich Security Main Office) in Berlin, where Brigadeführer Artur Nebe headed the Gypsy desk and acted on Himmler's behalf. He gave Mengele final approval to experiment on "qualified" Gypsies. One project dealt with the conversion of sea water to drinking water, which caught Nebe's attention. He "volunteered" Gypsy *Mischlinge* (mongrels [Nazi: Mixed Blood]) for these experiments without waiting for a specific request since he felt that they were "better suited" than Jewish subjects.

Mengele regularly entered the Gypsy quarter in Auschwitz to search for twins. His trips attracted large numbers of starving children because he spoke kindly to them and gave them candy. During these visits, Mengele noticed many cases of the fatal noma tumors among the Gypsies, which led him to conclude that the tumor's pathology was genetic and common to them. These observations contributed to the body of "scientific" information about Gypsies that was generated by the "research" of Nazi politicians, party functionaries, and social and medical scientists. In Mengele's case, he took a special interest in Gypsy twins, whom he had killed in order to make a special comparative "study" of Gypsy and Aryan eye coloration.[67] Another one of Mengele's "medical" experiments was to impregnate Gypsy women through artificial insemination and then do abortions at different stages of fetal development.

In May 1944, the camp's surviving Gypsies were transferred to

Buchenwald and scattered among its subordinate camps, where most perished. In all, 10,097 Gypsy males and 10,849 females were sent to Auschwitz. The few survivors came principally from Galicia. They had not been rounded up until the spring of 1944, and shortly after their arrival had been sent to Buchenwald.[68]

In other regions of Nazi Europe, the fate of Gypsies varied from territory to territory. On the eastern front, Gypsies were subjected to the actions of the *Einsatzgruppen*, who were given *explicit* orders to kill Gypsies[69] and who divided the occupied Soviet Union into four zones in order to facilitate their work. According to the *Einsatzgruppen* Operational Reports to RSHA headquarters in Berlin, Gypsies were classified as "criminal elements" and "asocials" who were a threat to public order and health. The activities of the *Einsatzgruppen* began with the invasion of the Soviet Union in the summer of 1941. Instructed to "kill all Jews, Gypsies, and Commissars" as they moved with front line units in Russia, they continued their indiscriminate executions until March 1943, when they were ordered only to kill "migrant" Gypsies and spare "nonmigrant" ones.[70] The former possibly referred to the Vesitka Roma, who camped in the forests, and the latter, the Foritka Roma, the more sedentary clans who settled on the outskirts of towns and villages, and resided in one location for at least two years. This differentiation contradicted the formula applied in Germany where wandering Gypsies, the Lalleri and the Sinti, were favored over the other Romani who were partly assimilated into urban society. Logical inconsistency notwithstanding, the order, however, came too late to save any significant numbers of Gypsies, since the *Einsatzgruppen* had already killed most Gypsies in their zones of operations. In eastern Latvia, where several Vesitka Roma clans lived, German authorities ordered all Gypsies to gather in Ludza, Rezekne, and Vilane in the summer of 1941. Gypsies in the latter two towns were shot in nearby forests, while those in Ludza were locked in a synagogue where they starved to death. The Germans used other methods to round up the more assimilated Foritka Roma in the rest of Latvia. They asked Janis Lejamanis, the head of Latvia's Gypsies, and Vanya Kochanowski, a university student, to compile a list of able-bodied Roma classified according to special skills. This provided them with the names and whereabouts of virtually all Gypsies with a fixed address. They were then able to make mass arrests and shoot the bulk of the Gypsies, especially women, children, the aged, and the sick.[71] The only ones spared were a few

Gypsy men with military experience whom they drafted into the army. Only a few Latvian Gypsies survived the war. The Germans also killed most of the Gypsies in Byelorussia and the Crimea.[72]

In southeastern Europe, the fate of the Gypsies was equally tragic. Their property had been seized by German military authorities soon after they occupied the area in May 1941.[73] The following month, General Franz Böhme, the "Plenipotentiary Commanding General in Serbia," asked permission to deport them, presumably to Auschwitz, to save the manpower and expense of keeping them in special camps.[74] The RSHA in Berlin agreed, but ordered the general to eliminate them, hoping to spare itself the trouble of organizing deportation transports. Böhme initially shied away from this solution, but was spared the embarrassment of circumventing orders from above by fortuitous events which "legitimized" his Gypsy executions. A spate of attacks on German occupation forces by Yugoslav partisans gave him his rationale: he could execute innocent Gypsies as hostages. He based his policy on arguments framed by his legal counsel, Staatsrat Harald Turner, head of the civil administration of the military government. In a 26 October *Rundschreiben* (memorandum) to all military unit headquarters, Turner stated that ". . . Gypsies . . . [like the Jews] are an element of insecurity and thereby a danger to public order and peace." In addition, he wrote, "The Gypsy cannot, by virtue of psychological and physical conditions, be a harmonious member of the community of nations."[75]

Beginning on 9 October, Böhme announced his new policy to use Gypsies as hostages. The next day, he ordered the mass arrest of all Jewish, Communist, and Gypsy men. One hundred would be shot for each German killed by partisans, and fifty for each German wounded. The killings were so successful that in less than a year, Turner proudly proclaimed that "Serbia is the only country in which the Jewish and Gypsy questions have been solved." A Belgian journal reaffirmed this fact on 13 November 1942, when it reported that all Gypsies in Serbia had been killed.[76]

In neighboring Croatia, a Nazi puppet state since April 1941, the Gypsy "question" was dealt with by its rulers. Immediately after it gained "sovereignty," the *Ustaša* (Croatian National Movement) government of Ante Pavelić initiated a vicious, genocidal crusade to rid Croatia of non-Croats, meaning, above all, Serbs, Jews, and Gypsies. The latter were designated as "nomads" and placed in twenty-two of Croatia's concentration camps. By the time that 500 Gypsies were sent to Auschwitz in November 1942, almost all of the 28,500 Croatian Gypsy prisoners had been murdered. By October 1943, only 200–300 Gypsies were still alive in Croatia,[77] barely 1 percent of the region's prewar Gypsy population.[78]

In Greece, the Gypsies suffered a fate similar to those in Serbia, though on a smaller, less systematic scale. Initially, the Germans seemed unconcerned about the Greek Gypsies. However, in response to increased activities by Greek partisans at the end of 1941 and early 1942, the military government introduced a hostage system. The first roundups included 300 Gypsies. Groups of fifty were then selected for execution. This practice continued throughout 1942 as resistance mounted, with very few survivors among these pools of hostages. In 1943, the military command issued an order to round up all Gypsies for immediate deportation to Auschwitz. Had it not been for the swift intervention of the prime minister and, especially, Archbishop Damaskinos, hundreds of Gypsies would have perished prior to the liberation of the country. Both men successfully appealed to the German military authorities to rescind the order, who by this time began to fear the postwar consequences of their crimes.[79]

This, and similar actions by the Nazis and their collaborators throughout Europe, had a dramatic impact on the Gypsy survival rate during the *Pořajmos*, though it varied from region to region. Of the 16,275 Gypsies recorded in the pre-1938 Reich, 14,325 were murdered, while about 12 percent survived. Entire communities were wiped out in Croatia, and only 1 percent of its Gypsies were alive after 1945. Gypsy communities in eastern Latvia, Byelorussia, Crimea, Serbia, and central Poland suffered equally high losses. There were also no Gypsy survivors from the death centers at Belsec, Chelmno, Majdanek, Sobibor, or Treblinka.[80]

Significant large-scale survival did take place among the Russian and Polish Xaladitka Gypsies. About 5,500 of Poland's 19,000 prewar Gypsies survived, primarily the Vesitka Roma, the forest clans whose life-style enabled them to hide in wooded areas unfamiliar to the Germans. Initially less visible than the urban-linked Foritka Roma, these wandering Vesitka clans stood a better chance of evading the urban-based *Einsatzgruppen* "hunting" expeditions sent into the countryside and its forests. Only betrayal by peasants or by partisan bands stood between these Gypsies and safety. There are, significantly, no such recorded incidents of unfriendly Polish, Byelorussian, or Ukrainian villagers or partisans providing the Ger-

mans with information about the whereabouts of Gypsies. Some Gypsies even joined underground resistance forces in Lublin and elsewhere. One factor that helped these Gypsies survive was their long-
standing suspicion of the *gadže* or non-Gypsy; while in hiding, they
kept their distance not only from the Germans but from the general
Polish population, mistrusting both and not relying on the good will
of anyone. Croatia's Gypsies were not as lucky since they were
trapped in a small area easily scoured by the *Ustaše* headhunters who
were determined to eliminate every Gypsy until the day that the war
ended. The German Roma were equally hard hit, particularly after
they lost Himmler's protection. Those drafted into the Wehrmacht
were eventually expelled and executed.

Given present research data, the total number of Gypsies killed by
the Nazi genocidal policy can only be estimated, ranging from a conservative low of 250,000[81] to a possible high of 500,000, out of an
estimated population of 885,000 European Gypsies in 1939.[82] One
source claims that 75 percent of Europe's Gypsies were killed by the
Nazis,[83] while others, using much higher prewar European Gypsy
population estimates, have claimed that 1 million to 4 million died in
the *Porajmos*.[84] Simon Wiesenthal, among others, has stated that up
to 80 percent of all Gypsies in Nazi-occupied Europe were exterminated; some scholars feel 70 percent is more accurate.[85] None of
this will be resolved without a systematic review of the sources and
careful statistical calculation. The data is available, but it will require
enormous scholarly analysis.

After the war, the fate of the Gypsies, as victims of a concerted effort to exterminate them, was subsumed in the overall charges of
"crimes against humanity." Though the policy of genocide of the
Jews also received no attention per se, its quantitative enormity in
terms of millions of victims and overwhelming documentation made
it impossible to avoid acknowledgment of this facet of the Nazis' extermination policies. The Gypsies' victimization, however, by virtue
of sparser evidence and less concerted efforts by the four Allied pros-
ecutions, became a mere footnote of the Nuremberg Trials. It was not
until 1962, during the Eichmann Trial in Jerusalem, that any Nazi was
charged with having perpetrated or participated in a specific crime
aimed at Gypsies per se, as stated in Article 11 of the Israeli charge
sheet.[86] During the examination of Nazi practices against the Gypsies,
from racial registration to mass shooting and gassing, the Israeli court
found Eichmann a major figure in what was defined as a program of

extermination of the Gypsies. Every act, including sterilization and medical experimentation, fit into the Nazi scheme of physically eliminating the Gypsy "race" from German-dominated Europe. Nevertheless, the court only accused Eichmann of "crimes against humanity" with respect to the Gypsies, stopping short of applying the word genocide to describe the crime of extermination, which it reserved for the Jews.[87] Jewish scholars of the Holocaust, however, have readily acknowledged the similarity of the Gypsy experience.

It was the express purpose of this essay to demonstrate that the Nazi policy vis-à-vis the Romani people was nothing short of systematic genocide from the underlying ideology and propaganda to the methodology of administering the rules and regulations of racial politics, to the execution of the means to achieve the ultimate goal of ridding Europe's populations of all Gypsies. On all levels, the Romani *Poŕajmos* qualifies as a bona fide case of genocide as defined by the United Nations, a crime that must be seen in the context of the grand revolutionary Nazi scheme of racial "purification."

Notes

1. Gisela Bock, "Racism and Sexism in Nazi Germany," p. 408.

2. Henry W. Shoemaker, "Banishment to Polynesia," pp. 158–60.

3. Ian Hancock, "Gypsy History in Germany and Neighboring Lands: A Chronology Leading to the Holocaust," a forthcoming article to appear in a special issue of *Nationalities Papers*.

4. *Reichsgesetzbuch*, 1934/1, No. 531.

5. Gabrielle Tyrnauer, "Germany and Gypsies," p. 178.

6. Hans-Joachim Döring, *Die Zigeuner im Nationalsozialistischen Staat*, p. 37.

7. Donald Kenrick and Grattan Puxon, *The Destiny of Europe's Gypsies*, p. 73.

8. Hancock, "Gypsy History."

9. J.S. Hohmann, *Geschichte der Zigeunerverfolgung in Deutschland*, p. 102.

10. Hancock, "Gypsy History."

11. Emil Brandis, *Ehegesetze von 1935 erläutet*.

12. For example see: Jean-Paul Clébert, *The Gypsies*, p. 31; and François de Vaux de Foletier, *Mille ans d'histoire des Tsiganes*.

13. For example see: Martin Block, *Zigeuner: Ihre Leben und Ihre Seele*, p. 54; Kenrick and Puxon, *Destiny*, pp. 28, 44, 46; and Vaux de Foletier, *Mille ans*, p. 61.

14. Hancock, "Gypsy History."

15. Heinrich Grellmann, *Die Zigeuner*, p. 7.

16. For example see: Kenrick and Puxon, *Destiny*, pp. 46, 50, 56, 60.

17. Bock, "Racism and Sexism," p. 401. The concept was introduced by Karl Binding and Alfred Hoche, *Die Freigabe der Vernichtung Lebensunwerten Lebens*.

18. Hancock, "Gypsy History."

19. Helen Fein, *Accounting for Genocide: National Responses and Jewish Victimization during the Holocaust*, p. 28.

20. Gabrielle Tyrnauer, *The Fate of the Gypsies during the Holocaust*, p. 19.

21. J. S. Hohmann, *Zigeuner und Zigeunerwissenschaft*, p. 201.

22. Tyrnauer, ''Germany and Gypsies,'' pp. 182–83.

23. Ibid.

24. Rüdiger Vossen, *Zigeuner: Roma, Sinti, Gitanos, Gypsies zwischen Verfolgung und Romantisierung*, p. 70.

25. Philip Friedman, ''The Extermination of the Gypsies,'' p. 153.

26. Ernst Klee, *Euthenasie im NS-Staat: die Vernichtung Lebensunwerten Lebens*, p. 64; and H. Buchheim, ''Die Aktion 'Arbeitsche Reich,' '' p. 191.

27. Tyrnauer, ''Germany and Gypsies,'' p. 179.

28. Hohmann, *Zigeuner und Zigeunerwissenschaft*, p. 201.

29. After the annexation of Austria in March 1938, the German authorities also used data on Gypsies compiled by the Austrian Government's Bureau for Combating the Gypsy Menace. Created in 1936 in the same spirit as the Third Reich's *Reichsburgergesetz* issued a year earlier, it was automatically integrated into similar organizations of the rest of the Reich after the March 1938 *Anschluss*, which made Vienna one of the three major assembly points for the Gypsy deportation to the General Gouvernement in Poland after the outbreak of World War II. See Raul Hilberg, *The Destruction of the European Jews*, pp. 137–38.

30. Kenrick and Puxon, *Destiny*, p. 89.

31. H. Kueppers, ''Die Beschäftigung von Zigeunern,'' p. 177.

32. *International Military Tribunal* (Nuremberg Documents): NG-558. Henceforth *IMT*

33. Ibid., PS-682; Vol. 33 (Red), p. 496.

34. Klee, *Euthenasie*, pp. 358–59.

35. Hilberg, *Destruction*, p. 295; and Klee, *Euthenasie*, pp. 358–59.

36. Klee, *Euthenasie*, p. 358.

37. Kenrick and Puxon, *Destiny*, p. 183.

38. Klee, *Euthenasie*, p. 361.

39. Erika Thurner, *Kurzgeschichte der nationalsozialistischen Zigeunerlagers in Lackenbach, 1940–1945*.

40. Germaine Tillon, *Ravensbrück*, pp. 27n, 31–32.

41. Ibid., pp. 105, 129, 240–41

42. Hilberg, *Destruction*, p. 137.

43. Yitzhak Arad, *Belzec, Sobibor, Treblinka: The Operation Reinhard Death Camps*, p. 151; Gideon Hausner, *Justice in Jerusalem*, p. 59.

44. Hausner, *Justice in Jerusalem*, p. 66.

45. Arad, *Belzec, Sobibor, Treblinka*, p. 151.

46. Hilberg, *Destruction*, p. 143.

47. Friedman, ''Extermination of the Gypsies,'' p. 154; and Martin Gilbert, *The Holocaust*, p. 244.

48. Fein, *Accounting for Genocide*, p. 140.

49. Kenrick and Puxon, *Destiny*, p. 88.

50. Jerzy Ficowski, ''The Fate of Polish Gypsies,'' p. 166; Gilbert, *The Holocaust*, pp. 251, 256.

51. Adam Czerniakow, *The Warsaw Diary*, pp. 346–47, 351, 364–68, 375.

52. Döring, *Die Zigeuner*, p. 152.

53. *Yad Vashem Studies*, vol. 7, pp. 177–78.

54. Jakob Wiernick, *A Year in Treblinka*, p. 35.

55. Gitta Sereni, *Into the Darkness*, p. 212.

56. Dov Freiberg, "Testimony" in Yad Vashem Archives, A-361.

57. Arad, *Belzec, Sobibor, Treblinka*, p. 153.

58. Robert E. Conot, *Justice at Nuremberg*, p. 375.

59. Friedman, "Extermination of the Gypsies," p. 154.

60. Döring, *Die Zigeuner*, pp. 215–18; Robert J. Lifton, *The Nazi Doctors: Medical Killing and the Psychology of Genocide*, p. 323; Gerald Reitlinger, *The Final Solution: The Attempt to Exterminate the Jews of Europe, 1939–1945*, pp. 125, 200, 488–89.

61. Tyrnauer, "Germany and Gypsies," p. 28.

62. Conot, *Justice at Nuremberg*, p. 375; and Benjamin B. Ferencz, *Less Than Slaves: Jewish Forced Labor and the Quest for Compensation*, p. 18.

63. Conot, *Justice at Nuremberg*, p. 375; and Rudolf Franz Höss, *Kommandant in Auschwitz*, pp. 139–40. For details see Anita Geiges and Bernhard Wette, *Zigeuner Heute*, pp. 254–58. There has been an uncorroborated report by an Auschwitz survivor that during the *Zigeunernacht*, Gypsies were not gassed but burned alive in the crematoria. (I owe this information to Professor Ian Hancock in a letter dated 26 February 1989.)

64. Dora E. Yates, "Hitler and the Gypsies," p. 164.

65. The most favored method was to arrest French and Belgian Gypsies on weekly market and seasonal fair days, as was the case in Lille, Höss, *Commandant of Auschwitz*.

66. Yates, "Hitler and the Gypsies," pp. 163–64.

67. Lifton, *The Nazi Doctors*, pp. 185, 348–49, 353, 357, 361–62, 460.

68. Ficowski, "The Fate of Polish Gypsies," p. 166.

69. Klee, *Euthenasie*, p. 367.

70. Hilberg, *Destruction*, p. 241, note 82.

71. Yates, "Hitler and the Gypsies," p. 160.

72. Friedman, "Extermination of the Gypsies," p. 156.

73. Ibid., p. 154.

74. Hilberg, *Destruction*, pp. 437–38.

75. *IMT*: NOKW-802.

76. *IMT*: NOKW-1486.

77. Fein, *Accounting for Genocide*, pp. 102–3; and Klee, *Euthenasie*, p. 358.

78. Yates, "Hitler and the Gypsies," pp. 62–63; Kenrick and Puxon estimate 500 survivors: *Destiny*, p. 183.

79. Yoannis Vrissakis, "Nazis and the Greek Roma: A Personal Testimonial," as told to Ian Hancock (five typed pages, no date).

80. Friedman, "Extermination of the Gypsies," p. 156.

81. Gilbert, *The Holocaust*, p. 824.

82. Friedman, "Extermination of the Gypsies," pp. 152, 156.

83. William A. Duna, letter to the U.S. Holocaust Memorial Council, 17 November 1989, p. 2.

84. Sylvia Puggiole, "Swiss Government Apologizes to Gypsies," documentary broadcast by National Public Radio, 5 December 1987; and Sylvia Sobeck, *Menschen zwischen Macht und Ohnmacht*, cited by Ian Hancock in "Uniqueness of the Vic-

tims: Gypsies, Jews and the Holocaust,'' *Without Prejudice*, vol. 1, no. 2, p. 55, note 41; Stephen Castles, *Here for Good: Western Europe's New Ethnic Minorities*, p. 197.

85. Simon Wiesenthal, letter to the U.S. Holocaust Memorial Council, 14 December 1984, cited by Ian Hancock in ''Uniqueness,'' p. 55; Margot Strom and William Parson, *Facing History and Ourselves*, p. 22; Wolf in der Maur, *Die Zigeuner: Wanderer zwischen den Welten*, p. 168; and Georg von Soest, *Aspekte zur Sozialarbeit*.

86. Hausner, *Justice in Jerusalem*, pp. 300–301.

87. Ibid., pp. 397, 424.

4

Albanian Gypsies
The Silent Survivors

JOHN KOLSTI

Introduction

Gypsies have lived among the Albanians for over 600 years.[1] Their arrival from Asia coincided with that of the Ottoman Turks, a larger Asiatic group that by the middle of the fifteenth century had changed the face of southeastern Europe. And, in the case of the Albanians several generations later, their faith. A people once predominately Roman Catholic now split into four distinct religious communities. By the middle of the nineteenth century, over half the Albanians in the Balkans had converted to the Sunni branch of Islam. One-quarter of the population had joined Shiite Bektashi brotherhoods, or communities of "Crypto-Christians," which did not share the fanaticism of their Greek Orthodox or Sunni Moslem neighbors.[2] Approximately 15 percent had come under the jurisdiction of the Greek patriarch in Istanbul, and fewer than 10 percent stubbornly held on to their Roman Catholic parishes in the north Albanian highlands and the plains below them that stretched toward Kosovo.

Background

By the nineteenth century, the four Ottoman vilayets, or provinces in European Turkey that were administered for the most part by Albanian Moslems, had become a refuge of sorts for Gypsy families that had either adopted Islam or had fled harsh persecutions and slavery in areas recently liberated from Turkish control, particularly the Romanian principalities. But Gypsies were not the only nomads in the Albanian vilayets.[3] Their caravans and tents were never far from Vlach[4] or Arumanian pastures, or settlements near Albanian market towns. Both groups endured physical and economic hardships not much different from conditions facing the Albanians themselves. Vlachs, Gypsies, and Albanians alike were ethnic minorities on the periphery of a crumbling empire. Sharing for the most part the patriarchal life-style of their neighbors, the Gypsies in Albanian lands probably came closest to finding a sense of equality with those around them. But it was the Albanians who had the most to lose from the collapse of that empire: namely, a compact territory in which they were a national majority. But it was not until the 1870s that they at long last "woke up" politically and began to regard themselves as a nation, a single people with a common ancestral and linguistic, if not cultural-religious heritage.

The creation of an independent Albania in 1920 put an abrupt end to Albanian dreams of political unity: nearly half of the Albanians (and perhaps as many Albanian Gypsies) found themselves in the situation they dreaded most before the war—as targets of a Slav majority all too eager to "settle accounts" with people they associated with centuries of Turkish terror. Nowhere else in Eastern Europe, perhaps, were Gypsies so closely identified with a despised minority. The harsh fate they shared in Serbia for nearly twenty years,[5] or until the occupation of Albanian districts by the Germans in World War II, was quite different from the relationships between Albanians and Gypsies in King Zog's, and later Mussolini's Albania. In Albania itself, policed as it was by a Sunni chieftain, little changed. The same Moslem beys and aghas continued to rule from their estates in the same efficient manner, long after the partitioning of European Turkey. Gypsy Christians, now members of an independent Albanian Orthodox Church, were still baptized and married, and still continued to worship standing next to the iconostasis at the front of the congregation.[6] Moslem Gypsies were still not appreciated inside the mosque or, for that matter, inside the burial grounds.[7] A feeble attempt by Ahmet Beg Zogolli to ban public dancing by Gypsies in the early 1920s was all but forgotten by the time Mussolini began to prepare to extend his financial control across the Adriatic. Gypsy goods were still welcome in the marketplace, and Gypsy settlements were still tolerated as were those of the Vlachs. Some settled Gypsies, an English observer noted,[8] had intermarried with local Turks and Moslem Gypsies in the coastal lowlands, losing over the years their Romani language and, as in the case of the Albanians, the "purity" of their race. But transient Gypsies, who no doubt earned the name *gurbati*, "beggars,"[9] continued to be feared, particularly the Moslem bands that passed through mountain districts, which had remained predominately Christian.[10]

In Albania's capital, its largest city with 25,000 inhabitants, a Gypsy *mahale*, or quarter, not only added color to the town's "oriental" appearance, but also contributed to its economic life. While Swire's opinion of King Zog's Tiranë and its inhabitants was hardly flattering—he described the capital as a "wretched and disgusting" city on the edges of which the croaking of bullfrogs from malarial swamps was "fit accompaniment to the plaintive music from the Gypsy quarter"—he provides us nevertheless with an interesting picture of settled Gypsies in the 1920s:

> These Cigans, as they are called, being no longer nomads, have lost their language, though they still tell the tradition that their forebears came over the sea from the direction of the sun (meaning Egypt). Their type is very swarthy and quite unlike the average Albanian, but in common with nomadic Romanies (Vlachs) their physique is poor. The men, when they must work, become hamals or blacksmiths or executioners or scavengers—it is the Gypsy who drowns the stray dog and carts away the refuse—tasks to which the Albanian will not stoop. There are many of them at the ports, where they work as stevedores and boatmen and porters. These women are stocky, hardworking, far neater than the Tirana Moslems, and they are often employed as servants, for the Albanian dislikes charing. Their noses are markedly semitic. Their intelligence is average, but they keep their houses much cleaner than the lowland Albanians. Nevertheless the latter despised them, so the old official class is afraid foreigners should think them Albanian.[11]

Fascist Albania

In the early 1930s, well before Italy annexed Albania and began "banishing" Italian Gypsy troops there,[12] Gypsy-phobia in Germany and Austria had already prompted discussions concerning the elimination of an Aryan subgroup whose soaring birthrate threatened to contaminate Aryan, or at least Teutonic blood. In 1940, as German troops began to deport Gypsy families to work camps in Eastern Europe, to areas occupied by them after the outbreak of the war, Mussolini began his ill-fated attack on Greece. His failure in Epirus and the subsequent German and Bulgarian occupation of Greece and Macedonia incorporated Albanian territory in the Balkans once again into the peripheral zone of a hostile empire, one in which favored national groups would (as in the case of Croatia) or would not (as in the case of Yugoslavia's Albanian districts) attempt to carry out the "final solution" of the Gypsy problem in southeastern Europe.

The collapse of Mussolini's military ambitions in the Balkans and the occupation of the Albanian hinterland by German and Bulgarian units eventually led to the realization of his plan to extend Italy's political as well as economic control across Albania's borders into Serbia and Macedonia. That is, to unite once again the former Ottoman vilayets of Shkodër, Janina, Manastir, and Ushkup (Skopje) into Greater Albania. Albanian Gypsies now came under Albanian, albeit fascist control, living on the estates, or *çifliqve*,[13] of landlords sympathetic to a government headed at one point by a member of the Frashëri family, a name all but synonymous with nineteenth century Albanian national and literary aspirations.[14] These were landlords who supported the formation of the *Balli Kombetar*, or National Front, whose government-backed units were sent into the field to fight Albanian and Yugoslav partisan brigades, but not to exterminate Gypsies.[15] In other words, conditions that enabled the *Ustaša* death battalions in Hitler's Independent State of Croatia to "out-Herod Herod" fortunately did not operate in Greater Albania. While conflicting figures make it impossible to say how many Gypsies lived in Greater Albania when it was created by Mussolini, or how many had become victims of the war by the time it disappeared from the map, it is safe to say that the survival rate of Albanian Gypsies was higher than the present governments of Albania and Yugoslavia would probably care to admit.

What saved Greater Albania's Gypsies, or at least spared them the slaughter that was carried out in former Austrian territories of Yugoslavia? Demographic factors certainly played a major role in their survival. As mentioned earlier, Gypsy groups were not the only ethnic minority in Albanian districts. Turkish *mahale* and scattered Vlach settlements made it difficult for the invader to sort out non-Slav or non-Greek elements in a population sharing centuries-long economic hardships and a common patriarchal life-style.[16] The confusion of languages spoken, and religious rituals observed, only compounded the difficult task of determining what groups comprised over 20 percent of the inhabitants of Greater Albania. The Albanian-speaking groups may have been included in a single nation-state, run by fascist governments in Tiranë installed first by the Italians and then by the Germans, but they came under the military control of three different armies of occupation. Italian troops, which were far from unpopular owing to Mussolini's pro-Albanian policies, continued to run most of Greater Albania. Bulgarian military units operated in Macedonia, reviving Bulgarian territorial claims to the former vilayets of Manastir and Ushkup. And German units in Serbia, where their hold was far less secure than in Croatia, had little reason to interfere in Mussolini's policies, which in fact had some support among the Albanians (and perhaps even among local Gypsies who had suffered equally under the Serbs). This was particularly the case in borderland areas next to Serbia, where Albanian SS units also operated.[17]

While the "final solution" to the Gypsy problem in Croatia was proceeding at a pace that even repelled German garrisons there, the social and political, rather than racial policies of Albania's fascist governments paid scant attention to the Gypsies who made up only an "insignificant part" of the total population. Albanian Ballist units and Bulgarian brigades were hardly motivated to pursue any wide-scale policy of deportation or extermination against the local Gypsies, since this would drive them into the mountains of central and southern Albania that, even before Mussolini's fall in the summer of 1943, had provided refuge for Albania's first partisan detachments. In fact, the Gypsies themselves moved onto the estates of the Ballists, who were motivated, for the most part, by the fear of an extension of Serbian military control into Albania and a return to the conditions that prevailed before the war under Yugoslavia's military dictatorship.[18] In a word, neither the Italians, their Bulgarian allies, nor Albanian nationalists were interested in or capable of destroying Albanian Gypsies, given their increasingly vulnerable situation before the Germans occupied the whole of Greater Albania after the fall of Mussolini and the withdrawal of Italy from the war.

German occupation of Greater Albania, which began in the summer of 1943, lasted less than one year. The subsequent withdrawal of German troops from northern Greece and southern Albania signaled the military survival of Albanian partisan units, which by the spring of 1944 were able to put more men and women into the field than the Germans and local fascists had available. The shrinking borders of the Third Reich in Eastern Europe, and the defection of Ballist and Gypsy troops during the partisans' drive north toward Montenegro and Kosovo, ended whatever deportation policy had been attempted: German troops had to move out of the area while fighting in Bosnia and Croatia intensified. Gypsy support for pro-German elements in Albania needs no apology.[19] Their identity may have fooled the Germans, but certainly not the Albanian fascists whose lands they had long worked. As in eastern Yugoslavia, Gypsy, Albanian, and Slav Moslems in Greater Albania shared a common enemy: namely, Serbs who equated Nazi occupation with centuries of Turkish terror. In the competition for recruits, it is difficult to believe the beys could not ''convince'' Albanian and Gypsy Moslems or Christians that they had nothing to gain from Tito's partisans in Herzegovina or Mihajlović's *Četniks* in Serbia. In other words, Albanian Gypsies played an active part in their own struggle for physical survival.

Of all the ethnic minorities in the Balkans, including the Vlachs, the Gypsies were perhaps the best prepared physically to avoid getting caught in open areas, and able to fight to save their families, particularly since partisan commanders had promised Albanian Gypsies what the Albanians had been granted under the Italians and Germans: schools in their own language, and social and political rights—human rights—unthinkable in prewar Yugoslavia. For the Albanian nationalists, one step backward after the events of 1944 was impossible; for their Gypsy neighbors, a first step forward seemed a reality. In an area that had long been a place of refuge for Balkan Gypsies, their ability to survive as individuals or family groups centered around a number of ethnographic, political, geographic, and cultural factors that effectively blunted Nazi racial policies directed against them. While Albanian Gypsies suffered from local hatreds directed against or diverted toward them, their survival rate in southeastern Europe was proportionately higher in former Ottoman territories than in lands that had been under Austrian domination. What is interesting is the fact that in territories controlled by fascists before the war started (Albania, Romania, and Bulgaria), Gypsies continued to be ''neglected,'' a situation that certainly did not result in areas occupied by German troops at the start of the war. One must ever be reminded, however, that no matter how ''light'' Gypsy losses were in Greater Albania, regardless of whether they were racially motivated, premeditated, or accidental, they were all the more tragic owing to the ''insignificance'' of their number in relation to the total population.[20]

Physical extermination, however, was not the only problem faced by the Gypsies of Albania. Even before a new socialist order was established in Tiranë, they had already seen their numbers dwindling as a result of their own reaction to changing political boundaries and territorial claims by new nation states around them. They lacked, or at least failed to express, a common national cause. They were illiterate and uneducated, having only the ''gift of tongues'' that seemed even to their polyglot neighbors to have miraculous powers—it was believed, for example, that crumbs from a Gypsy woman's bag would cure stuttering problems.[21] They adhered to different, antagonistic religious communities, which made the substance of their religious convictions even more suspect than those of Albanian Bektashi brotherhoods. They were as familiar with vendettas as the highland clans among the Albanians. They either spoke Romani or did not, and those that had not long given up their nomadic wanderings, opting instead to settle in tents outside market towns, moved into cities to sell their goods and services. With a decline in the number of Romani-speaking Gypsies, the long process of social and economic integration, which continued in King Zog's Albania, would be accelerated after the war in Europe reached its turning point, and after Moslem Albanians and Gypsies in increasing numbers opted to join Yugoslav-supported partisan units operating in Kosovo and central Albania. The process would be declared ''official'' after the war was over, and a drive toward cultural assimilation in New Albania would begin.

Postwar Albania

When the war ended, the Gypsies, no doubt along with the Vlachs and smaller minority groups, were among the first ''casualties'' of the peace. If the Gypsies had contributed little as a group to the Albania of Ahmet Beg Zogolli, or to the Serbia of Nikola Pašić, they had even less to add to the Stalinist ''citadel'' of Enver Hoxha or Alexander Ranković's Kosovo. While the Albanians ended the war with their borders intact and a degree of recognition as a nationality, if not a separate nation in the Socialist Republic of Serbia, the Gypsies, who had no ancestral lands or cultural-historical legacies in European Turkey or the Middle East, ended the war with next to nothing.[22] If the Croats had gained temporary privileges as a national group under the Germans, and the Albanians in Greater Albania unprecedented rights under the Italians, the Gypsies who survived the fighting in Albania had to "pay a price" for their assimilation into the new social and political order of a nation-state whose population, as a result of losses and migrations across borders, had become even more homogeneous than it had been before 1920. With officially recognized nationalities to worry about, particularly the Greeks in the towns of southern Albania and scattered Slav groups along its Montenegrin and Serbian borders, Albania did not need the Gypsies or the Vlachs to complicate further the job of building a new society.

Conclusion

Where physical extermination had never been an option in Albania or Greater Albania for "solving" the Gypsy problem, as it was defined in central Europe, and where deportation to work camps and death camps in German-occupied Yugoslavia and central Europe had proved impossible, the only course remaining after the war was one of assimilation of "silent" minority children[23] into a Soviet-model school system, and, ultimately, into the mainstream of Albania's highly centralized economic system. The centuries-long Ottoman legacy of disease and illiteracy, regional and religious rivalries, along with a certain tolerance for nomadic groups as well as "oriental" *mahale* in the towns, not unlike ethnic enclaves in our own cities, was bulldozed into the ground along with other remnants of this ageless society. Buried, too, was the "unnoticed all-pervading neglect"[24] that had made it possible for at least some "pure" Gypsies living away from the towns to preserve their mother tongue among other people with whom they were closely identified.

It remains to be seen and documented, in national archives, in the market place, and in the home, how Albanian Gypsy survivors of the Holocaust survive in the memory and language of their children and grandchildren.

Notes

1. They found refuge in the Byzantine Empire in parts of ancient Illyria and Macedonia that had sheltered the Albanians and Vlachs from Slavic migrations in the sixth and seventh centuries and later from the Crusaders and the Turks. A Gypsy settlement near Prizren was noted for the first time by an English traveler in 1699. *Kosovo Kosovo*, p. 234. This is a lengthy bilingual study of the history of the Albanian districts of Serbia.

2. The Bektashis (more than any other religious community to which Albanian Gypsies belonged—they belonged to all four) associated the idea of nation with that

of language, not religious belief or civic ceremony. Not unlike the Gypsies themselves, Albania's dervish orders, whose origins are also traced back to Turkey and Persia, remained outside the influence of the Pope, the Patriarch, and even the Porte.

3. Acceptance of Gypsy groups in Albania was helped not only by the mix of linguistic and religious communities in the area, but by a nomadic life-style that long preceded their arrival. Jean-Paul Clébert, *The Gypsies*, p. 96.

4. For information on the Vlachs and a study of their treatment by historians in and outside the Balkans see T.J. Winnifrith, *The Vlachs: The History of a Balkan People*.

5. After World War I, Albanians and Albanian Gypsies living in districts acquired by Serbia no longer had either the Porte or the Great Powers (who drew the political boundaries) to protect them. In the 1920s, what schools there were in the area were Serbian. Deportation to Turkey of local Moslems (regardless of ethnic background), not economic or cultural assimilation, suited Serbian racial policies. Indeed, in 1963, a Serbian medical student at Belgrade University thought that the words *ciganin* and *šiptar*—from the Albania word *shqipëtar*, "Albanian"—referred to one and the same group. *Kosovo Kosovo*, pp. 191–93. For an excellent, comprehensive survey of the Albanians and their experience under Pašić and Ranković before and after World War II see Ramadan Marmullaku, *Albania and the Albanians*; and Anton Logoreci, *The Albanians: Europe's Forgotten Survivors*.

6. As described to me in a personal interview. Why local Gypsies seemed to enjoy preferential treatment at the mass was not made clear, although fear of them may have contributed to the "respect" they received.

7. As told to me by a Sunni Moslem, whose opinion of the dervishes is little different from that of the Gypsies, neither being taken seriously. Centuries earlier, local officials in Turkey were not against collecting taxes from Gypsies, even from Moslem families whose religion was "still worth a . . . tax discount." For early Ottoman policies toward ethnic and religious groups see Peter Sugar, *Southeastern Europe under Ottoman Rule, 1354–1804*, p. 103. See also Tihomir Djordjević, *Naš narodni život*, p. 320.

8. Joseph Swire, *King Zog's Albania*. Except for rather romantic notions of who "real Albanians" and "real Gypsies" are, Swire's impressions of Albania and the Albanians are invaluable, given the general lack of information and interest in "the most backward country of Europe." For a fair and impartial study of the Albanians between 1804 and the rise of Ahmet Beg Zogolli see Charles and Barbara Jelavich. *The Establishment of the Balkan National States, 1804–1920.*

9. Damodar P. Singhal, *Gypsies: Indians in Exile*, p. 71.

10. As told to me in a personal interview. Settled Gypsies who were integrated into the religious life of a Christian district and its economy simply were not a serious problem, something that could not be said of non-Christian intruders—Gypsy, Albanian, or Turk.

11. Swire, *King Zog's Albania*, p. 196.

12. Donald Kenrick and Grattan Puxon, *The Destiny of Europe's Gypsies*, p. 108. See also Pyrrhus J. Ruches, *Albania's Captives*, p. 142. Gypsies, not surprisingly, almost get lost in this curious book which places "real Albanians" as far away as possible from traditionally Orthodox areas in the southern half of the country. An excellent study of the Holocaust in Mussolini's empire notes that the exiling duty in Albania was carried out to spare Jews as well as Gypsies, moving them away from

German units in Italy, Croatia, and Serbia, and keeping them away from local fascist detachments that supported them. See Susan Zucotti, *The Italians and the Holocaust: Persecution, Rescue, and Survival.*

13. "On every estate between Elbasan and Berat," that is, north and south of the Shkumbi River in central Albania, the traditional dividing line between Gegs to the north and Tosks to the south. Djordjević, *Naš narodni život,* p. 310.

14. Particularly the brothers Sami and Naim Frashëri, the latter a Bektashi-be whose Persian-inspired poetry mythologized the bond between the Albanians and their ancestral pasture lands and mountains.

15. And against "Northern Epirotes," Ruches notes, tracing the Ballist slogan "digj shtëpi të bënë Shqiperl" (burn a house and build Albania) to a Bektashi monastery in Gjirokastra in south Albania.

16. While invaders may have had trouble sorting out the ethnic groups in Albania, this hardly could have been the case for the local beys or Shiite brotherhoods.

17. One motivating factor behind popular support for Ballist and Albanian SS units was fear of a partisan victory. *Kosovo Kosovo,* p. 205. A partisan victory would mean a Serbian victory and the end of Albanian majority in the former Turkish districts of Kosovo and Metohlja. For an excellent study of the fate of national minorities victimized by World War II, and the peace that followed it, see Raymond Pearson, *National Minorities in Eastern Europe, 1848–1945,* p. 217. On a larger scale, the SS and fascist units protected German escape routes from Greece, particularly after Italy withdrew from the war, as outlined in Stefanaq Polo and Alex Buda, et al., eds., *Historia e popullit Shqiptar,* vol. 2, pp. 697–711. No mention of Gypsy involvement in these units is made, but their role in later partisan activity is, not surprisingly.

18. It was not until January 1943 that Albanian partisans, convinced that "there would be no turning back to the old ways," went into action against the Italians, as did Albanian Gypsies, to whom Tito's advisers had also made "vague promises." *Kosovo Kosovo,* p. 211.

19. See Kendrick and Puxon, *Destiny,* p. 120. The survival rate of Gypsies under the Italians and local fascist supporters contrasted sharply with their near extermination in German occupied Croatia and Serbia.

20. Some put it as high as 80,000, or 2.75 percent of the population thirty years after the war. See Grattan Puxon, "Roma: Europe's Gypsies," p. 13.

21. Djordjević, *Naš narodni život,* vol. 3, p. 124. Volumes 2 and 3 in this series contain over 150 pages of material on the folklore of and about Yugoslavia's Gypsies.

22. Whatever the "historical necessities" of Albania's wartime collaboration with the Italians and, after the fall of Mussolini, Tito's partisans were, all for the purpose of preserving the nation if not the state (Greater Albania), the cost is estimated at 7.3 percent of the population killed or wounded. Albania's unidentified "nomads" no doubt shared this fate. See Ndreçi Plasari and Shyqri Ballova, "Politique et Stratégie Dans la Lutte Antifasciste de Libération Nationale du Peuple Albanais (1939–1944)," p. 22.

23. "Silent" except for an oral traditional literature that remained unrecorded, its language incapable of competing for equality in Albanian and Greek schools.

24. Puxon, "Roma," p. 5.

5

The Gypsy Historical Experience in Romania

DAVID CROWE

In the long course of the Gypsy experience in Eastern Europe, none has been worse than that in Romania. Within several centuries after Gypsies entered the medieval provinces of Wallachia and Moldavia, they began to be enslaved, a condition that lasted until the mid-nineteenth century. Although slavery was not a condition peculiar to Gypsies or the Balkans at the time, the deep-seated, dehumanizing prejudice that has characterized the historic Romanian relationship with Gypsies produced a socioeconomic caste system that resulted in the "social death" of Gypsies as Romanian slaves, and, after Gypsy emancipation, created an atmosphere of antagonism and prejudice toward the Romani that has caused them to be looked upon as worthless and dishonest "all-purpose scapegoats."[1]

While it is impossible exactly to pinpoint when Gypsies entered Romania's historic provinces, Wallachia and Moldavia (the Danubian Principalities), most evidence points to their presence there by the late eleventh century. Initially, the Gypsies found a place for themselves in these medieval kingdoms as metalsmiths and craftsmen. By the thirteenth century, they began to be enslaved for a variety of economic, military, social, and possibly racial reasons.[2] The first precise historical documentation identifying the enslavement of Gypsies in the region comes from the court records of the first Hapsburg Archduke, Rudolf IV (1339–1365), and of medieval Serbia's great emperor, Tsar Stephen Dušan (*Silni*, the Mighty; the Lawgiver, 1331–1355), who both set aside 20 percent of their kingdoms' Gypsy population as the property of the church and the nobility.[3]

During the same period, Wallachia under the Grand Voivode and Prince, Basarab (1317–1352), and Moldavia under Prince Bogdan (*Bogdan Voevoda Moldaviensis*) began to emerge as autonomous political entities through wars of independence.[4] Several years later, Wallachian records indicate that Prince Vladislav Vlaicu (1364–1377) gave forty Gypsy families and land to the new monastery at Vodita.[5]

Over the next century, Gypsy slavery became institutionalized in the Romanian provinces, and abundant historical records document the Gypsies' plight. The most significant factor affecting the enslavement of Gypsies at this time was warfare. In the aftermath of his campaigns against the Ottoman Empire in northern Bulgaria in 1461–1462, the Wallachian ruler, Vlad IV Tepes (the Impaler), brought back 11,000–12,000 "Gypsies (or Gypsy-like people)" to his capital where he tortured and killed some for his entertainment.[6] Vlad IV's contemporary in Moldavia, Stephen the Great (1457–1504), brought 17,000 Gypsies back from his campaigns in Wallachia in 1471 to use as slave labor. His move, however, simply strengthened a practice supported by law, which, for example, stated that any Moldavian that got a Gypsy pregnant and wanted to marry her would lose his status and have to become a slave. Later, "any Moldavian who married a gipsy himself joined the ranks of the 'robi.' "[7]

In 1503, Wallachia and Moldavia became direct vassal states of the Ottoman Empire. Politically, to gain the support of Christian religious leaders, particularly the Orthodox ones, "the *millet* system of autonomous self-government under religious leaders" arose, which saw these figures cement themselves to the Sultan, since the system gave them more authority over their followers than previously under Christian leaders. Financially, these provinces were treated as "tax farms" by Turkish officials, who were allowed to keep a percentage of the taxes they collected. While private cultivation of land was encouraged in the Ottoman Empire as long as proper taxes were paid, peasants increasingly lost their ability to move about freely because of growing labor shortages in the sixteenth century. Another factor of Ottoman social and economic life was the division of urban society into guild systems along job-skill lines, which indirectly helped to solidify Gypsy craft specialization.[8]

The era of Ottoman domination of the Danubian Principalities was characterized by the increased integration of Gypsy slavery with the growing enserfment of the peasant class. The Orthodox church, long an important landowning institution in Wallachia and Moldavia, now enjoyed a special status under the Turks, while the nobility, encouraged by the raw stability and institutionalized greed of Ottoman rule, joined together "to reinforce the feudal regime by *robot* and *corvée* and payment in kind." Gypsy slavery and general peasant serfdom now become the cornerstone labor institutions in the Romanian countryside.[9]

However, unlike the peasants, the significance of the Gypsies in the two provinces came not from their farming abilities, even though there were Gypsy farm workers, but from their important talents as craftsmen. Their skills in various areas of metallurgy were such that they had a "virtual monopoly in smithing," and in many areas of Wallachia and Moldavia they "were almost the only artisans."[10] In time, Gypsy slaves were categorized according to who owned them and the type of work that they did. Referred to as *sclavi*, *scindromi*, or *robie*, they were known as either *ţigani de casaţi* (house slaves) or *ţigani de ogor* (field slaves). Domestic Gypsy slaves owned by the crown or the state were then divided according to whether they were owned by noblemen (*sclavi domneşti*), the Court (*sclavi curte*), or rural land owners (*sclavi gospod*). Crown slaves were known according to their principal jobs: the *aurari* or *rudari* (gold washers), the *ursari* or *oursari* (bear trainers or "exhibitors of animals"), and the *lingurari* (spoon carvers). Another category of Gypsy domestic slaves were the *laişei*, which included the *lautari* or *laoutari* (musicians or "fiddlers"), who did most of the skilled, nonagricultural work on the estate.[11] Contemporary Balkan Gypsy clans take their names from those given to them during this period, such as the *kirpači* ("basketmakers"), the *kovači* (Magyar, blacksmith) or *sastrari*, the *zlatari* ("goldwashers"), the *čurari* ("sieve-makers"), and the *chivuţe* ("whitewashers"). The Romanian Orthodox church also had Gypsy slaves, the *sclavi monastiveşti*, who were divided into the *vatraşi* (household slaves) and the more artistic *laişei*.[12]

Because of the Gypsy slave's value as a laborer and a craftsman, laws were passed both to restrict their movement and to prevent runaway slaves and illegal Gypsy slave trading. In 1560, for example, the Voivode of Wallachia protested the kidnapping and resale of Gypsies to the Sultan. A century later, the 1646 laws issued by the Moldavian ruler Basil the Wolf (Vasile Lupu) had sections relating to various crimes and punishments by and for Gypsy slaves, including wealth gained through sorcery. Article 8 stated, for example, "Si le Tsigane d'un propriétarie, y est-il dit, ou sa femme, ou son enfant ne vole qu'une, deux ou trois poules, une oie ou toute autre bagatelle, il liu sera pardonné."[13]

Over the next hundred years, the status of Gypsy slaves in Wallachia and Moldavia was affected by the general decay that had set in throughout the Ottoman Empire. Because of continual foreign intrigues in the area, a Phanariote line of Greek rulers dominated the provinces from 1714 until 1821. The period is marked by tremendous political instability and exploitation of the countryside so severe that peasants began to flee the provinces.[14] Though some efforts were made to reduce the labor burdens of the peasants to stop their flight into Transylvania and elsewhere, they were later revoked. Constantine Mavrocordat, who ruled Moldavia and Wallachia on ten separate occasions during this period, tried desperately to better the plight of the peasants during his reign of Wallachia from 1744 to 1748. He outlawed serfdom there in 1746 and three years later in Moldavia. The Moldavian Assembly took notice at this time "that some landlords have been in the habit of selling serfs [*vecini*] like slaves [*robi*], treating them like gypsies, . . . separating children from their parents and transferring them from one place to another." It ruled in the law, *Act pentru desrobire ţeranilor in Moldavia* (6 April 1749), that these practices involving serfs had to stop. On the other hand, Mavrocordat reaffirmed the status of Gypsy slaves in his Uricariul of 1749 that stated that "Les tziganes sont complément asservis et doivert avec femmes et enfants servir d'une maniere permanente leurs maîtres," though he sponsored legislation eight years later that decreed that Gypsy children could no longer be sold apart from their parents.[15]

In the midst of such instability, some noblemen had begun to complain "that the word 'service' does not differ from 'slavery,' " which had led to the selling of serfs as slaves. With distinctions blurred between the two groups, intermarriage between Gypsies and non-Gypsies had now also become a problem. A number of conflicting laws were passed in the second half of the eighteenth century, which initially tried to qualify free and slave conditions of such unions, but gradually moved toward completely outlawing them. In most instances, restrictions saw such marriages as un-Christian and immoral.[16]

By the 1770s, Wallachia and Moldavia were scenes of international intrigue as Austria and particularly Russia sought to take advantage of

Ottoman weakness to build up vital spheres of influence there. The increased Western interest and presence in the two provinces paved the way for some positive reforms along Western lines and stimulated a hint of Romanian national feeling.[17]

Ongoing conflicts between Turkey, Russia, and Austria, however, neutralized these changes, while the French Revolution and the Napoleonic Wars created new prospects for significant reform in the Principalities. Unfortunately, Turkish rule during this latter period reached a spiritual nadir, and was, for the two provinces, an era as that of "lowest degradation." At the point when Romanian noblemen felt strong enough to approach the French to strengthen their interests in the region, Russia occupied both areas. Russia's move was grudgingly approved by Napoleon in his secret agreement with Tsar Alexander I at Erfurt on 12 October 1808, and remained in force until 1812. The Russian military occupation "devoured" the provinces, which, according to one observer, gave it the "appearance of a desert. . . ." This was followed by nine more years of unsteady rule that ended in a series of complex revolutionary events that saw native rulers replace the Phanariote princes in 1822.[18]

The new governors "found the Principalities in a lamentable state, . . ." and the peasants so beaten down by decades of oppression that they had sunk into "a sort of natural stupor and apathy. . . ." However, any significant change in their plight did not begin until several years later, when Russian forces once again occupied the provinces during another conflict with Turkey. It is at this juncture that the first significant changes were made in the plight of the Romanian peasants and Gypsies in the nineteenth century. Pavel D. Kiselev, the Plenipotentiary President of the Divans of Wallachia and Moldavia, sought "to construct a social base of support for Russian power among the peasants" with reforms designed to "eliminate the most offensive abuses which local officials inflicted upon the peasants. . . ."[19] Unfortunately, the reality is much less positive. Though Kiselev's reforms, embodied principally in his *Règlement Organique*, did bring about better government and improve general conditions in "public life," those affecting the peasant were mixed and, at least in their eyes, created "the slavery of labour service." Its clauses dealing with Gypsies better defined their status and strengthened their owners' control over them.[20]

On the other hand, there were also provisions to create a "fund . . . for redeeming the Tsigans from vagrancy, and obliging them to build houses and dwell in them.''[21] Though it has been argued that Kiselev ''was sickened by the concept of slavery on moral grounds,'' he was not inclined to free them. When some Gypsies attempted to bribe him with gold if he would emancipate them, he told them angrily that they would ''remain as slaves forever.'' In fact, if his views on the Russian serf question are any indication of his true feelings on Gypsy slavery, then the most that can be said is that he ''hoped to correct the abuses'' and ''soften the impact of bondage on the population'' within the context of Russian imperial designs in the region.[22]

Regardless, the overall impact of these reforms did begin to change the status of Gypsy slaves, and can be seen as ''le prélude de la liberation des Tsiganes.'' Barbu Stirbei, a member of the group that helped write the *Règlement Organique* and later a reformer in his own right as Prince of Wallachia, unsuccessfully proposed abolition of Gypsy slaves in 1834 after the negative reaction to his sale of 3,000 *robi* to renovate his palace. Three years later, Alexandru Ghica, the Prince of Wallachia from 1834 to 1842, freed all of his Gypsy slaves and granted them equality with other peasants working for him, though this only affected 5,582 families out of a total Gypsy population estimated to be between 150,000 and 500,000.[23] In 1844, Mihai Sturdza, the Prince of Moldavia, supported legislation that freed both monastery and state Gypsy slaves. The Wallachian church followed suit three years later.[24]

In 1848, a series of European-style revolutionary outbursts, stimulated by events in France, swept through the Romanian Principalities and revived talk of Gypsy emancipation. Weak in Moldavia, the Wallachian revolutionary movement forced Prince Gheorghe Bibescu to appoint a new cabinet on 23 June, which prompted the Russians to force his resignation two days later. By 8 July, the new government, now in flight, outlawed Gypsy slavery and ''set up a committee to see that this decision was enforced.''[25] Turkey moved into the provinces several months later, followed by a Russo-Turkish occupation of both provinces that lasted until 1851. In 1853 Russia reoccupied the area because of a conflict with Turkey, and the following year was replaced by Austria, which remained there until 1857 because of the Crimean War. In the midst of foreign occupation, Gypsy slavery returned, even though the native princes implemented significant reforms that improved the plight of the peasants. The *robi* were reemancipated in Moldavia in late 1855 and in Wallachia several months later in anticipation of the Crimean War peace discussions at Paris that some hoped would lead to the unification of the provinces.[26]

Though the major powers vigorously discussed Romanian autonomy, they decided to wait until a special commission could look specifically at the issue before taking this step. As a result of the conclusions reached by this body in 1857, it was decided to unite both provinces into the United Principalities of Moldavia and Wallachia. According to the Convention of Paris (1858), each state would be autonomous with a separate ruler, but remain under Turkish suzerainty. Article 46 of the new accord assured the "personal liberty" of everyone in the United Principalities, which paved the way for general Gypsy emancipation. This was not fully realized, however, until the implementation of the Agrarian Law of the Principalities' reform-minded ruler, Alexandru Ioan Cuza, on 26 August 1864, which gave liberty and land to all sedentary Gypsies and other peasants.[27]

Unfortunately, these gains often went unrealized in the era before World War I. Many Gypsies fled Romania after emancipation for fear of reenslavement if the political system collapsed as it had in 1848. Those that remained were often forced to reattach themselves to the estates or monasteries that had held them in captivity. Many of their problems stemmed from the fact that post–1864 Romania was a nation dominated by wealthy landowners who increasingly turned their affairs over to a rural middle class driven by quick agricultural profits at any cost. Peasant dissatisfaction erupted in a rebellion in 1888 that prompted a new Land Law the following year that did little to address the peasant desire for more land and, in fact, introduced a "Golden Age of irresponsible landlordism" in which "the peasant found himself as much exploited, as fatally tied to the soil, as in the vanished days of serfdom."[28] Peasant discontent once again exploded in 1907 in a rebellion that verged on rural warfare with an estimated 10,000–11,000 deaths. New legislation was passed to better the plight of the peasant, yet never effectively came to grips with the core problem for Gypsies and non-Gypsies—the vast power of the landowning class.[29]

Combined with these difficulties was the problem of anti-Gypsy prejudice. Despite reports that showed that "the gipsy is altogether a better labourer than the Wallack . . ." and did not deserve the criminal reputation that surrounded the Romani, one observer concluded, after praising their skills as musicians, artisans, and craftsmen, that if you treated "them . . . as your fellowmen and fellow-

citizens, . . . you will make nothing of them. Such is their character.''[30]

Despite this atmosphere, a sense of Gypsy ethnic self-awareness
began to emerge, supported by similar movements regionally. In the
fall of 1879, for example, a conference was held in Kisfalu, Hungary,
to discuss ways to achieve Gypsy political and civil rights throughout
the Continent. Though ridiculed in the press, it stimulated a greater
sense of ethnic identity for them. Nothing better underlines this sentiment than a Gypsy memorial service held before the newly erected
statue of Mihail Kogălniceanu, regarded as the Gypsy emancipator,
several days after it was unveiled in 1913.[31]

The outbreak of the First World War the following year found
Romania on the sidelines. In 1916, convinced of an Entente victory,
the government signed the Treaty of Bucharest (27 August) that
promised Romania Transylvania, Bukovina, the Banat, and part of the
Hungarian Plain if the Allies won. When the war ended, Romania
received most of this territory to strengthen it as a democratic island
against Bolshevism. With these acquisitions, Romania's minority
population rose from less than 10 percent of the total before the war
to over 28 percent of it afterward.[32] Of this number, 133,000 were
Gypsies, who made up 0.8 percent of the total population. A decade
later, this figure increased to 262,501 (1.5 percent of the population),
with 101,015 (0.6 percent) listing Gypsy as a language preference.[33]

At a distance, there was hope that the status of Gypsies in postwar
Romania would improve since, as a *quid pro quo* for its new acquisitions, the government was forced to guarantee minority rights in a
number of international agreements it signed after the war as well as
in its own laws and the 1923 Constitution. Their true fate, however,
was linked to the desire of the government to ''Romanize'' its new,
large minority population, to the plight of the peasants vis-à-vis land
reform, and to lingering anti-Gypsy sentiment.[34]

From the beginning, one of the principal goals of the leaders of
Greater Romania was ''to convert the new territories into integral
components of a homogeneous nation state.'' What followed were
policies of ''integral nationalism'' that had a detrimental effect upon
all of the country's minorities. Also affecting rural Gypsies was the
breakup of many large estates which resulted in the redistribution of
over 12 million acres to 1.5 million families and villages. Though
some Gypsies benefitted through the acquisition of land, they often
had little practical farming experience. In addition, many of the gains

made by the peasant as a result of these changes were partially countered by export duties and taxes initiated by the government to pay for industrializing the country. Across the board, life for the Romanian peasant was among the harshest in Eastern Europe during the interwar years, and is perhaps best reflected in the saying that "Our mountains bear gold, we go begging from door to door."[35]

These conditions, which worsened after 1929 because of the Depression and increasingly oppressive government policies, only strengthened traditional prejudices against the Gypsies. To some Romanian peasants, Gypsies were "untouchables" who were considered less valuable than farm animals.[36] These attitudes were fortified by written observations that described "filthy and miserable" Gypsy camps located on "waste ground" at the edge of "towns and villages." Males were seen as indolent and lazy, while young Gypsy women were thought to be a blend of "wildness and unconscious grace."[37] On the other hand, there was a distant, romantic view of the Gypsies that centered around their music and their mysterious, nomadic life-style.[38]

The Gypsies were also affected by the fact that officials felt that, unlike many of the country's other minorities, they had neither a "protective state," a "history," nor a " 'culture' and 'civilization' through written languages" to justify their claims to minority rights. As a result, their status in interwar Romania was comparable to that of the Jews, who, though they played a much different role in Romanian society, were treated as second class citizens and subjected to increasing abuse, particularly in the 1930s.[39]

Despite this atmosphere, some Romanian Gypsies formed a local organization in Clabor, while others used the rights granted them to enter universities. In 1930 a Gypsy journal, *Neamul Tiganesc* (The Gypsy Family), was begun, followed three years later by the General Association of Roma in Romania. Although it only existed for a year, it published two newspapers, *Glasul Romilor* (The Voice of the Roma) and *O Rom*, and advocated, among other things, adoption of a national holiday to celebrate Gypsy emancipation. Its leaders also began to discuss plans to create "a library, a hospital, and a university for Rom." It was also actively involved in planning a Gypsy World Congress in Bucharest in the fall of 1933 which brought together Gypsies from throughout Europe. The congress, which opened with the theme "United Gypsies of Europe," adopted a program that advocated efforts to stimulate Gypsy ethnic consciousness in league with greater demands for national minority rights. The following year, a national Gypsy congress meeting in Bucharest created the *Uniúnea Generála a Romilor din Românía* (General Union of Roma of Romania). Led by Gheorghe Nicolescu, it advocated an assimilationist policy and an end to nomadism.[40] Unfortunately, the growing oppression of King Carol II's regime forced the Gypsies and other minorities to adopt a "low profile" to preserve the gains they had already made.[41]

By the late 1930s, Romania, like many of its East European neighbors, had drifted into the fascist camp. The new constitution of 1938 paid little attention to minority rights, while the Minority Statute of 4 August 1938 was viewed as little more than a "piece of propaganda" meant primarily for "German . . . consumption."[42] Within a year after the outbreak of the Second World War, Romania saw some of the territory that it had acquired between 1918 and 1920 returned to the USSR, Bulgaria, and Hungary. King Carol tried to stifle public outcries over these losses by more stringent policies against groups like the Gypsies and the Jews. His successor, Ion Antonescu, intensified such efforts in his new "Nationalist Legionary State."[43] Officially, Gypsies, like Jews, were considered no better than "Mice, rats, crows . . ." and, according to Antonescu, should be eliminated.[44]

In 1941 Romania and Germany created the province of Transnistria as a "model Romanian settlement through large-scale Romanian colonization," a euphemism for an area that was to become a dumping ground for Gypsies, Jews, and other racial undesirables from Romania and other countries. Over the next two years, authorities shipped 25,000 Romanian Gypsies to Transnistria, where many died. Harsh living conditions prompted some Gypsies to escape, and many eventually made their way back to Romania. Those that remained in Romania suffered from harassment, though even this subsided by 1943 as the country's leadership, increasingly suspicious of their ties with Germany, tempered these policies with an eye toward a separate peace settlement with the Allies.[45] Antonescu was overthrown on 23 August 1944, and replaced by King Michael who remained in power until 1947. War losses for the Gypsies of Romania totalled between 36,000 and 39,000, though some feel that this number is too conservative.[46]

During the three-year interval between 1944 and 1947, the Soviet Union, backed by the Red Army, was able to engineer the gradual communization of the country. It was aided by a revitalized Communist party that grew from less than 1,000 in 1944 to 217,000 the following year.[47] In this period of rapid growth, Gypsies and other minorities joined this movement and acquired local and regional party positions. These moves fit in with Stalin's efforts between 1944–1947 to use "the national minorities as a means for undermining anti-communism in Romania."[48]

On the other hand, Moscow's hand-picked prime minister and head of the National Democratic Front, Petru Groza, gave only lip service to the concept of strong minority rights.[49] This trend continued with the advent of the Romanian People's Republic on 30 December 1947, which, though it specifically guaranteed ethnic rights in its constitutions of 1948 and 1952, "subordinated" them "entirely to the goal of building socialism." Over the next decade, programs designed to nationalize the economy, develop heavy industry, collectivize agriculture, and indoctrinate the nation were coupled with the "indirect attempts at assimilation" of the country's minority communities.[50]

Gypsies, however, have not received the same official recognition as other minorities and are not treated like other ethnic groups in Romania. This, in part, reflects a historic "ambivalent attitude toward the larger Gypsy minority" and the inability of the country's rulers to decide whether they were a "class" or a "racial phenomenon." This indecisiveness was strengthened initially by low postwar demographic statistics and the lack of any outside pressure to force the Romanian government to grant Gypsies the same privileges afforded the Magyars, the Germans, the Jews, and other "cohabiting nationalities." This position has also been fortified by negative public attitudes toward the Gypsies and growing embarrassment over their life-style vis-à-vis a "modernizing and communizing Romania."[51] The Gypsies, who are not viewed as civilized, have, according to official policy, first to adopt a more settled, cultured Romanian life-style before they can begin to be given normal minority rights. This would bring the Gypsies more in line with the agrarian-oriented, hard-working Romanian social value system. Romanian officials feel that only through integration and adoption of Romanian values can the Gypsies shake their image as nomadic outsiders, whose life-style and moral values run contrary to that of the Romanian nation.[52]

These attitudes, blended with the dramatic economic and social transformation of the country, have had a significant impact upon the Gypsies. In the countryside, individual Gypsy farmers were forced onto collectives as were nomadic Gypsies who had occupations other than farming. "In addition, large numbers of Gypsies settled in the cities and became manual workers."[53] This process, in turn, affected Gypsies in other ways. Although there were some Gypsy intellectuals in the interwar period, their numbers were not significant enough to open doors to the professions for others. Consequently, in the period between 1956 and 1966, there was a decline in the number of Gypsies in the professions. On the other hand, these policies had a significant impact on Gypsy illiteracy, one of the principle barriers to any type of upward mobility in Romanian society. In 1956, 37.7 percent of all Gypsies over eight were illiterate. Within a decade, though, almost "all Gypsies twelve years or over were in primary schools. . . ." This was, however, only a beginning since the Gypsies were woefully underrepresented in mid-level and higher education.[54] Another effect of these policies was a separation between the better educated Gypsies who had chosen to " 'switch' nationality in order to achieve upper social mobility" and those less educated who clung to their traditional culture and language. This caused a higher percentage of Gypsies, principally from the latter group, to declare Romani as their primary language in 1966 (58.8 percent) than in 1956 (46.1 percent).[55]

As a result, the Gypsies remain "inadequately integrated" into Romanian society, while "large minorities in this group remain extremely traditional in socioeconomic lifestyle and cultural values."[56] Part of the problem, of course, deals simply with time. The other problem, prejudice, is more deeply ingrained into the fabric of Romania's peasant-oriented society, and is the most difficult barrier to overcome, particularly in light of the traumatic social and economic upheavals that have shaken the country since World War II. Traditionally, Romania had one of the largest peasant populations in Eastern Europe.[57] The complex political, economic, and social policies adopted by the country's Communist rulers since 1945 have dramatically changed the rural : urban balance from 23.4 percent urban : 76.6 percent rural in 1948, to 42.7 percent urban : 57.3 percent rural in 1974. These changes, however, have not dramatically altered the peasant-based attitudes toward the Gypsies, and in some instances have "exacerbated old differences."[58]

One of the hallmarks of the Communists, particularly under Nicolae Ceauşescu, has been an effort to transform the value system of the Romanian farming class through a blend of "orthodox Marxism and nationalistic traditionalism in policy making." The new system emphasized a keen sense of Romanian nationalism blended with an active commitment to the state, work, and family. Though unsuccessful in most instances, these new ideals, combined with the natural animosity and stereotyping of Gypsies throughout the country, has kept alive and encouraged an "ethnic hierarchy" that deals with the Gypsies as an inferior race or class.[59]

These feelings are so deeply ingrained in the Romanian mind that the term *Ţigan* is synonymous with someone who is "worthless and shiftless."[60] These attitudes, which hark back to the period of Gypsy slavery, are so pervasive that they blur ethnic distinctions. Romanians will refer to someone as a Gypsy because of certain behavioral characteristics, regardless of whether they are a Gypsy or not. There are reported cases where Romanian villagers saw Gypsies as responsible for the evils of collectivization, industrial abuse, and general economic mismanagement. In other settings, Gypsies were seen as opportunists who moved, along with other minorities, into areas left by German settlers after World War II. In the assault on government headquarters in Bucharest on 18 February 1990, protesters blamed the violence that accompanied the attack on Gypsies.[61]

Despite these feelings, Romanians are officially quite embarrassed by the Gypsy situation, and foreign contact with Gypsies is discouraged.[62] Romania's new national government has tried to be sensitive to the needs of the country's various minorities, though the plight of the Gypsies is complicated by their rising numbers. While it is impossible to get an accurate count of the number of Gypsies in the country, some estimates range as high as 760,000 to one million.[63] In light of other minority groups' population declines over the past twenty five years vis-à-vis the increase in the size of the Romanian population, the plight of the Gypsy in Romania is, at best, an uncertain one.[64] Perhaps the best clue to their fate can be seen in the lives of those who have been able to blend more fully into Romanian society. Some, such as Meron Niculescu, the president of the Romanian Academy of Sciences in the 1970s, and Ion Voicu, a director of the Romanian National Philharmonic Orchestra, were Gypsies. Others have been able to integrate successfully into Romanian village settings, and even marry non-Gypsies, though these situations are more the exception than the rule.[65] However, no real changes will take place until the Romanian government decides to grant the country's Gypsies the same rights and privileges afforded its other minorities. Yet even this premise is shaky, given the general uncomfortable atmosphere toward these ethnic groups. Regardless, until that is done, Romania's Gypsies will continue to live in the shadows of Romanian society without a concrete identity.

Notes

1. Sam Beck, "The Origins of Gypsy Slavery in Romania," p. 58; idem, "The Emergence of the Peasant-Worker in a Transylvanian Mountain Community," p. 375, note 4; John Kifner, "A Country Is Haunted," p. A6; Ian M. Matley, *Romania: A Profile*, p. 189.

2. Beck, "Origins of Gypsy Slavery," p. 55; Ian Hancock, *The Pariah Syndrome: An Account of Gypsy Slavery and Persecution*, pp. 13–14; P.N. Panaitescu, "The Gypsies in Wallachia and Moldavia: A Chapter of Economic History," pp. 64–65.

3. Hancock, *Pariah Syndrome*, p. 16; Victor S. Mamatey, *Rise of the Hapsburg Empire, 1526–1815*, p. 4; Fred Singleton, *A Short History of the Yugoslav Peoples*, pp. 25–26.

4. Andrei Oțetea, ed., *A Concise History of Romania*, pp. 166–72; R.W. Seton-Watson, *A History of the Roumanians*, pp. 26–30.

5. Oțetea, *Concise History of Romania*, pp. 168–69; Panaitescu, "Gypsies in Wallachia and Moldavia," p. 65; Hancock notes a controversy surrounding the question as to whether the terms used in these documents, *acingani* and *cbngarije*, actually refer to Gypsies, Hancock, *Pariah Syndrome*, pp. 11–12, 16; for an excellent overview on Gypsy origins in this part of Europe, see Andrew Arjeh Marchbin, "A Critical History of the Origin and Migration of the Gypsies," pp. 52–74.

6. Several sources list 1445 as the date for Vlad IV's campaigns in Bulgaria. He did not come to power as prince until 1456, and in 1462 was forced from his throne and into exile in Hungary until 1476 when he briefly regained his crown before his death. Beck, "Origins of Gypsy Slavery," p. 56; Hancock, *Pariah Syndrome*, p. 22; Oțetea, *Concise History of Romania*, pp. 192–93; Seton-Watson, *History of the Roumanians*, pp. 40–41; Stanford Shaw, *History of the Ottoman Empire and Modern Turkey*, Vol. I: *Empire of the Gazis: The Rise and Decline of the Ottoman Empire, 1280–1808*, p. 64.

7. Beck, "Origins of Gypsy Slavery," p. 56; Hancock, *Pariah Syndrome*, p. 15; Ifor L. Evans, *The Agrarian Revolution in Romania*, p. 51; M. Gaster, "Mixed Marriages," p. 226; Seton-Watson, *History of the Roumanians*, p. 44; for more documentary evidence on fourteenth- and fifteenth-century Romanian Gypsies, see C.J. Popp Serboianu, *Les Tsiganes*, pp. 45–47.

8. Shaw, *History of the Ottoman Empire, Volume I*, pp. 59, 73, 122, 155–57; for more on the significance of slavery in the Ottoman Empire, see H. Inalcik, "Servile Labor in the Ottoman Empire," pp. 25–52.

9. Panaitescu, "Gypsies in Wallachia and Moldavia," p. 67; Shaw, *History of the Ottoman Empire*, pp. 151–52; Seton-Watson, *History of the Roumanians*, p. 52; for an excellent discussion of the development of serfdom in Transylvania during this period, with some comments on slavery, see David Prodan, "The Origins of Serfdom in Transylvania," pp. 1–18.

10. Beck, "Origins of Gypsy Slavery," pp. 57–58; Panaitescu, "Gypsies in Wallachia and Moldavia," p. 69.

11. Hancock, *Pariah Syndrome,* pp. 16–17; Panaitescu, "Gypsies in Wallachia and Moldavia," p. 69; Serboianu, *Les Tsiganes,* pp. 62–63, provides extensive coverage on the *lautari* in Wallachia and Moldavia.

12. Hancock, *Pariah Syndrome*, pp. 7, 17; for more on Gypsy tribal designations, see Jean-Paul Clébert, *The Gypsies*, pp. 69–71; see also Serboianu's breakdown of the various tribal categories of Gypsies in Wallachia and Moldavia, *Les Tsiganes,* pp. 53–57; and William G. Lockwood, "Balkan Gypsies: An Introduction," pp. 95–96, also has an extensive list of Romanian Gypsy tribes.

13. M. Gaster, "Rumanian Gypsies in 1560," p. 59; Seton-Watson, *History of the Roumanians*, pp. 74, 80; Hancock, *Pariah Syndrome*, pp. 22, 24; for administrative purposes, Gypsies were divided into three categories by the time of Basil the Wolf: (1) *laişei (laïechi)*, (2) *vatraşi (vatrachi)*, (3) *Netotsi*, the "demi-sauvages et demi-nus," Serboianu, *Les Tsiganes*, pp. 42, 51–52.

14. Oţetea, *Concise History of Romania*, pp. 251–62; Seton-Watson, *History of the Roumanians*, pp. 126–30.

15. Evans, *Agrarian Revolution,* pp. 22, 51; Hancock, *Pariah Syndrome*, p. 24; Oţetea, *Concise History of Romania,* pp. 261–63; Seton-Watson, *History of the Roumanians*, pp. 140–42.

16. Beck, "Origins of Gypsy Slavery," p. 57; Hancock, *Pariah Syndrome*, p. 25; Seton-Watson, *History of the Roumanians*, p. 142; "Two Rumanian Documents Concerning Gypsies," pp. 181–82.

17. Oţetea, *Concise History of Romania,* pp. 264–66; Seton-Watson, *History of the Roumanians*, pp. 152, 156–57.

18. Oţetea, *Concise History of Romania,* pp. 266–67; Seton-Watson, *History of the Roumanians*, pp. 158, 160–61, 164; the Russians invaded the Danubian Principalities in November 1806 after the Turks removed two pro-Russian governors, at French instigation, several months earlier. At Tilsit the following year, Napoleon convinced the Tsar to withdraw his forces there while he worked to gain peace between Turkey and Russia. However, if the negotiations failed "within three months," Napoleon agreed that France would help Russia drive the Sultan from the area. W.G. East, *The Union of Moldavia and Wallachia, 1859,* pp. 8–9; Alan Palmer, *Alexander I: Tsar of War and Peace,* pp. 122–23, 142–43, 161; Stanford Shaw and Ezel Kural Shaw, *History of the Ottoman Empire and Modern Turkey,* Vol. II: *Reform, Revolution, and Republic: The Rise of Modern Turkey, 1808–1975,* p. 17.

19. W. Bruce Lincoln, *Nicholas I: Emperor and Autocrat of All the Russias*, p. 189; Seton-Watson, *History of the Roumanians*, pp. 199, 201.

20. Oţetea, *Concise History of Romania,* p. 304; Seton-Watson, *History of the Roumanians*, pp. 209–10; for a more concise view of Kiselev's career and his evolving attitudes on the status of Russian and Romanian peasants, see Henry H. Hirschbiel, "Kiselev, Pavel Dmitrievich (1788–1872)," pp. 41–44; Serboianu, *Les Tsiganes,* pp. 48–50.

21. Alex Russell, "Classification and Numbers of Wallachian Gypsies in 1837," p. 150.

22. Hancock, *Pariah Syndrome*, pp. 27–30; Hirschbiel, "Kiselev," p. 42.

23. Oţetea, *Concise History of Romania,* pp. 307–8; Serboianu, *Les Tsiganes,* pp. 48–50; Seton-Watson, *History of the Roumanians,* pp. 207–8; Hancock, *Pariah Syndrome,* pp. 31–32, 34, uses the higher figure, while the lower one is used by W.R. Halliday in "Roumanian Gypsies," p. 143; David Mitrany, *The Land and the Peasant in Rumania: The War and the Agrarian Reform (1917–1921),* p. 50n; and by William Wilkinson, *An Account of the Principalities of Wallachia and Moldavia,* p. 169. Istvan Deak notes in his "The Revolution of 1848–49 in Transylvania and the Polarization of National Destinies," p. 122, that there were 70,000 Gypsies in Transylvania in the mid-nineteenth century.

24. Hancock, *Pariah Syndrome,* p. 34; Panaitescu, "Gypsies in Wallachia and Moldavia," pp. 71–72; Evans, *Agrarian Revolution,* p. 34, says that Crown and Church slaves were freed in Wallachia in 1844, and in Moldavia in 1845.

25. Oţetea, *Concise History of Romania,* pp. 327–30; Seton-Watson, *History of the Roumanians,* pp. 220–24; for an excellent, concise look at the direct French impact on Wallachian and Moldavian intellectuals at this time, see Raymond Pearson, *National Minorities in Eastern Europe, 1848–1945,* pp. 86–87, 127–28.

26. Hancock, *Pariah Syndrome,* pp. 34–35; Oţetea, *Concise History of Romania,* pp. 340–43; Seton-Watson, *History of the Roumanians,* p. 229; for an interesting view of Gypsy family and clan life during this period, see M. Gaster, "Bill of Sale of Gypsy Slaves in Moldavia, 1851," pp. 68–81; Evans, *Agrarian Revolution,* p. 34.

27. East, *The Union,* p. 51; Oţetea, *Concise History of Romania,* pp. 348–54; Panaitescu, "Gypsies in Wallachia and Moldavia," p. 72; Seton-Watson, *History of the Roumanians,* pp. 262–63, 310; for more details on the Convention's negotiations, see T.W. Riker, *The Making of Romania: A Study of an International Problem, 1856–1866,* pp. 141–80; details of the Agrarian Law are found in ibid., pp. 458–59.

28. Hancock, *Pariah Syndrome,* pp. 37–38; Oţetea, *Concise History of Romania,* pp. 363, 383, 385, 389–90; Seton-Watson, *History of the Roumanians,* pp. 319–21, 367–69.

29. Mitrany, *Land and Peasant in Rumania,* p. 62; Oţetea, *Concise History of Romania,* pp. 398–400; Seton-Watson, *History of the Roumanians,* pp. 385, 388–89.

30. Alex Russell, "Roumanian Gypsies," p. 154; T.W. Thompson, "Gypsies in the Mezoseg of Transylvania," p. 194; T.W. Thompson, "Gypsy Prisoners at Szamos Ujvar, Transylvania," pp. 195–96.

31. Hancock, *Pariah Syndrome,* p. 45.

32. David Crowe, *World War I and Europe in Crisis (1914–1935),* pp. 12, 46; Elemer Illyes, *National Minorities in Romania: Change in Transylvania,* p. 34; Seton-Watson, *History of the Roumanians,* p. 566.

33. Illyes, *National Minorities in Romania,* pp. 34–35; in his *Contemporary Romania and Her Problems,* pp. 187–89, Joseph S. Roucek states that there were 285,000 Gypsies in Romania in 1920, with 225,000 in the Regat, and 60,000 in the new areas added after World War I. Other specialists place 136,844 Gypsies in Transylvania in 1925; for information on the Gypsy contribution to the Romanian language, see Frederick Kellogg, "The Structure of Romanian Nationalism," p. 22.

34. Illyes, *National Minorities in Romania,* pp. 86–91; Milton G. Lehrer, *Transylvania: History and Reality,* pp. 233–35; Zsombor de Szász, *The Minorities in Romanian Transylvania,* pp. 405–8.

35. Evans, *Agrarian Revolution,* p. 159; Mitrany, *Land and Peasant in Rumania,* p. 225; Oţetea, *Concise History of Romania,* p. 433; Pearson, *National Minorities,* p. 167; Hugh Seton-Watson, *Eastern Europe between the Wars, 1918–1941,* pp. 87–97; 200–201, 273–74.

36. Frederick H. Barth, *A Transylvanian Legacy: The Life of a Transylvanian Saxon,* p. 168; B. Gilliat-Smith, ''Reviews,'' p. 139; Seton-Watson, *Eastern Europe,* pp. 201, 204, 208.

37. E.O. Hoppe, *In Gypsy Camp and Royal Palace: Wanderings in Rumania,* pp. 42, 44–45.

38. Charles Upson Clark, *United Roumania.* p. 291; Hoppe, *In Gypsy Camp,* pp. 50–52.

39. Sam Beck, ''Ethnicity, Class, and Public Policy: Ţiganii/Gypsies in Socialist Romania,'' p. 27; Stephen Fischer-Galati, ''National Minorities in Romania, 1919–1980,'' pp. 198–99; Joshua Starr, ''Jewish Citizenship in Rumania (1878–1940),'' pp. 66–68; Nicolas Sylvain, ''Rumania,'' p. 499.

40. Hancock, *Pariah Syndrome,* p. 45; Donald Kenrick and Grattan Puxon, *The Destiny of Europe's Gypsies,* p. 205; Jean-Pierre Liégeois, *Gypsies: An Illustrated History,* pp. 145–46.

41. Beck, ''Ethnicity, Class, and Public Policy,'' p. 27; Oţetea, *Concise History of Romania,* pp. 457–60; Pearson, *National Minorities,* p. 168; Seton-Watson, *Eastern Europe,* p. 213.

42. Illyes, *National Minorities,* pp. 93–94.

43. Stephen Fischer-Galati, ''Fascism, Communism, and the Jewish Question in Romania,'' pp. 170–71; *Hitler's Ten Year War against the Jews,* pp. 86–89; C.A. Macartney and A.W. Palmer, *Independent Eastern Europe,* pp. 424–27; Sylvain, ''Rumania,'' pp. 400, 504–5.

44. Kenrick and Puxon, *Destiny,* p. 128; Stephen Fischer-Galati takes a much more temperate view toward King Carol II and Antonescu in his *The New Rumania: From People's Democracy to Socialist Republic,* pp. 13–16.

45. Julius S. Fisher, ''How Many Jews Died in Transnistria?'' p. 99; Julius S. Fisher, *Transnistria: The Forgotten Cemetery,* pp. 134–37; P.N. Panaitescu, ''The Gypsy Flower-Sellers of Bucarest,'' p. 77; Pearson, *National Minorities,* p. 199; Joseph B. Schechtman, ''The Transnistria Reservation,'' pp. 178–81, 188.

46. Christian Bernadac, *L'Holocauste Oublié: Le Massacre des Tsiganes,* pp. 412–13; Ian Hancock, ''Uniqueness of the Victims: Gypsies, Jews and the Holocaust,'' pp. 54–57; Kenrick and Puxon, *Destiny,* p. 130; Pearson, *National Minorities,* p. 200.

47. Stephen Fischer-Galati, ''The Communist Takeover of Rumania: A Function of Soviet Power,'' pp. 310–20; Richard F. Staar, *Communist Regimes in Eastern Europe,* p. 185.

48. Beck, ''Ethnicity, Class, and Public Policy,'' pp. 27–28; Mary Ellen Fischer, ''Nation and Nationality in Romania,'' p. 506; Fischer-Galati, *The New Rumania,* pp. 5–6; Illyes, *National Minorities,* pp. 102–3.

49. Walter M. Bacon, Jr., ''Romania,'' pp. 167–68; Illyes, *National Minorities,* p. 104.

50. Ibid., pp. 99, 113–15; Trond Gilberg, ''Ethnic Minorities in Romania under

Socialism," p. 439. This article also appeared under the same title in Bernard Lewis Faber, ed., *The Social Structure of Eastern Europe: Transition and Process in Czechoslovakia, Hungary, Poland, and Yugoslavia*; Fischer, "How Many Jews?" p. 506; one Romanian author referred to this process as "the homogenization of the social structure of the population" and saw it as a form of "social levelling," Ion Blaga, *Romania's Population: A Demographic, Economic and Socio-Political Essay*, p. 89; George Schöpflin states that "it appears that the Rumanian party's policy is to satisfy the minorities through industrialization . . . and that demands for other rights by the minorities are subordinate to the economic programs," in *The Hungarians of Rumania*, p. 9.

51. Beck, "Gypsies in Socialist Romania," pp. 20–22, 31–33; Robert R. King, *Minorities under Communism: Nationalities as a Source of Tension among Balkan Communist States*, pp. 146–48.

52. Sam Beck, "The Romanian Gypsy Problem," pp. 102–3; Trond Gilberg, *Modernization in Romania since World War II*, p. 210; for a historic overview of this Romanian aversion to "foreigners," see Ruth Benedict, "History as It Appears to Rumanians," pp. 413–15.

53. Gilberg, "Ethnic Minorities in Romania," pp. 441, 449.

54. Ibid., pp. 443, 447–48, 460–63.

55. Ibid., pp. 452–53, 463; Paul S. Shoup, *The East European and Soviet Data Handbook: Political, Social, and Development Indicators, 1945–1975*, p. 53; in 1956, 65 percent of the Gypsies "were in Transylvania, and 10 percent in the Banat; 66,882 (0.38 percent of the total population) stated that Gypsy was their mother-tongue, which make Gypsies the fourth largest linguistic minority. However the numbers of Gypsy nationality were only 43 percent of the 1930 figure," K.M. Petyt, "Romania: A Multilingual Nation," p. 91; see Schöpflin, *Hungarians of Rumania*, p. 4, for a breakdown of the 1966 Transylvanian Gypsy population by *judet* [county]; Gilberg, *Modernization in Romania*, p. 223.

56. Gilberg, "Ethnic Minorities in Romania," pp. 445, 449–50, 452, 454.

57. Seton-Watson, *Eastern Europe*, p. 75.

58. Trond Gilberg, "Rural Transformation in Romania," p. 102; Gilberg, "Ethnic Minorities in Romania," p. 459; in 1956, only 17.3 percent of the Gypsies were urbanized, a figure that rose to 26.5 percent a decade later, Gilberg, *Modernization in Romania*, pp. 216, 231.

59. Beck, "Ethnicity, Class, and Public Policy," pp. 20, 23; Gilberg, "Rural Transformation in Romania," pp. 94, 110–13.

60. Ian M. Matley, *Romania: A Profile*, p. 189.

61. Sam Beck, "Indigenous Anthropologists in Socialist Romania," p. 267; Beck, "Emergence of the Peasant-Worker," p. 375, note 4; David A. Kideckel, "Economic Images and Social Change in the Romanian Socialist Transformation," p. 405; Kifner, "A Country Is Haunted," p. A6.

62. Beck, "Indigenous Anthropologists," p. 265; Nebojša Bato Tomašević and Rajko Djurić, *Gypsies of the World: A Journey into the Hidden World of Gypsy Life and Culture*, pp. 182–87.

63. Jean-Pierre Liégeois, *La Scolarisation des Enfants Tziganes et Voyageurs*, p. 12; Grattan Puxon, "Roma: Europe's Gypsies," p. 13; Tomašević and Djurić, *Gyp-*

sies of the World, p. 182. Vladimir Pelesky, "Die Zigeunerfrage in den Ost- und Südosteuropäischen Staaten," p. 618, estimates there were 400,000 Gypsies in Romania in 1970.

64. Staar, *Communist Regimes,* p. 198.

65. Liégeois, *Gypsies*, p. 77; Erica F. McClure and Malcolm M. McClure, "Factors Influencing Language Variation in a Multilingual Transylvanian Village," p. 207.

6

Damnation of the Outsider
The Gypsies of Croatia and Serbia in the Balkan Holocaust, 1941–1945

DENNIS REINHARTZ

> I confess that I feel somewhat guilty towards our Romani friends. We have not done enough to listen to your voice of anguish. We have not done enough to make our people listen to your voice of sadness. I can promise you we shall do whatever we can from now on to listen better. . . . I remember what happened in the "night of the gypsies,". . . That night will remain with me as long as I live. Throughout the kingdom of the night a whisper of fire ran through from man to man, from child to child. We heard just one word—they are burning the Gypsies.
>
> Elie Wiesel[1]

As Yehuda Bauer pointed out in his *A History of the Holocaust*, the Gypsy, like the Jew in Europe before the coming of World War II, traditionally was viewed as "the stranger," "the outsider," "the eternal other," and "the symbol of foreignness, of dark and evil forces. . . ."[2] In the Balkans and elsewhere, Gypsies and Jews historically were wrongfully linked together in popular belief and scholarly investigation. The same incorrect linkage is made even in Gypsy poetry, for example, "The Gypsy and the Jew":

The gypsy and the Hebrew,
Together were exiled,
From their country that they knew,
Their characters defiled.

As both of them had a part,
In that scene so long ago,
When a man dear to our heart,
Was sacrificed you know.

It was then the men of wealth and power,
Exiled them from their land,
Why, up to this very hour
The world cannot understand.

Now from that day in Bethlehem,
The earth has been their home,
The Hebrew and the gypsy man
Are both destined to roam.[3]

This popular, negative stereotype, centered on his alien life-style and the Gypsy's vulnerability as a member of a minority on the fringes of European society, led to the wholesale slaughter of as many as 500,000 in the hysteria of the Holocaust.[4]

While some of the attitudes and much of the hatred that contributed to the attempted destruction of the Roma have largely disappeared, the popular images generally have not. And next to the six million Jews and several million others who perished in the Holocaust, the agony of the Roma continues to be overlooked.[5] The purpose of this essay is to explore the fate of this people in two of the most monstrous, bloody theaters of the World War II Holocaust—Croatia and Serbia—in a effort further to understand the Roma, but also, as Elie Wiesel pledged, to make people listen better to their "voice of anguish and sadness," sounding out of the depths of the horror of the Holocaust.

The fragmentation of Yugoslavia into various zones of occupation and collaborationist states after the Axis invasion and conquest of April 1941 dictates that the plight of the Gypsies in these areas be examined separately. Since there was no significant Gypsy population in Slovenia, this essay will center around the Gypsy Holocaust in Croatia and Serbia.

There has been a continuous Roma presence in the Yugoslav lands since the thirteenth century. In most areas, except Montenegro, the Roma of prewar Yugoslavia were largely sedentary and well established in villages, often for centuries. But as Nebojša Bato Tomašević relates in the new book *Gypsies of the World*, they were still often treated as "outsiders":

> I remember how as a child living in Cetinje, the modest, mountain-ringed capital of Montenegro, I often passed the time, whilst playing truant from school, in warring with the Gypsies. Unlike other parts of Yugoslavia, in which they have had their villages for centuries, not a single Gypsy settlement was or is to be found on the territory of Montenegro. However, Gypsy nomads, called *Guberti* in this region, used to make their way across this rugged country in the fall. In groups of about fifty, ragged, wild-looking, with long beards and hair and a multitude of small children milling around the donkeys loaded with cauldrons, pots and pans, long tent-poles and tattered bedding, they moved slowly towards the scattered mountain hamlets around Cetinje. They dared not enter the town itself as the police carefully watched their every move and severely punished any attempt to disobey the ban. We children had been brought up by mothers and grandmothers on stories of Gypsies' evil deeds, of kidnapped white children, blinded so they could beg, of roaming at night through graveyards, of cannibalism, black magic and the evil eye, by which they could make a healthy man fall ill, go mad or die. For us, Gypsies represented the same kind of evil as the Turks had done for our fore-fathers. In the true spirit of our warrior tradition, by which the enemy had to be repulsed in an organized manner whenever and wherever he appeared, the children from my street developed a strategy for disturbing their progress, attacking from safe, inaccessible points when they least expect us.
>
> On some vantage point, some projecting rock on a hillside under which the Gypsies had to pass along a narrow, winding path, we took it in turns to stand guard, armed "to the teeth" with rocks and stones. We awaited their arrival with impatience, piling ammunition up in front of us.
>
> Then we would see the leader of the Gypsy tribe, some twenty yards ahead of the rest. This was always a strong, vigorous young man who inspired confidence in the Gypsies and respect in all others. With the experience of "seasoned" fighters, we would let him pass and then, raising a terrible din, hurl our stones at the followers. Surprised by our attack, they would falter and scatter in alarm, mothers shrieking to their children to take cover behind the pack animals,

while the men regrouped behind some rock to await developments.

Their leader would dash back to them within moments and, together with the other Gypsies, start shouting in a tongue we children could not understand—added proof, it seemed to us, that they were the devil's own brood.

Realizing they could not pass us without a few bloodied heads while we were entrenched behind our rock, the leader would reach for his gun and, followed by several Gypsy youths, charge uphill towards us. We would allow them to come quite close, and then let fly with our stones. The leader then would fire a couple of shots in our direction, a serious warning that it was time for us to leave the field to the "better armed enemy" but knowing we could lie in wait again, somewhere else, with maybe more success.[6]

The Independent State of Croatia

When World War II broke out, many Gypsies in Croatia and Slovenia sought refuge in Italy, where they were interned and deported to Sardinia. Others were detained at Puglia, though many escaped. Some, like the Gypsy hero from Vicenza, Walter Catter, eventually joined the Partisans. Those who entered Italy after the creation of the fascist Independent State of Croatia in 1941 were sheltered in detention camps by the Italians in order to keep them from recrossing into Yugoslavia in search of relatives. Many of them were furnished with Italian identity cards to put them further beyond the reach of the Nazis and *Ustaše* until 1943. Those caught in the German dragnet after this period were sent to camps in Austria for extermination. Near the end of the war, many Gypsies liberated from Croatian concentration camps again sought refuge in Italy.[7]

When the *Ustaša* fascist satellite of Croatia was created by the Axis in April 1941, its diverse population of 7.5 million Croats, Serbs, Moslems, and others included 28,000 Gypsies, many of whom were nominally Orthodox or Moslem.[8] Proportionally, the greatest genocide of the Holocaust was not in Nazi Germany, but in its loyal ally, the *NDH* (*Nezavisna Država Hrvatska*, or Independent State of Croatia). Between 1941 and 1945, approximately 75,000 Serbs, 60,000 Jews, and 26,000 Gypsies, among others (10 percent of the population of the *NDH*), perished as a result of the racial policies and programs of the Independent State of Croatia.[9]

The Croatian people's vague traditions of racism took more concrete forms under the *Ustaše* and the *NDH*. World War II Croatian

Aryanism, which asserted the racial superiority of the Croats over their fellow South Slavs, Jews, Gypsies, and others and implied racial kinship with the peoples of Western Europe, is a complex, contradictory, and alien phenomenon in modern Balkan history. Yet it was at the core of the Croatian Holocaust because it was an essential part of the *Ustaša* ideology of the *NDH*. But was Aryanism basic to and representative of Croatian nationalism? Probably not.

Milovan Djilas has correctly characterized the *Ustaša* ideology as ''an amalgam of primitive Croatian nationalism with modern fascist totalitarianism . . . militant separatism to fascism to total anti-Serbianism.''[10] In a recent article, Pedro Ramet briefly traced the evolution of the Croatian ideology from the early nineteenth century through the Second World War. He pointed out that nineteenth-century Croatian nationalism branched into two distinct, but closely related forms. The most significant was traditional and mainstream nationalism that emphasized the uniqueness of the Croats while recognizing their shared South Slavic heritage. It was exemplified by liberal movements like the Illyrianism of Ljudvet Gaj (1809–1872) and later Croatian Yugoslavism, and it contained few really racist tendencies. Less important was the more extreme, primitive ''exclusivist Croatian nationalism'' which triumphed temporarily with the *Ustaše* and the *NDH*.[11]

In the nineteenth century, the militant Croatian separatism of men like Eugene Kvaternik (d. 1871) and Ante Starčević (1823–1896) was initially a response to Magyar pretensions to historical Croatia, which was transferred to Serbian, Pan Slav, and/or Yugoslav pretensions in the twentieth century by Ante Pavelić (1889–1959), the founder of the *Ustaše*. Starčević has been called the ''father of racism'' in Croatia and the ''ideological father'' of the *Ustaše* principally because of his influence on Pavelić and the genesis of its ideology in the *Frankovci* wing of Starčević's ''Party of the Right [Law].'' After Starčević's death, his Jewish-born son-in-law, Josip Frank, took over his movement and made it the more extreme ''Party of the Pure Right [Law],'' with Pavelić an important member. While it is uncertain whether most Croats accepted the post–World War I Kingdom of Serbs, Croats, and Slovenes as ''their state,'' few supported the reactionary *Frankovci*. Regardless, between the two world wars, the Croatian Peasant party best represented the nationalist views of the majority of Croats. In exile from the growing Yugoslav royal dictatorship, Pavelić's outlook hardened, especially when he was placed under a death sentence in absentia by King Alexander in 1929, the same year Pavelić organized the *Ustaše* in Italy with help from Mussolini and Admiral Miklos Horthy, the fascist dictator of Hungary. It was in the pronouncements of the *Ustaše* that its extreme racist tendencies crystallized, eventually leading to Croatian Aryanism. For example, on 1 June 1933, more than a year before the *Ustaša-IMRO* (Internal Macedonian Revolutionary Organization) assassination of King Alexander and French Foreign Minister Louis Barthou in Marseilles, Pavelić made public the "Principles of the *Ustaša* Movement." The Eleventh Principle declared that in the national and state affairs of Croatia "nobody who is not by birth and blood a member of the Croatian people can make any decisions . . . no foreign people or state."[12] Yet despite its threatening propaganda and terrorist acts, the *Ustaše* goals of secession and independence came only under the auspices of the Axis in the second year of World War II in Europe. After the fall of Yugoslavia and the German occupation of Zagreb, Pavelić and the *Ustaše* leaders were brought in from all over Axis Europe and given local control in Croatia. The result was the *NDH* under the fascist *Ustaše* with Pavelić as the *Poglavnik* (leader), and the Italian Duke of Spoleto, who had never set foot in the *NDH*, as King Tomislav II.[13]

On 19 April 1941, only days after its founding, the *NDH* enacted its first racial laws. Eventually, under this Nazi-modeled legislation, the Croatian "definitions," except for those concerning the Gypsies, were more inclusive than their German counterparts, thereby reflecting the southeast European polyglot. But as in Germany, in the *NDH*, the Roma, due to their foreign appearance, strange customs, language, semi-nomadic existence, and lack of regular employment— generally offensive asocial behavior to Aryans—were considered "aliens outside the national community." Being Serbian Orthodox, Jewish, or Roma was equated with Orientalism in the *NDH*, but not being an "Aryan" Moslem, for the *Ustaše* needed the support of the *NDH*'s 750,000 Moslems (mostly in Bosnia and Herzegovina) to counter its 2.5 million Serbs and other non-Aryan peoples. Yet, since the Gypsies' origins were in India, they were more Aryan than the Moslems, Croats, and even the Germans.[14]

Article 1 of the "Decree Regarding Race Membership" of 30 April 1941 stated that "a person of Aryan descent is one who derives from ancestors who are members of the European race union, or who derives from descendants of such union outside Europe." Gypsies were defined officially in Article 4 as those having two or more Gypsy grandparents. In contrast, to be considered a Jew one had to have three or more Jewish grandparents. Article 2 also further discriminated against the Gypsies. It required special permission from the Ministry of Interior for marriages between Aryans and anyone having one second lineage ancestor who was a Gypsy or two who were Jews. The *Ustaša* delineations of a Gypsy were even more specific than those of the Nazis which equated Gypsies and Jews in all cases. Proof of racial origins was established on the basis of birth/baptismal and marriage certificates of parents and grandparents. Questionable cases were decided by the Ministry of Interior upon recommendations from the Race Political Committee.[15]

Under Decree No. 13–542 of the Ministry of Interior, all Gypsies had to register with the police on 22–23 July 1941.[16] Thereafter, Gypsy enterprises and other property were confiscated and turned over to individuals of "Aryan origin" (the *Ustaše* and their followers), regardless of qualifications, under the Office of Nationalized Property of the NDH. In 1941–1943 most of Croatia's Gypsies were put in *Ustaša*-manned concentration camps like Tenje, Jasenovac, and Stara Gradska in the *NDH*. By the summer of 1942, like their counterparts from occupied Serbia, growing numbers were also being transported to the Third Reich for "medical" experimentation and more systematic extermination at Auschwitz and other camps outside Yugoslavia.[17] Leo Laufer, a Jewish survivor of many of the camps, has related his encounter with the Roma in Birkenau in October 1944:

> I remember in *Lager D*, where we were, next to us was *Lager E*. This is where the Gypsies lived. You know the stories written about the Gypsies. And I remember so vividly the Gypsies, when we remember them, were more privileged than us Jews in Birkenau. And what I say, why they were more privileged, we were admiring them, that they had the opportunity of living in the barracks with their families, their children, their wives, old ones, young ones, that were all together. And with us was only men. We were only young men. They were privileged to live. And we always said how beautiful maybe it would have been if you would have your parents together, our brothers and sisters and be together. And we really admired them for quite a while. And it was kindly, I would say maybe sentimental. I remember when we used to come home from work, we used to open up the back door and listen to some of their songs cause it was just

the next barrack over, like Camp D and Camp E. And they used to sing melodies, mostly, I believe from Rumania and Hungary and so on. And we really admired them. And it was something that, you know, we felt toward them. But then when the last transport and the people from Lodz came from my city, when they liquidated the Lodz ghetto, in one night when we got up in the morning there wasn't one Gypsy left. Children, men, women, grandfathers, totally gone, totally gone. And when we went to work in the morning, we could still see. The chimneys were going like rockets. We could smell it; we could feel it. Of course we had the feeling that this is what happened to them—little did we know that the same night we came home from work that the Jewish people from Lodz were the ones who replaced the Gypsies, in the same barracks.[18]

Many Gypsies also were executed outright in reprisal for Partisan and *Četnik* activities in the *NDH*.[19] At his war crimes trial in Zagreb, Andrija Artuković, the former *Ustaša* Minister of Interior and Minister of Justice, was remembered by a witness, Jelena Rasovic, as having said in a speech at Sremska Mitrovica Prison that the *Ustaše* "had killed the black Gypsies, and all that was left was to kill the white Gypsies [Serbs]."[20]

Usually the Roma were not welcome among the Serbian nationalist *Četniks*, and as a result of the atrocities committed against the Roma in Croatia and Serbia, many of them joined the Partisans. But sometimes, especially in the mountainous regions, they formed their own resistance groups apart from the Partisans and *Četniks*, and on occasion fought them as well as the Axis forces. Nevertheless, for their contributions, an autonomous Gypsy region in Macedonia was considered in post–World War II Yugoslavia, but was never realized.[21]

German-Occupied Serbia

In 1941 there were approximately 150,000 Roma in Serbia with about 10,000 of them in Belgrade. For several days before the actual Axis invasion of Yugoslavia on 6 April 1941, the Germans mercilessly bombed the Gypsy quarter in Zemun across the Sava River from Belgrade. Soon after the occupation began, all Gypsies were required to wear yellow "*Zigeuner*" armbands at all times in public and were treated like the Jews.[22]

In a memorandum of 26 October 1941 to local German commanders in Serbia, Staatsrat Harald Turner, the chief of civil administration and an *SS Gruppenführer* under General Franz Böhme, the commander of all German troops in Serbia, stated the basic occupation policy toward the Gypsies:

> The Gypsy cannot, by reason of his inner and outer makeup [*Konstruktion*], be a useful member of international society [*Völkergemeinschaft*]. . . . As a matter of principle it must be said that the Jews and Gypsies represent an element of insecurity and thus a danger to public order and safety. . . . That is why it is a matter of principle in each case to put all Jewish men and all male Gypsies at the disposal of the troops as hostages.[23]

By March 1942, the Semlin *Judenlager* on the Semlin Exposition Grounds outside Belgrade already contained about 10 percent of the city's Gypsies, and more were arriving daily from the city and the rest of Serbia. Croatian *Ustaša* were brought in to guard the Gypsies at Semlin under German supervision.[24]

In occupied Serbia, Gypsies were defined by the Germans as those having at least three Gypsy grandparents. "Mixed bloods" (*Mischlinge*) were those who had one or two Gypsy grandparents and were married to Gypsies. In Serbia, they equated the Roma with the Jews.[25]

At Semlin, the Gypsies generally were degraded and had their valuables taken from them by the *National Socialist Volkswohlfahrt* (*NSV*). As in other Serbian camps, they were forced to do the most demeaning work, particularly gravedigging. The frequent German execution of Gypsies and Jews spared Serbs from arbitrary retaliation by the invaders, which might have damaged the "interests" of the German occupation. Gypsies, Jews, and other hostages were executed at a ratio of 100:1 for every German soldier killed in Serbia. In 1942, Turner reported with pride that "In the interests of pacification, the Gypsy question has been fully liquidated. Serbia is the only country in which the Jewish question and the Gypsy question have been solved."[26] Yet, although during World War II some 20,000 Gypsies perished in the Semlin camp alone, the Germans, their allies, and their collaborators only effectively controlled about one-third of Serbia's Roma population. Many of the rest fled, hid, evaded, or joined the resistance.[27]

Conclusion

The magnitude of the historic discrimination against the Roma as "outsiders" prior to the Second World War contributed to their suffering more severely than any other group in the Holocaust in Croatia and Serbia. Although they were often wrongly associated with the Jews, the Roma usually were considered to be even more lowly, less human, and suffered commensurately. They truly were a forgotten people. Allied intelligence reports of the time either failed to mention them or categorized them as "others." [28]

However, despite their losses in Serbia and Croatia, the Gypsies of Yugoslavia came out of the war better than elsewhere in the Balkans or Eastern Europe. Today, there are approximately 800,000 of them, and they are a constitutionally recognized nationality with all the rights thereof. But even in contemporary Yugoslavia, what is official is not always actual, especially with regard to the resurgence of Serbian nationalism and discrimination against ethnic Albanians. Yet, after Tito's death, Grattan Puxon, the general secretary of the World Romani Congress, paid him tribute for his efforts:

> The death of President Tito was a profoundly sad event for Roma both inside and outside Yugoslavia. As the architect of the post-war multi-national state, he succeeded—perhaps better than any other statesman—in carrying into practice the principle of equality between different nationalities co-existing within the same country. And his blend of socialism, non-alignment and limited private enterprise has been applauded and copied.[29]

Despite these gains, the agony of the Roma in Croatia and Serbia during the Holocaust should make us all, as Elie Wiesel has pledged, "listen better."

> The upright stone stares angrily
> with clenched fists and a great curse.
> From within a hidden voice
> tries to send out a song.
>
> The roads we still travel
> wait to hear.
> The Gypsies await the call
> together with their horses.
>
> But they are quiet, all are asleep.
> Our brothers lie among the flowers
> and no one knows who they are
> or on which road the victims fell.

Hush, Gypsies! Let them sleep
beneath the flowers.
Halt, Gypsies!
May all our children have their strength.
—Dimiter Golemanov[30]

Notes

1. These words were spoken recently at a ceremony honoring the Gypsy victims of the Holocaust in Washington, D.C., sponsored by the United States Holocaust Memorial Council, which was chaired by Wiesel. See "Gypsies Hear Pledge of Aid on Holocaust," *New York Times*, 7 September 1986.

2. Yehuda Bauer, *A History of the Holocaust*, pp. 46–47; also, see Benno Müller-Hill, *Murderous Science: Elimination by Scientific Selection of Jews, Gypsies and Others, Germany, 1933–1945*.

3. Damodar P. Singhal, *Gypsies: Indians in Exile*, p. 158.

4. Josef Koudelka, *Gypsies;* Jeremy Noakes, "Social Outcasts in Nazi Germany"; and *New York Times*, 17 September 1986.

5. For example, three recent studies on World War II in the Balkans, while dealing specifically and even extensively with the Jews, make no mention of the Gypsies. See Mihai Fatu and Mircea Musat, eds., *Hortheyist-Fascist Terror in Northwestern Romania September 1940–October 1944*; John L. Hondros, *Occupation and Resistance: The Greek Agony, 1941–1944*; Marshall L. Miller, *Bulgaria during the Second World War*.

6. Nebojša Bato Tomašević and Rajko Djurić, *Gypsies of the World: A Journey into the Hidden World of Gypsy Life and Culture*, pp. 7–8.

7. Bauer, *History of the Holocaust*, p. 337; Donald Kenrick and Grattan Puxon, *The Destiny of Europe's Gypsies*, pp. 108–11.

8. Ibid., p. 112.

9. Edmond Paris, *Genocide in Satellite Croatia, 1941–1945: A Record of Racial and Religious Persecutions and Massacres*, p. 9; in comparison, only 25,000 of Germany's 30,000 Gypsies perished, Noakes, "Social Outcast," p. 18.

10. Milovan Djilas, *Wartime*, pp. 11–12.

11. Pedro Ramet, "From Strossmayer to Stepinac: Croatian National Ideology and Catholicism," pp. 123–39.

12. Stejpan Hefer, *Croation Struggle for Freedom and Statehood*, p. 108.

13. Dennis Reinhartz, "Holocaust kao poslanje" [An Extreme of the Holocaust], pp. 27–28; Dennis Reinhartz, "Aryanism and the Independent State of Croatia, 1941–1945," pp. 19–25.

14. Raul Hilberg, *The Destruction of the European Jews*, vol. 1, p. 438 and vol. 2, pp. 708–17 and Noakes, "Social Outcast," pp. 15–18.

15. "Decree Regarding Race Membership," p. 1.

16. *Hrvatski Narod* [Croatian Nation], p. 7; Tilman Zulch, *In Auschwitz Vergast, Bis Heute Verfolgt: Zur Situation der Roman (Zigeuner) in Deutschland und Europa* [Gassed in Auschwitz, Pursued to the Present: About the Situation of the Roma (Gypsies) in Germany and Europe], pp. 89–146.

17. For a recent study on Jasenovac, see: Antun Miletić, *Koncentracioni Logor Jasenovac 1941–1945* [The Jasenovac Concentration Camp 1941–1945].

18. Diane Plotkin, "Historiographic Analysis of a Survivor's Narrative: The Story of Leo Laufer," pp. 10–11.

19. Hilberg, *Destruction*, vol. 2, pp. 711–13.

20. Larry Keller, "Witness Ties Artuković, Killing . . ." p. 6.

21. Kenrick and Puxon, *Destiny*, pp. 111–19.

22. Christopher R. Browning, *Fateful Months: Essays on the Emergence of the Final Solution,* p. 71; and Kenrick and Puxon, *Destiny*, pp. 111–15.

23. Browning, *Fateful Months*, p. 54; Hilberg, *Destruction*, vol. 1, p. 438.

24. Browning, *Fateful Months*, p. 71; Kenrick and Puxon, *Destiny*, pp. 117–18.

25. Kenrick and Puxon, *Destiny*, p. 115.

26. Ibid., p. 119.

27. Browning, *Fateful Months*, pp. 51–53; Hilberg, *Destruction*, vol. 1, p. 439; Kenrick and Puxon, *Destiny*, pp. 115–19.

28. For example, see: Great Britain. *Foreign Office Weekly Political Intelligence Summaries*, no. 83, p. 15; no. 87, p. 15; no. 96, pp. 15–16; *Correspondence of the Foreign Office*, Great Britain: Public Records Office. FO371, R7914/1068/92, p. 7; FO371, R5331/850/92, pp. 15–16.

29. Grattan Puxon, "Tito and the Future of Roma," p. 5; idem, "Gypsies: Blacks of East Europe," pp. 460–64.

30. Singhal, *Gypsies*, pp. 128–29.

7

The Gypsies of Czechoslovakia

JOSEF KALVODA

The 1952 edition of the *Dictionary of the Czech Language* defines Gypsy as follows: "gypsy—a member of a wandering nation, a symbol of mendacity, theft, wandering, . . . jokers, liars, imposters, and cheaters."[1] This definition was published two years after the Czechoslovak government outlawed any form of discrimination on the basis of color.[2] As far as this writer recalls, the above definition expressed the popular understanding of the Gypsies as a group in Czechoslovakia in the 1930s. Despite the persecution of the Gypsies during the war and the popular sympathy for them because of it, prejudice against them has not disappeared, and one can find it reflected in the official press as well as in ordinary conversation. It is evident from official publications that Gypsies are seen to pose certain problems for the regime and the society.[3]

Historical Background

Why the Gypsies left their original homeland in northern India around 1000 A.D. is not known. They reached Europe via Asia Minor and the Balkans. By the end of the fourteenth century relatively large numbers of them had settled in the Danubian area, working as smiths, cobblers, horse traders, and the like. By and large the Gypsies were incorporated into the social and economic order by the rulers of the various principalities.[4] The early history of Gypsies in Western

Europe was different. Groups traveled west from Hungary and Bohemia, wandering in the guise of penitents on pilgrimages. They attracted attention because of their unusual appearance and letters of safe-conduct from the Holy Roman Emperor and sometimes the Pope. They made a living by begging, telling fortunes, performing magical tricks, trading horses, peddling, and thieving. These activities were compatible with their nomadic life-style, since the Gypsies did not establish permanent residence or ties to the local communities. Originally protected guests, the Gypsies became outlaws. They were expelled as undesirables from one jurisdiction to another, their bad reputation preceding them. Several countries in Western Europe passed laws for their expulsion.[5]

The Czech lands of Bohemia, Moravia, and Silesia belonged to the Holy Roman Empire and the general attitude of the people and the government toward Gypsies resembled that of the rest of Europe. Gypsies were considered a worthless and undesirable element that had to be ignored or expelled. Thus Gypsies in the western part of today's Czechoslovakia led a nomadic life. They had the reputation of thieves and parasites who played violins and sang their songs around campfires in the evenings while preparing their meals. In today's Slovakia, which belonged to the Hungarian Crown until 1918, as in the Danubian area and the Balkans, Gypsies were sometimes permitted and sometimes forced to settle. They performed valuable services and were not persecuted.[6]

Following the outbreak of fires in Prague in 1541, blamed on Gypsies who were suspected of being paid mercenaries of the Turks, legislation against them was passed in Bohemia. This first attempt to drive the Gypsies from Czech territory was followed by several other efforts. In the seventeenth century, many Gypsies were hanged from trees along the border to discourage others from entering the country. In Czech districts, signs warned that hanging awaited Gypsies if they moved across the border; in Slovakia, warnings were tempered by announcements that Gypsies who agreed to settle within three weeks of crossing the border would be spared this fate.[7]

Persecution of Gypsies ceased in the eighteenth century when the rulers of the Hapsburg Empire attempted to assimilate Gypsies into the peasantry and make them productive and useful subjects. Local authorities were instructed to supervise the settlement of wandering Gypsies and to build houses for them in the villages. Gypsies were expected to enter useful occupations, build roads, and work in the

fields and forests. Masters were instructed to beat Gypsies if they refused to work or worked badly, and to see to it that they "waste no
time on music."[8]

Gypsies were prohibited from returning to their nomadic life-style
and were not allowed to own horses. They were prohibited from
speaking Romani and wearing outlandish clothes, while their children
had to be instructed in the Christian religion. In an effort to convert
Gypsies to a new way of life, they were renamed *Neubauern* (new
peasants) or *Ujmagyar* (new Hungarians). With the death of Emperor
Joseph II in 1790, however, the policy lapsed, and in the Czech lands
the Gypsies returned to their wagons. In Slovakia, however, most
Gypsies settled on the outskirts of villages. The men worked as farm
workers, smiths, or musicians, and the women as servants in
households.[9]

During the nineteenth century, Gypsies resisted assimilation and
maintained their cultural identity. In Czech districts, Gypsies were
considered a nuisance and were required to register with the
authorities, whose gendarmes tried to get them out of their jurisdiction as quickly as possible, usually escorting them to the borders of
their districts. In Slovakia, Gypsy settlements grew larger due to a
high birthrate and the building of new huts, or shanties.[10]

With the establishment of the Czechoslovak Republic in
1918–1919, the status of the Gypsies changed. Like the Jews, they
were recognized as a separate nationality in 1921. This, however, did
not change their behavior or reduce complaints made by peasant organizations: they are a burden on the peasantry; they have nothing and,
there- fore, they beg or steal, and it is difficult to control them; they
are not afraid of jails, since imprisonment merely improves their
living conditions; they commit crimes, especially in wintertime, in order to escape the pangs of hunger. Thus taxpayers had to support
Gypsies for whom jails were convenient shelters.[11]

Although there was a pogrom in western Slovakia in 1928 that
resulted in the death of six Gypsies, including two young children—a
reprisal for pilfering crops from fields—it was a rather isolated case.
Similar outbreaks of violence occurred in Austria, Germany, and
France. In a way, it was a peasants' revolt against the Gypsy way of
life, and sentences imposed by the courts were lenient.[12] In retrospect,
it appears that those events were a prelude to the atrocities of World
War II.

The Nazis intended to purge Europe of Gypsies and Jews by progressive stages. The Gypsies in Germany and in territories occupied by the German army were victims of "the final solution." Those in countries allied with the Third Reich were to suffer a similar fate. First the Gypsies of Germany and Austria were arrested in three major waves (in 1939, 1941, and 1943) and were sent to concentration camps. Since most of the Gypsies in Western Europe were accustomed to nomadic life, some of them managed to escape to Spain or remain in hiding. Yet between 500,000 and 600,000 Gypsies perished.[13] In contrast to the large amount of literature that deals with the Jews, the persecution of Gypsies and their extermination in Nazi Germany and other countries has remained mostly undocumented.[14]

Most Gypsies in the Czech lands of the Third Reich (Sudetenland from October 1938 and the rest from March 1939) shared the fate of the German Gypsies and were exterminated as a distinct group in the gas chambers. In Slovakia, however, the more numerous Gypsies survived the war. Although they were subjected to severe discrimination, excluded from restaurants, cinemas, parks, and public transportation, or forced to move their shanties further away from towns and villages or to build new, isolated settlements, the Gypsies were not exterminated.[15]

Only a handful of Gypsy families survived the Nazi era in Czech districts, and with the arrival of the Communist-led National Front government, they were looked upon with great sympathy by the Czechs. The Slovak Gypsies left their settlements in large numbers and moved into Czech areas from which Germans were expelled. This was the first time that Gypsies entered the labor market and worked as unskilled workers among the Czechs. The government encouraged Gypsies to seek employment in cities and villages, and emphasized the great opportunity that was opened for them in the new Czechoslovakia. But the Gypsies still led separate lives, and in Czech urban areas they congregated in ghettos. Because their cultural habits were markedly different, they were not assimilated into society.[16]

In Slovakia, the growth of the Gypsy settlements was temporarily checked by the departure of the migrants. However, due to very high natality among them as well as the large number of migrants returning home from Czech territories, the size of the Gypsy population began to swell. Since there were greater opportunities for material improvement in the former Sudetenland, and since many of the Gypsies considered Slovakia to be their home, movements to and fro were on the increase. The traditionally nomadic Gypsies, commonly called

"Vlachs," continued to move across the country in their horse-drawn carts and remained more or less free from any control.[17]

The Gypsies under Socialism

In contrast to the multinational state that existed before World War II, Czechoslovakia in 1945 was restored as a state of the Czechs and Slovaks, and there was no place in it for the Gypsies as a nation or even as an ethnic group. The situation did not change after the communist takeover in 1948. The Gypsies were merely a markedly different people whose birthrate substantially exceeded that of the Czechs and Slovaks. At that point, the government began openly to advance the basic premise of the undesirability of preserving Gypsy identity and a way of life that was not compatible with the new socialist order.

It decided to eliminate "the primitive old Gypsy way of life with all its bad habits."[18] The way to do that, the policy makers believed, was to disperse the Gypsies, destroy their social life, and to assimilate them in the general population. Official spokesmen claimed that the integration of Gypsies was in their own best interest.

Without doing much research, and with some deliberation, the Central Committee of the Communist party of Czechoslovakia decided in October 1958 to end the wandering of Gypsies, and the government launched a crash campaign to settle and assimilate Gypsies throughout the country. A law was passed on "the permanent settlement of nomads," though Gypsies were not specifically named in it.[19] The law affected some 6,000 ethnically distinct Vlachs (Arumanians), the few surviving Czech Gypsy families, and the migrant Gypsies. It directed the local authorities to provide comprehensive assistance to the Gypsies ("persons who lead a nomadic way of life"), in order to enable them to lead a sedentary life, with suitable employment and accommodations, and to use educational means to turn them into orderly, working citizens. The penalty for those disobeying the law and continuing their nomadic ways, in spite of being offered help to settle permanently, was imprisonment ranging from six months to three years.

Government spokesmen insisted, however, that Law 74, which in 1958 deprived the Gypsies of the right to travel and carry on their former way of life, was not directed at any one group but at "persons who wander from village to village avoiding honest work and living in a disgraceful manner, even when they have permits to reside." It was also claimed that this action was supported by both whites and Gypsies.[20] Drastic measures were taken to end nomadism; wheels were removed from Gypsies' carts and wagons, and in some cases horses were shot. These actions, however, did not end nomadism, because Gypsies from other countries, particularly Yugoslavia, reportedly migrated to Slovakia.[21]

Housing for the immobilized Gypsies varied considerably. Some continued to live in their own carts, which were now without wheels, while others were moved by well-intentioned public officials into new, modern apartments. As should have been expected, the Gypsies were hostile to the idea of giving up their caravans and did their best to preserve their traditional communal life around the campfire. Behavior of Gypsies in modern housing projects—for example, playing and singing around campfires in the evenings—did not improve relations between newly settled Gypsies and their neighbors, who probably had themselves waited years for similar housing. According to one report, there were many complaints that "gypsies remove the stove from the kitchen outside the house, where they later cook, using as fuel the flooring, door, and window frames, and sometimes even the rafters and ceiling, so that the house was soon uninhabitable."[22] For most Gypsies, however, no housing was provided.

In the campaign of implementing the 1958 act on permanent settlement of nomadic people, the media reported on the Gypsies' high rate of criminality, incest, and illegitimacy. The Gypsies were presented as different from the rest of the society, as people who relied on cunning, and who frequently changed domicile in order to avoid punitive controls of the state. Their folk tales, it was noted, glorified the ability to fool not merely individuals but the whole of society. The media stressed the need to integrate the Gypsies into the society at large and change their habits, denying them the right to national identity and the right of ethnic survival. A Czech periodical put it as follows: "Under socialism it is totally unthinkable to build some 'socialist and national' Gypsy culture from the fundamentals of something which is very primitive, backward, essentially often even negative and lacking in advanced tradition. . . . The question is not whether the Gypsies are a nation but how to assimilate them."[23] Reacting to complaints about Gypsies being allocated apartments right away, while many newlywed Czechs or Slovaks had been on waiting lists for ten years,

Svobodné slovo responded on 20 October 1967: "They are like us, and yet they are different."

Although, as early as 1947, the Communist party's announced goal was to integrate the Gypsies into the rest of the population and to raise their economic, social, and cultural levels to those of the Slavs, the measures taken in 1958 to implement this goal proved to be inadequate.[24] The campaign to integrate the Gypsies failed on several counts. Czech employers, when in need of labor, ignored regulations and gave jobs to "registered nomads" without seeking approval beforehand. Local governments were preoccupied with other matters and did not keep track of the movements of Gypsies, who continued their journeys back and forth between their homes in Slovakia and workplaces in Czech districts. In Slovakia, the local authorities were reluctant to disperse the Gypsy population by providing housing for them outside their settlements. When Gypsies returned from the Czech lands with savings, they built houses (without first obtaining permits) in settlements which usually lacked electricity, adequate sanitation, and sometimes even potable water. Thus many new houses and shanties, despite official prohibitions against building them, were added to settlements already designated for demolition.[25]

According to a report from eastern Slovakia, the region with the largest Gypsy population in the country, the plan to eliminate settlements by 1970 was not fulfilled and could not be fulfilled because 70,000 Gypsies still lived in shanties, and their situation was deteriorating due to the high birthrate and the steady increase in population. It was reported that "each adequate well and toilet had to serve over two hundred Gypsies," and that the lack of basic amenities was reflected in the high rate of infant mortality and tuberculosis, which were "more than double the national average."[26]

Since the local authorities failed to carry out the policy of assimilation and dispersal of the nomads, the government created the National Council for Questions of the Gypsy Population in 1965.[27] The council's task was to enforce full employment of able-bodied Gypsies, liquidate Gypsy settlements, and disperse and resettle the inhabitants. With local authorities reluctant to get involved and force the Gypsies to adopt a new way of life, the council's foremost charge was to coordinate official actions since many vacancies in menial occupations, such as street cleaning, road maintenance, and garbage collection, were being filled by political outcasts and by Gypsies, the country's most nonpolitical stratum. Gypsies from large settlements in Slovakia had to be moved to small towns and villages in Czech areas. In all, there were 1,266 large Gypsy settlements, officially termed "undesirable concentrations," in Slovakia, with 10,589 families living in 8,587 shanties.[28] Thus 64,096 persons, representing 39 percent of the Gypsy population in Slovakia, were to be relocated. In addition, the restriction on free migration, which had previously applied only to "registered nomads," was now extended to all Gypsies. Only those Gypsies included in the planned resettlement were permitted to move. As a Gypsy spokesman sarcastically put it, "They plan how many there should be in each village: horses, cows, and Gypsies."[29]

The local authorities were advised to classify Gypsies into three groups, and then decide which of them should be relocated first. In the first group were those who no longer lived in Gypsy concentrations and who were just one step away from full assimilation. These were to be helped to make the transition to complete assimilation where they lived. In the second group were those who worked regularly and whose children attended school. These Gypsies were most adaptive and they had to be spread as thinly as possible throughout the country. In the third group were

> . . . the most backward and wretched part of the gypsy population. They live a typical gypsy life in a gypsy concentration. They work irregularly, or not at all. They do not send their children to school nor do they take much care of them and it cannot be said of them that they have attained any cultural level, for they live in filth and from their numbers are recruited parasites and criminals. Among them are included many chronically ill or feeble people drawing sickness benefits who do not even want to be cured because their illness brings them an income without work. The solution to the problem of assimilating gypsies from this group will be very demanding.[30]

For these Gypsies, basic amenities in the settlements were to be improved, and their resettlement carried out later.

Classification of the Gypsies was done arbitrarily by government officials, and there was no right to appeal any decisions. In fact, the Gypsies were not even informed of their classification. In practice, this did not matter, since Czech local authorities refused to accept their quotas on the grounds that they had no available accommodations. Thus fewer than 500 Gypsy families were transferred to Czech districts in the first three years of the program. In the same time span, unplanned migration was double that number. In 1968 the government realized the failure of previous policies and decided tentatively to allow Gypsies to take a hand in planning their own future.[31]

The Prague Spring and the Nightfrost

When censorship was abolished during the "Prague Spring," many of the former taboos—including bad governmental policies, political and religious persecution, and incompetence of government officials—were publicly discussed. Taking advantage of the unexpected developments, educated Gypsies, or Roma, as they called themselves, began to write disapprovingly about policies aimed at the liquidation of their nation: namely, the forced assimilation and the denial of their ethnic identity. Their demands, especially for official recognition of their nationality and the right to form an organization, were endorsed by some non-Gypsy individuals and periodicals. The widespread prejudice against Gypsies was denounced by the media, and even some scholars began to be concerned about the status of the Gypsies and their problems.[32] Among the latter, the most articulate defender of the Gypsies' right to their identity was a sociologist, Milena Hübschmannová. She rejected the official policy presented by Jaroslav Sus in his book, *The Gypsy Question*, which proposed unconditional assimilation as the only solution for the question. The "reactionary nature of Gypsy folklore" and Gypsy heritage, Sus wrote, were not worthy of preservation; the Gypsies had to be assimilated along the lines of the governmental decree of 1965.

Hübschmannová pointed out that traditionally a small minority of Gypsies led the nomadic way of life and that the majority were settled in Slovakia, working as blacksmiths and musicians. After the country underwent radical socioeconomic transformation following the war, the Gypsies were forced to work as ditch diggers or unqualified laborers in construction, road maintenance, street sweeping, and the like. Resettled Gypsies were denied the opportunity to join relatives in other districts, and a large number of them were sent from Slovakia to ecologically devastated northern Bohemia. She stressed that the Gypsies have characteristics acquired at birth (their looks), in their families (their language), and from living in a group that does not share its values with the rest of the society. And, since the 1960 Constitution recognized the minority status of the Hungarians, Poles, and Ukrainians, Hübschmannová believed, the Gypsies should also be granted ethnic or national status.

It should be pointed out that in 1957 the government refused requests from Gypsy spokesmen to form their own association; but in 1958, the Communist party of Czechoslovakia issued a statement suggesting that the Gypsies constituted a special, socioethnic group, which had to be ministered to in a special manner. Then, in January 1968, the government permitted the establishment of the Union of Gypsy-Romanies, which consisted of two organizations—one in Czech districts and one in Slovakia.[33] The union was funded by the National Front and maintained offices in each region and district. Membership in the union grew swiftly: over 5,000 people had joined by the time of the organization's first national conference in 1969. Within two years, the Czech and Slovak organizations attracted both the poorer Gypsies and the small but influential Gypsy intelligentsia, which had been regarded as totally assimilated. They published their own magazines and promoted festivals of Romani song and dance. Young Gypsy musicians and pop groups appeared on television singing in Romani. The media increasingly referred to Gypsies as "Rom." Interest in Gypsy culture was reflected in published articles by sociologists and demographers.[34]

The union raised some political issues that had long been avoided by the Communist party and the government. Miroslav Holomek, president of the state-wide organization, advanced the concept of a separate Gypsy nationality, arguing in 1969 that the Gypsies fulfilled all the Marxist-Leninist conditions for designation as a nationality in a socialist state.[35] Yet they had not received any special status from the government until 1958, when it designated them a "socioethnic group." Furthermore, from 1948 to 1965, Gypsies were excluded from the official Czechoslovak census.

Holomek argued that Gypsies had preserved their own national identity for centuries, and that they were denied nationality status for the sake of political expediency. Since they were not recognized as a nation, the Gypsies were not respected and their opinions were not heeded.[36] He felt the integration policies of the government were artificial and doomed to failure because dispersion and migration quotas served administrative needs, not those of the Gypsies. Similar opinions were voiced by Gypsy scholars, such as Eva Davidová and Milena Hübschmannová. The latter argued that the Gypsies did not fade away under socialism because they are a nation: that is, they possess a national consciousness.[37]

The Soviet invasion of Czechoslovakia and subsequent "normalization" in the early 1970s ended the union's effectiveness at arguing Gypsy interests. The associations were disbanded in 1973 on the grounds that they had "failed to fulfill their integrative function."[38] Among the real reasons for abolishing the union were its confused finances, political changes resulting from the Soviet invasion in 1968, and, above all, the Gypsies' demands for recognition of their nationality status. The government decided to return to resettling Gypsies.

In the years 1972–1981, 4,000 shanties in Slovakia were demolished and 4,850 families were relocated. In 1983, there were still 400 Gypsy settlements in Slovakia, with 3,018 shanties housing 21,622 persons, that is 10.5 percent of the Gypsy population in the state.[39] The Czechs resisted the resettlement policy, since most of the Gypsies from Slovakia had been moved to Bohemia and Moravia. Local authorities resented taking in the Gypsies because of previous experiences with them. Gypsies who did not want to move often packed up and returned to Slovakia, leaving living quarters in disrepair. This, in turn, caused resentment among housing-hungry Czechs and the taxpayers.

In the 1970s and 1980s, government propaganda held up fully employed, productive, successful, and assimilated "citizens of Gypsy origin" as role models for the Gypsies at large, stressing opportunities existing in the socialist society. Although Davidová, Hübschmannová, and other scholars continued to write as much about Romani culture as editors and censors were willing to print, no public demands for the recognition of Romani nationality or ethnicity were made in the press. The party-controlled mass media would not feature such demands and supported the official government policy on the Gypsies. When the World Romani Congress in Geneva made an appeal to the Czechoslovak government to recognize the national minority status of the Gypsies just as they had been recognized in Hungary and Poland, the leading Communist party daily, *Rudé právo* (21 June 1986), rejected the request. It condemned the international organization and others in the West for the charge that Gypsies were being discriminated against in Czechoslovakia. Instead, it featured success stories of assimilated Gypsies who had made it in the new, socialist society. Those Gypsies who were unwilling to change life-styles and adjust to a socialist society were victims of a capitalistic way of thinking and vestiges of the past, the party's daily claimed.

Culture and Religion

The Gypsies are a special ethnic group whose traditional religion forms the core of their culture. They attempt, through their religious practices, to secure for themselves success in their endeavors, to turn away danger, illness, and misery, and to attain love and security.[40] When asked about their religion, most Gypsies profess to be Roman Catholics; some of them, especially in eastern Slovakia, are Orthodox. Atheists or agnostics are very rare. Because of its particularly impressive religious services, the Roman Catholic church, with its vivid ceremonies and striking colors, appeals to them.

The Gypsies adopted Christianity because they did not want to appear too different from the people among whom they moved. In addition, the fear of the unknown, death, and natural phenomena, and the inability of their original, natural-animistic faith to give answers to fundamental questions of man's origin and the afterlife, led them to embrace, at least formally, though often superficially, Roman Catholicism or Orthodoxy.

According to a study of Gypsies living in the town of Trebišov in eastern Slovakia conducted in the 1950s,[41] the Gypsies adopted only those Catholic practices that corresponded to their expectations and/or benefited them in some way. For example, a religious wedding ceremony was, for some families, merely a formality. Only their own marriage ritual was valid, and the fact that the Gypsy community approved the match. In Trebišov, the average age of girls marrying was fourteen, while boys were between fourteen and eighteen. More well-to-do Gypsies, however, already in the 1950s, were married in either a church or civil ceremony. As they put it, they took "the oath," mindful of certain material benefits such as a dowry, natal care, and child support from the state.

The Trebišov Gypsies adopted all religious holidays, to which they added some of their own traditional practices, particularly during Easter, Christmas, and the Feast of Saint Stephen three days later. The most celebrated religious holiday, however, was the day of the Mother of God in August. It was at the warmest time of year and was celebrated outside the home for two whole days and nights. The holiday reflected the Roma's joy of summer, ties with families, and the whole community. It was a special time for visiting relatives.

Almost all of the Trebišov Gypsies believed in Jesus. Their images of God and Christ reflected their own qualities, imaginations, and values. They believed that God sent a strong man, Jesus, to earth so that he would cleanse the world. Superstition, too, was a part of the popular religion of the Gypsies. Popular rituals were based on a belief in positive effects of magic. Since positive results, regardless of the cause, sometimes occurred, the Roma of Trebišov by and large believed in them.[42] Many of the superstitions were related to pregnant women who had to observe certain prescriptions and prohibitions. Almost all women believed that when a pregnant woman saw some food for which she had an appetite, and did not get it or could not buy it, the child would "leave her," that is, she would have a miscarriage. When a Gypsy woman found herself in such a situation, the best thing for her to do was to take or steal the food in order to prevent the loss of her unborn child. Also, pregnant women did not wear any kind of necklace lest the cord twist around the neck of the unborn child and choke it. After the birth of a child, its mother would place various amulets on the child's hand, usually a red ribbon or red beads, for its protection.

Many of the Trebišov Roma still believe that a dead person is not completely dead for three days and that death merely "entered him." This belief is reflected in the custom of family and friends "keeping watch" over the deceased, whose coffin is open in his house for three days and nights. They sit next to the deceased, tell tales, recount anecdotes and humorous incidents, drink, and play cards. If during the "night watch" a man or a boy staring at the dead person fainted, it was said that the individual "looked into the face of death," and that this in itself could be a cause of death.

According to Davidová, even in the late 1950s, many of the Trebišov Roma believed that some people had "two souls" and that this became evident after death. The second soul does not give peace to the deceased and the latter visits his or her survivors at night. As the story goes, at night a man comes back to sleep with his wife who may even get pregnant by him. While some members of the younger generation, especially those who have moved away from the Gypsy communities and intermarried, have made a break with the past and abandoned family rituals, the overwhelming majority of those who consider themselves Roma continue to observe traditional religious customs.

Education, Economic Status, Demography, and Assimilation

In the decade 1965–1975, the Gypsy population doubled to more than 250,000 persons,[43] though some estimate the number to be as high as 300,000.[44] Since Gypsies continue to have large families and the status of some of them has improved, it is likely that the Gypsy minority will continue to grow. One child in eleven born in Czechoslovakia is a Gypsy.[45] Thus Czechoslovakia has one of the world's largest Gypsy populations. About one-third of the Gypsies still live in dire poverty in shanties in segregated settlements in Slovakia. In Slovakia in the early 1980s, Gypsies, who make up 4 percent of the population, accounted for 24 percent of the charges for parasitism, 50 percent of robberies, 60 percent of petty thefts, 75 percent of charges for endangering the morals of youth, and 20 percent of all crimes committed.[46]

Government efforts to turn Gypsies into productive workers seem to have been successful to some extent. In 1970, 66.3 percent of the males and 41.2 percent of the females of working age were employed, while by 1981, 75 percent of all male and female Gypsies had jobs. In 1983 in Slovakia, 83.4 percent of employed Gypsies were in construction.[47] This was, indeed, seasonal work, which allowed them to move from place to place. But since temporary laborers had to live in barracks, they could not take their families with them. An overnight visit of a wife could result in the loss of wages or even a job.[48]

The level of education among migrant workers is very low and illiteracy is still a significant problem among adults. Children are required to attend schools, but absenteeism among them is very high and their performance is seldom on a par with other pupils, since they are not proficient enough in Czech or Slovak. Gypsy children living in the settlements hear only Romani until they start school; but lately the number of children attending nursery schools has increased.[49]

Since Gypsy children in general lack the necessary language skills, they are often sent to "special schools," institutions whose students generally are mentally impaired. In such cases their potential is squandered. More recently, some communities have established special kindergartens for Gypsy children to provide language training in Czech or Slovak.[50] Although these children are better prepared for school, they still often lag behind the other students in their performance. They have to use textbooks that lack any mention of Gypsies and provide no examples with which they can identify. Nor do

Czech and Slovak teachers provide them with role models. Many of the poorly motivated students are not promoted or leave school prematurely. In the 1970s, three-quarters of the children failed to complete their basic education, and the present generation of Gypsies will, most likely, repeat the experience of their parents.[51]

The Czechoslovak government has published detailed statistics on education of the Gypsy children in the 1980s.[52] While in 1980, 17.1 percent of the Gypsy pupils were in "special schools" already mentioned above, 2.6 percent of all other children were placed in these institutions. In 1985, the number of Gypsy children in these schools increased to 27.6 percent, while the percentage of other students remained the same. The performance of Gypsy children in regular elementary schools was poor. In 1980, 15.34 percent of them failed grades 1–4, while only 0.94 percent of the other children did as poorly. The situation has not improved since then. One reason for their poor performance is their high truancy rate. In 1980–1985, the school attendance of Gypsy children averaged 75.1 percent; all other children attended school 97.3 percent of the time.

The usual explanations for the existing situation are that Gypsy children do not know Czech or Slovak well enough, they lack motivation, and do not adapt well. In addition, many Gypsy children get poor marks because of their behavior, especially in schools with a large Gypsy enrollment.[53]

While the Czechs are approaching a population growth rate of zero (it is considerably higher among the Slovaks), the Gypsy minority continues to grow. Gypsies under the age of fifteen comprise about 50 percent of the Gypsy population, whereas less than 45 percent of the population is of working age. In Czechoslovakia, poor people tend to have large families; Gypsies, most of whom are poor, often have from seven to twelve children. Despite the fact that the infant mortality rate for Gypsies exceeds twice that of the rest of the population (40 to 50 deaths per 1,000 live births), in the 1980s the annual statewide increase in Gypsy births was 2.6 percent. It has been noted that about 20 percent of all Gypsies born in the country are mentally retarded. These data indicate the low level of prenatal care of Gypsy women.[54]

The government's practice of advising women to have abortions and paying for the abortions and/or sterilization has been questioned by a group of several hundred individuals known as "chartists." In January 1977 they signed a proclamation on human rights, appealing to the government to comply with the Helsinki Accord of 1975 which had been duly ratified by Czechoslovakia. Charter 77 issued many documents on violations of human rights and various issues, including one on Gypsies.

The document on the "Situation of the Gypsies in Czechoslovakia,"[55] issued in December 1978, states that the Gypsies are "the least protected group of citizens in Czechoslovakia," that they are deprived of a right of association, and that the public is mostly indifferent to their plight or openly hostile to them. The Gypsies represent a *de facto* Third World culture existing in a European culture; they are a significant minority in the country, and yet the government does not recognize them as a national group. On the contrary, the aim of the government is to eliminate them as a group through various policies of assimilation. In violation of the state constitution, they are forced to register and prohibited to move freely. Furthermore, the document asserts, the housing of the great majority of Gypsies is totally inadequate. About 30 percent of them are illiterate, and their children are forced to attend Czech or Slovak schools where they are told that Gypsy culture does not exist.

According to the document, the Gypsy minority is undergoing a process of social disintegration, which has no comparison in the history of the Gypsies. An increasing number of them are sentenced to long prison terms. Children are taken away from their parents and are placed in state institutions and foster homes. Gypsy women are urged to undergo sterilization, and their consent is often obtained by suspicious means. The document refers to the practice of government-subsidized sterilization of Gypsy women as *genocide*. Gypsy women often resort to abortions because they are unaware of other birth control methods. Consequently, among Gypsy women the incidence of abortions is higher than the average for the female population as a whole, which is 1.64 per female.[56]

Although Gypsy fertility declined considerably during the 1970s, it is much higher than the national average. Between the years 1970 and 1980, the number of females aged 15–49 increased by 43.8 percent. It was 58.4 percent in the Czech Socialist Republic (CSR) and 37.9 percent in the Slovak Socialist Republic (SSR), while the total increase of women of that age was less than 1 percent in the CSR and 8 percent in the SSR. According to published statistics, in 1980 the average number of live births for a currently married Gypsy woman was 21 percent lower than in 1970 (CSR 23 percent, SSR 19 percent). Thus, when a Gypsy woman reached fifty years of age in 1980, her average number of live births in the CSR was 5.5 children and in the SSR 6.2 children. In 1980 the national average was 2.27 children for a woman who reached the age of fifty.[57] Since the state guarantees six months of maternal leave with full pay and considerable child support paid for eighteen years, some Czechs and Slovaks believe it "pays" for many Gypsy women to have large families.[58]

In absolute figures, there were 219,554 Gypsies in Czechoslovakia in 1970, and 288,440 in 1980, out of a total population of 15,277,000.[59] As Czech demographers point out, however, not all Gypsies were included in these statistics.[60] Since Gypsies are not recognized as a national group, the official statistics refer to them as individuals of Gypsy *origin*. The offices of local administration maintain a "Gypsy Register." Determination of who is a Gypsy is based on "common knowledge, characteristic life-style in multi-generational families with a great number of children, and inadequate knowledge of the language of society," according to *Demografie*, a governmental publication.[61] Thus it is the local officials who determine whom to include in the "Gypsy Register," and their decisions are often arbitrary. *Demografie* has noted an inaccuracy in official census figures, suggesting: "In view of the fact that the Gypsies are not considered a nationality, no ascertainment of their mother tongue has been made; the census takers have to base their findings on special characteristics of persons included in the groups of Gypsy population."[62] The periodical reports that the number of Gypsies registered with local authorities was 306,246 in 1980, while the official census conducted in the same year gave the figure 288,440.[63] It is "obvious," states the same source, "that the census of 1980 did not account for all the Romas." In 1980, for example, in the seven districts in Prague, there were 537 more Gypsies (11 percent) in the "Gypsy Registers" than in the official census. During the preceding decade, the number of Gypsies living in Prague almost doubled.[64] In 1986, as reported in *Rudé právo* (23 April), the number of Gypsies in the whole country reached 345,000. A further increase in the number of Gypsies will be recorded in the 1990 census.

It has been noted that fertility is higher among Gypsies in Slovakia than in the Czech lands. In Bohemia and Moravia, Gypsies increased their percentage in the population from 0.61 in 1970 to 0.86 percent in 1980, while in Slovakia the increase was from 3.51 percent to 4.00

percent. Since the birthrate of the population at large is considerably lower than that of the Gypsies, their percentage in the total population of the country is likely to increase in 1990.[65]

In view of the fact that more than 53 percent of Gypsies live in Slovakia, it is hardly surprising that Gypsies, having been denied nationality status but required to declare a nationality, chose Slovak, usually involuntarily. According to the 1980 census, 75 percent of Gypsies "opted" for being Slovaks, 15 percent Hungarians, and 10 percent Czechs.[66] Thus Gypsy identification with Czechs is lowest, and many of the Gypsies resettled in northern Bohemia still cling to their "Slovak nationality." Slovaks, incidentally, are the largest national minority in the Czech republic.[67]

A study conducted in western Bohemia in the Cheb (Eger) district, which has a large Gypsy population, shows that Gypsies are not easily assimilated. Fourteen different ethnic backgrounds have been identified in that district; all the groups have been assimilated, except for the Gypsies. Only 19 percent of them were counted as "assimilated," the rest characterized as migrating from place to place, sporadically working, and taking poor care of their children. Among the children born in maternity wards, every seventh child was a Gypsy. Several of the Gypsy mothers, the study shows, attempted to stay in confinement as long as they could, and in some cases left the clinic without their children. One-third of the mothers abandoned their children.

In 1982–1983, in the "special school" in Cheb, more than 50 percent of the children were Gypsies. In the whole district, 50 percent of the Gypsy children attended the "special schools," while 27 percent were not promoted to the next grade. Gypsy children starting school did not know Czech and 63 percent of them had to repeat the first grade. (The law does not allow for repeating the grade the second time.) The study confirms that Gypsy children in the higher grades had a poor command of the language and got below-average grades. Sadly, their parents seemed to show no interest in the education of their children. It has been noted that poor performance in school affects pupils' behavior: Gypsies feel isolated, are shy, suspicious, dishonest, and unwilling to work.[68]

The high work mobility, crime rate and juvenile delinquency, sexual behavior, low economic status, and low level of education of most Gypsies have contributed to the continuation of deep-seated prejudice against them in the society at large. Yet the level of skills of some

Gypsies has increased considerably, as Imrich Farkaš, the chief commissar of Gypsy matters in Slovakia, reported:

> We have already got a not insignificant number of tractor drivers, welders, locksmiths, butchers, waiters, cooks, noncommissioned and commissioned army officers, members of the police force and even miners. Gypsy women work as hairdressers, waitresses, beauticians, teachers, nurses, cashiers, etc. Soon there will be no line of work left without Gypsy participation.[69]

While this assertion by one government official is true, it applies only to a minority of Gypsies who are fully integrated. It was also reported that 368 Gypsy males and 68 females held elective positions in the People's Committees in 1982.[70] They undoubtedly got elected to local governments in communities with a large Gypsy population, but their participation in politics at higher levels is very limited. Only a few of them have reached the top strata of society.

Governmental efforts at total cultural assimilation of the Gypsies are not likely to succeed, and most Gypsies will manage to maintain their traditional life-styles and identity. Given the general attitudes of the new generation of Gypsies, discussed above, it is likely that most of them will only increase the ranks of the country's indigent and criminal population. "Assimilated," educated, and prosperous Gypsies will probably continue to be only a small minority.[71]

Postscript

This essay was completed before the November 1989 "velvet revolution" in Czechoslovakia. In part due to the new president Václav Havel's general amnesty and the release of recidivists, criminal activity in Czechoslovakia increased during the first months of 1990. The newly won freedom also made visible groups of people called "Skinheads" and "Punks." (The terms are used in Czech and are not translations.) These two groups have been involved in violence against people of darker skin, Gypsies in particular. Incidents have occurred even in Prague. On 1 May 1990, citizens of Gypsy-Romani origin left the Wenceslas Square as soon as members of the two above-mentioned groups appeared, but two dark-skinned tourists from Canada were attacked, and had to be hospitalized.[72] Most attacks on Gypsies-Romas by "Skinheads" and "Punks" have taken place in northern Bohemia where there are larger concentrations of Gypsies. The latter have staged demonstrations to protest these attacks and have demanded protection against racial intolerance. As reported by the Czech Ministry of Interior, the growth of racial intolerance is due, in part, to the large percentage of crime perpetrated by Gypsies-Romas. Although the Gypsy-Romani make up only 1.26 percent of the population in the Czech lands, their share in criminal activity has been 15.6 percent, and as high as 48 percent of assaults with robberies. The Czech Ministry of Interior and the police have announced that they will take action against all perpetrators of violent crimes, racial intolerance, propagation of fascism and its symbols, and mass actions leading to violence on groups of citizens.[73]

Notes

1. František Trávníček, *Slovník jazyka českého* [Dictionary of the Czech Language] (1952), p. 145.

2. Tomáš Grulich and Tomáš Haišman, "Institucionální zájem o cikánské obyvatelstvo v Československu v létech 1945–1958" [Institutional Interest in the Gypsy Population in Czechoslovakia in the Years 1945–1958], p. 74.

3. *Demografie*, published by the Federal Statistical Office, Prague, has carried many articles about Gypsies and their status in the society. See, for example, two articles by Miroslav Holomek (11, 3 [1969]); an article by Stanislav Kier in the same issue; articles by Michal Bulíř (29, 1 and 4 [1987]); Jiří Hana (29, 2 [1987]); Pekárek, Prášilová, and Cifka (21, 4 [1979]); Vladimír Polášek (21, 4 [1979]); Václav Sekera (17, 4 [1975]); Vladimír Srb, (10, 3 [1968], 11, 4 [1969], 26, 2 [1985], 30, 7 [1988]); Rudolf Tancos (11, 3 [1969]). See also the articles in *Český lid* by Grulich and Haišman (73, 2 [1986]); Antonín Robek (73, 2 [1986]); Renata Weinerová (73, 2 [1986]); Naděžda Zuzánková (69, 2 [1982]), to list but a few.

4. See Willy Guy's essay in Josef Koudelka's *Gypsies*. There is no pagination in the book.

5. Ibid.

6. Ibid.

7. Ibid.

8. Ibid.

9. Ibid.

10. Ibid.

11. Ibid.

12. Ibid.

13. Jan Yoors, *Crossing*, p. 34.

14. Ibid. See also Ctibor Nečas, *Nad osudem českých a slovenských cikánů v létech 1939–1945* [On the Fate of Czech and Slovak Gypsies during the Years 1939–1945], p. 180.

15. At the end of World War II about 100,000 Gypsies lived in Slovakia. Ruthenia, the easternmost province of pre–World War II Czechoslovakia, with a very large

Gypsy population, was occupied by Hungary in March 1939 and was incorporated into the Soviet Ukraine in 1944–1945. Some Gypsies from Ruthenia moved to Czechoslovakia after the war.

16. Based on personal observations of this writer, who lived in Czechoslovakia until November 1948. See also Guy.

17. Guy.

18. Ibid.

19. Law 74/1958, passed in October 1958, deprived "nomads" of the right to travel and carry on their former occupations. According to the *New York Times*, 26 October 1958, the number of wandering Gypsies was 40,000; according to Milena Hübschmannová, 11,820 ("Co je tak zvaná cikánská otázka" [What Is the So-called Gypsy Question?]).

20. *New York Times*, 26 October 1958, p. 7.

21. Anna I. Duirchová, "Glimpses of the Rom: Excursions in Slovakia."

22. Guy. In personal conversations with people who resided in the same buildings with Gypsies, this observation has been corroborated. This writer was told about urine dripping from the ceilings, etc. The sanitation habits of many Gypsies have fostered a negative attitude toward them on the part of Czechs who live in their neighborhoods.

23. *Demografie* 4, 1 (1962): 80–81.

24. "Cigáni," *Encyklopedia Slovenská*, p. 321.

25. Guy.

26. Ibid.

27. Hübschmannová, "Cikánská otázka," p. 115.

28. Vladimír Srb, "Cikánské obyvatelstvo v roce 1967" [The Gypsy Population in 1967], p. 270.

29. Guy.

30. Ibid.

31. Ibid.

32. See *Literární Listy*, 18 April and 25 July 1968; Hübschmannová, "Cikánská otázka," pp. 105–20.

33. Guy. Also, *New York Times*, 3 November 1968, p. 18.

34. Vladimír Srb, "Ustavující sjezd svazu Cikánů-Romů v ČSR v Brně" [The Founding Congress of the Alliance of Gypsies-Romani in Czechoslovakia in Brno].

35. Miroslav Holomek, "Současné problémy Cikánů v ČSSR a jejich řešení" [The Current Problems of Gypsies in Czechoslovakia and Their Solution], p. 205.

36. Hübschmannová, "Cikánská otázka," p. 109.

37. Ibid., p. 115.

38. Guy.

39. Imrich Farkaš, *Pravda* (Bratislava), 23 September 1982, p. 5.

40. My comments on "Culture and Religion" are based, to a great extent, on Eva Davidová, "Lidové náboženství třebišovských Cikánů-Romů koncem padesátých let 20. století, před rozpadem jejich tradiční komunity" [Popular Religion of Trebišov Gypsies-Romas toward the End of the 1950s, before the Break-up of Their Traditional Community], in *Slovenský národopis* (Bratislava), 1, 36 (1988). The whole issue contains essays on various aspects of ethnocultural and socioeconomic life of the Roma in Czechoslovakia. Other essays relevant to this topic are Arne B. Mann,

"Obyčaje pri umrtí Cigánov-Rómov v troch spišskych obciách" [Customs during the Death of Gypsies-Romas in Three Spiš Communities], pp. 192–201; Elena Lacková, "L'udové liečenie olašských Rómov východnýho Slovenska v minulosti" [Popular Medical Treatments of Olsš's Romas in Eastern Slovakia in the Past], pp. 203–8. Personal observations are included.

41. Davidová, "Lidové náboženství," pp. 93–103.

42. For a more detailed discussion of customs, traditions, and superstitions related to death and burial of Gypsies, see the essay by Mann, "Obyčaje"; and for more information on treatment of illnesses and related practices the essay by Lacková, "L'udové liečenie."

43. Guy.

44. Grattan Puxon, "Roma: Europe's Gypsies." According to this source the total Romani population in Europe in 1970 was 3,918,000.

45. Guy.

46. Jaroslav Mesko, *Pravda* (Bratislava), January 28, 1983, p. 4.

47. David J. Kostelancik, "The Gypsies of Czechoslovakia."

48. Guy.

49. Farkaš, *Pravda* (Bratislava), 23 September 1982, p. 5.

50. Zdena Štěpánková, *Rudé právo*, 23 May 1984.

51. Guy.

52. Michal Bulíř, "Školní docházka cikánských dětí v létech 1980–1985" [School Attendance of the Gypsy Children during the Years 1980–1985], pp. 86–89.

53. Jiří Hana, "Vybrané problémy cikánské etnické skupiny v okrese Cheb" [Selected Problems of the Gypsy Ethnic Group in the Cheb District], pp. 167–71.

54. "Prague against Gypsies," *Time*, September 15, 1986.

55. "Dokument 23 o situaci Cikánů v Československu," *Listy* (Charter 77 document) (2, 47 [1979]). The full text in English is in *Human Rights in Czechoslovakia*, pp. 15–170.

56. Zuzanna Finková, "Zištovanie plodnosti cigánskych žien" [Ascertaining Fertility of Gypsy Women], p. 340.

57. Vladimír Srb, "Změny v reprodukci Československých Romů 1970–1980" [Changes in the Reproduction of the Czechoslovak Romas, 1970–1980], pp. 305–8.

58. Stefanie Písaříková, *Rolnické noviny*, 20 November 1969. Actually, having many children is a part of the traditional Gypsy culture. The alleged Gypsy saying is: "The more children, the less expensive is life."

59. Vladimír Srb, "Některé demografické a kulturní charakteristiky cikánského obyvatelstva v ČSSR 1980" [Some Demographic and Cultural Characteristics of the Gypsy Population in the Czechoslovak Republic in 1980], pp. 161–78.

60. Srb, "Změny v reprodukci," p. 305.

61. Srb, "Charakteristiky," p. 161.

62. Ibid.

63. Ibid.

64. *Demografie* 30, 4 (1988), p. 374.

65. Srb, "Změny v reprodukci," p. 308.

66. Srb, "Charakteristiky," p. 170.

67. For statistics on population see Josef Kalvoda, "National Minorities in Czechoslovakia, 1919–1980." pp. 108–59.

68. Ibid., p. 170. In an article on Gypsy children in kindergartens, "Cikánské (romské) děti v mateřských školách" [Gypsy (Romani) Children in Kindergartens], Michal Bulíř published detailed statistics on the increase of Gypsy children's enrollment in kindergartens. In 1972 1.14 percent of the children attending these schools were Gypsies; in 1986 the percentage increased to 3.33 percent. In absolute figures the number of Gypsy children in kindergartens was 4,515 in 1972 and 22,240 in 1986. Thus in the 1980s a majority of Gypsy children of kindergarten age were enrolled in school, and in 1986 4,254 of them were in special classes for Gypsy children.

69. *Pravda*, 23 September 1982, p. 5.

70. *Pravda*, 28 January 1983, p. 4.

71. Ibid.

72. "Dělaji nám ostudu" [They Are Giving Us a Bad Name], p. 6.

73. "Roznodně proti násilí" [Resolutely against Violence], p. 4.

8

The Gypsies in Hungary

DAVID CROWE

There have been Gypsies in Hungary for over 650 years. Historical records indicate that they entered Hungary between 1416 and 1417 from Transylvania (Siebenburgen) during the reign of King Sigismund (1387–1437), though linguistic evidence indicates that Gypsies had begun to settle there earlier. In 1423, Sigismund granted the Gypsy leader Ladislas and his followers certain rights of transit, and they began to flock to Hungary. Most settled on the outskirts of villages or towns, and became prominent in some parts of the country as blacksmiths.[1] From the outset, they were subjected to varying degrees of discrimination. In the eighteenth century, Empress Maria Theresa (1740–1780), after Pope Clement XIII granted her the right to become Apostolic ruler of Hungary, adopted policies designed to force the Gypsies to assimilate into Hungarian society. She outlawed use of the word *Cigány* and decreed that Gypsies in the future be called "new citizens," "new peasants," or "new Hungarians." In 1780, the government placed 8,388 Gypsy children in schools where they became wards of the state, and another 9,463 in foster homes. Within a few years, all of the children had run away from the schools or the families. The Gypsies responded with some outbreaks of violence in certain areas, though in most instances they simply left Hungary for other parts of Europe.[2]

In 1782, local authorities tried and executed a large number of Gypsies for cannibalism, a charge later proved false by the new Emperor, Joseph II (1780–1790). On the other hand, Austria's Enlightened Despot continued the spirit of many of his mother's restrictive Gypsy policies. Once settled in villages, the authorities slowly monitored their activities and movements. Other laws over the next fifteen years removed privileges to Gypsy leaders that had been granted in the fifteenth century, gave economic rewards for mixed marriages, and continued to encourage the removal of children from Gypsy families. As a result, Hungary's Gypsy population of 43,609 in 1780 dropped to 30,241 over the next three years, and did not fully recover from these policies until the mid-nineteenth century.[3]

From the time that statistical data has been collected, it has always been difficult to determine the exact number of Gypsies in Hungary because of their traditional nomadic life-style and the atmosphere of prejudice that made them hesitant officially to identify themselves as Gypsies. A census in 1851 indicated that there were 83,769 in Hungary and Transylvania, a figure that increased to 95,500 sixteen years later. However, a purely Gypsy census done in 1873 indicates a population of 214,000, while a national census in 1880 showed only 97,200, a figure that dropped to 91,603 a decade later. In 1893, authorities conducted the most thorough Gypsy census to date that contained ethnographic and statistical data. It showed Hungary's Gypsy population to be 274,940: 88 percent (243,432) were settled, 7.5 percent (20,462) were semi-nomadic, and 3.25 percent (8,938) were nomadic, with 38.10 percent speaking Hungarian, 29.97 percent speaking a Gypsy tongue, and 24.39 percent Romanian. The latter figure represents the large wave of migration into Hungary from Romania during the end of the nineteenth century.[4]

A general census in 1910 identified 147,599 Gypsies in Greater Hungary, while a similar survey in 1930 showed only 14,473 in post-Trianon Hungary, a figure disputed by Gabor Kemény, who estimated that there were 100,000 Gypsies still there. In 1938, parliamentary member Gyozo Droby guessed that there were 130,000 to 150,000 Gypsies scattered throughout the nation. These discrepancies, particularly after 1920, reflect the powerful influence of magyarization on all minorities in Hungary, as well as the continued spirit of anti-Gypsy sentiment.[5]

Between 1938 and 1941, Hungary's minority population expanded substantially because of its large territorial acquisitions during this period. Although it is difficult to determine how many Gypsies came into Hungary at this time, Hungary's general minority population increased from 7.9 percent of the total population in 1930 to 22.5 percent of the total ten years later. One study indicates that there were about 100,000 Gypsies in Hungary in 1939, while another states that there were only 57,776 there two years later.[6]

In 1940 Hungary passed a law that ordered all Gypsies from its newly acquired Yugoslavian territory to leave the country. In February 1941, plans were made to intern all Gypsies who had no job, though the scheme was not initially carried out. Some arrests and internments of Gypsies did occur, though a full-scale program of Gypsy persecution did not take place until German forces occupied Hungary in 1944. They shipped over 31,000 Gypsies to various concentration camps outside Hungary. The bulk of them were sent to Auschwitz, which had 20,946 Gypsy prisoners at one time or another. On 2 August 1944, the Germans decided to eliminate the camp's remaining 4,000 Gypsies, though hundreds more were shipped there for immediate extermination in the fall of 1944. Approximately 28,000 to 32,000 Hungarian Gypsies died in the Holocaust.[7]

The status of Gypsies in immediate postwar Hungary is difficult to ascertain, particularly in light of the atmosphere of forced transfers and rising political unrest. At Stalin's instigation, Hungarian officials, in the shadows of Soviet occupation forces, were pressured, despite opposition by noncommunist officials, to do everything possible to destroy the ethnic fabric of the country through the forced expulsion of its German and Slovak minorities. In addition, a spirit of Stalinist internationalism evolved that emphasized ethnic and minority identity as a form of "bourgeois ideology."[8]

This spirit contradicted the Hungarian Communist party's minorities policy statement that "assured the nationalities living in Hungary of equal rights and promotion of their 'progressive culture,' " as well as its "support for 'cultural exchange and free contacts with their mother-tongue nations in the neighboring countries.' " It also compromised Article 49 of Hungary's new constitution of 20 August 1949, which made "discrimination . . . against any citizen on the grounds of . . . religion or nationality . . . illegal" and guaranteed "to all nationalities living within its borders the possibility of education in their natural tongue and the possibility of developing their national culture."[9] Consequently, in the census of 1949, where nationality was based on language, only 21,387 people claimed to be Gypsies, though some specialists feel, if nationality had been the criteria, 31,000–37,000 individuals would have claimed Gypsy ancestry.[10]

The death of Joseph Stalin on 5 March 1953 saw the gradual evolution of a more tolerant minorities policy in Hungary, particularly after the Hungarian Revolution in October 1956. Linked principally to the plight of Hungarian minorities in other East European countries, an atmosphere emerged that helped create official concern over the conditions of the country's ill-defined Gypsy population. In the fall of 1958, the Political Committee of the Hungarian Communist party issued a resolution that committed it to a policy of active, legal support for the development of minority culture and education, and emphasized the importance of each minority's national organization in these efforts.[11] The government also created a *Cigányszövetség* (Gypsy Council) in the same year, but dissolved it in 1960. Results published from an official census at that time show that Hungary's official Gypsy count had risen to 25,633, though unofficial estimates placed the figure at 200,000.[12] Although it is difficult to determine exactly why the government chose to dissolve the Gypsy Council in 1960, it was probably because of the difficulty in creating a viable organizational structure for a group that, unlike other minorities, had no settled traditions or official organizational history. This, combined with deep prejudice toward the Gypsies throughout Hungary, prompted Budapest to develop a policy that was different from those for other minorities because of the peculiar needs of this group. On 20 June 1961, the Central Committee decreed that Hungary's Gypsies did "not constitute a national minority," but must have the same developmental and constitutional privileges as other groups. The resolution noted several times that the greatest barrier to the "assimilation, social, economic, and cultural advancement of the Gypsies," particularly in rural areas, was a "phalanx of prejudice."[13]

For a number of years, the Hungarian press featured stories on the plight of the Hungarian Gypsy in an effort to combat anti-Gypsy prejudice. In an article in *Népszabadság* on 27 August 1958, the author noted that rural prejudice sometimes made it difficult for them to obtain adequate housing. This, combined with similar official feelings on the local level, forced the Gypsies to live outside the villages in shacks. The following year, the same paper condemned Hungarian workers for verbally attacking Gypsies, which it attributed to a "discredited, inhuman, racial theory. It is not the Gypsies' original sin," it stated, "but their centuries-old oppression and exclusion from society, which makes them live, still today, on the fringes of society." Another article castigated discriminatory hiring practices that the author related to apartheid toward what some regarded as the "Brown Hungarian." In a sawmill in Eger, for example, workers were able to slow down efforts to hire Gypsies. An article in the same newspaper four years later described their seasonal work and virtual impoverish-ment during the winter, and wondered how they survived.[14]

In many ways, though, these articles fortified the centuries-old stereotypical view of Gypsies throughout Hungary. Sociological studies begun during this period discovered a depth of prejudice, par-ticularly in the countryside, where 80 percent of Hungary's Gypsies lived, that would seemingly affect any government efforts to aid them. In the village of Átány, where Gypsies had lived since the eigh-teenth century, villagers, who felt the Gypsies had "been created dif-ferent" and referred to them as "carrion-eating people," forced them to live on unwanted village land away from the center. They were given menial jobs unwanted by the villagers. On the other hand, Gypsy bands and musicians had a significant role in all important celebrations, while stories about the "origin of the Gypsies" were considered an integral part of the area's local history. Villagers also allowed them to be married or baptized by the Lutheran minister and to be buried in the churchyard, despite the fact that the local Gypsies were Catholics.[15]

Elsewhere, slang with anti-Gypsy overtones was commonly used. Phrases such as "a Gypsy's friend is a Gypsy"; "it has gone to Gypsy Alley" (cigányútra ment) or "to swallow something the wrong way"; "to dress somebody in Gypsy trousers" (felhúzni a cigánynadrágot) or "to give somebody a licking"; "this is not how they beat Gypsies" (nem úgy verik a cigányt) or that is not the way to do something, are some examples of anti-Gypsy terminology used in common Hungarian speech.[16]

Consequently, any policy designed to integrate the Gypsy more deeply into Hungarian society had to be sensitive to this prejudice. One of the cornerstones of efforts to end Gypsy social isolation was a 1964 "housing development plan" that ordered the destruction of the worst Gypsy settlements. Living conditions in those worthy of preser-vation would be improved, though ultimately they would be replaced by newer homes.[17] Over the next ten years, officials did an extensive survey of Gypsy conditions throughout Hungary and discovered, in the midst of an ongoing Gypsy population boom that saw figures reach 320,000 in 1970, that there were 2,100 Gypsy settlements throughout the country, with 126,000 Gypsies living in what Secre-tary of State Lajos Papp described as "shanty towns." Almost half did not have a well, while two-thirds had no electricity.[18]

The official plan enabled Gypsy families to borrow money from the government to build new homes. In addition, local governments could also extend credit to Gypsies for similar purposes. The national scheme required that a Gypsy head of family who had "worked steadily for two years," and had, according to the county he lived in, saved 6,000–10,000 forints, could borrow 60,000–80,000 forints on a twenty-five-year note to build a new house. Between 1964 and 1975, the Government issued 700 million forints in loans to the Gypsies, while between 1965 and 1970, 2,500 new Gypsy homes were built with a portion of these funds.

Authorities also discovered serious housing problems in urban areas, particularly in Budapest, whose Gypsy population was estimated to be 65,000 by 1974. Nationwide, 3,000 apartments were opened to Gypsies, while officials in the capital halted Gypsy settlement in the city. Most, however, lived in slums on the capital's periphery. Over 50 percent of the dwellings were habitable, though 2,350 had "no running water," and 1,500 had no electricity. Consequently, officials throughout Budapest's suburbs were ordered to make apartments available to Gypsies near their slum sites.[19]

According to government officials, efforts to rehouse Gypsies have been quite successful. The number of Gypsies living in slum dwellings dropped from 126,000 in the late 1960s to 28,000 a decade later, a figure disputed by outside experts, who estimate the latter figure to be 100,000. Part of the difference could be the dramatic growth of the Gypsy population during this period.[20]

There have also been some integration success stories in other parts of the country, particularly where housing needs have been coupled with labor development programs for semi-skilled Gypsy workers. In the Baranja mining area in southwest Hungary, which had a Gypsy population of 13,000 in the early 1960s, officials opened positions for Gypsy male workers, and encouraged them to become active in local government bodies.[21] Another example of successful integration was in the northern province of Nograd near Budapest, which traditionally has had one of the highest concentrations of Gypsies in Hungary. Between 1965 and 1975, Gypsies built 500 new homes, while 70 percent of the female Gypsies have acquired regular jobs, considerably above the national average of only one-third of all Gypsy males employed in 1961. The city of Nogradmeyer, where one-third of the population is Gypsy, they run a foundry, long a Gypsy specialty, which in 1975 had

240 workers and an annual revenue of 32 million forints. Three Gypsies also held seats on the town council.[22]

Unfortunately, these successes are more the exception than the rule. Only about 1.5 percent of Gypsy laborers were skilled by the late 1970s, and most held menial or unskilled positions. Some of the difficulties centered around local prejudice, which forced Gypsies to find work far from home, though much of it was due to lack of job training and education. The latter has been one of the major concerns of the government, and the education of Gypsy children one of the cornerstones of its efforts more fully to integrate Gypsies into Hungarian society. Authorities, however, have discovered that there are immense difficulties in creating an effective educational plan for Gypsy children.[23]

One of these difficulties, literacy, has always been a problem for Hungarian Gypsies, and has hurt their ability to integrate more completely into Hungarian society. At the beginning of the twentieth century, only one in four hundred nomadic Gypsies was literate, while only three or four in one hundred semi-nomadic Gypsies could read or write, and 93.5 percent of settled Gypsies ''were illiterate.''[24] By 1964, 30 percent of Hungary's Gypsies were literate and only 39 percent of school-age Gypsy children could read or write. In 1970 studies showed that 70 percent of the country's elderly Gypsies had never gone to school, and half of those between 35 and 39 had no formal education. On the other hand, younger Gypsies have benefitted greatly from government programs, with 14 percent of those born between 1953 and 1957 never having any schooling, a figure that drops to 10 percent for those born between 1957 and 1962.[25]

Even in school, though, there are still serious problems. Unlike other minorities, who were given their own network of institutions and classes in some cases, authorities decided to attempt to integrate Gypsy children directly into Hungarian schools, despite the fact that in 1970, 89 percent of Hungary's Gypsy children were Vlach, and often entered schools knowing only thirty to forty Hungarian words. This put them two to three years behind their Hungarian counterparts, and some teachers often treated them as retarded. Discouraged and often misunderstood, 50–60 percent of the Gypsy children were dropping out of the public school system by 1970.[26] Consequently, Hungarian officials began to create special classes and to open a limited number of schools exclusively for

Gypsy children to deal with their special needs.[27]

In 1972 they also began a special project at the Gypsy school at Ráckeve to study the linguistic problems of six- to nine-year-old Gypsy school children, who were drawn from a Gypsy community on the city's periphery, and a less assimilated settlement farther away. As a result of this and similar programs, authorities have tried to make teachers more aware of Gypsy educational problems, have created smaller, special classes for them, and, in one case, have developed special classes for five-year-old Gypsy kindergarten children to help them develop better Hungarian language skills prior to entering the public schools.[28]

Unfortunately, problems still exist today despite the fact that 71 percent more Gypsy children reach the eighth grade in school than in 1970–1971. According to Hungarian figures, the "ratio of Gypsy pupils in need of care in institutions for handicapped children is 28.5 percent and that of mentally defective Gypsy children is 31 percent." About half the children in welfare centers are also Gypsy, while 10 percent of them are "physically or mentally retarded." In addition, a large percentage of Gypsy children will only complete the lower grades in school. Some of the principal reasons for these failures are Gypsy home life and family resistance to school attendance.[29]

As the government moved to improve housing and educational opportunities for the Gypsies, it also upgraded Gypsy representative bodies. After the dissolution of the *Cigányszövetség* in 1960, the Gypsies, unlike other minorities, had no formal national representative body. In 1968 the government created a special Gypsy Interministerial Commission under the Council of Ministers to work with various agencies that dealt with Gypsies, though they have held few seats on this body, and had very little impact on its decisions.[30]

In August 1974, the Patriotic People's Front (PPF), the country's political party, invited delegates from the World Romani Congress (*Comité International Rom*) War Crimes Commission to Budapest to commemorate the thirtieth anniversary of the destruction of the Gypsy prisoners at Auschwitz. The two hundred delegates used the occasion to demand that the Hungarian government create a "National Romani Organization" for Gypsies. Two days later, authorities announced the creation of a consultative *Cigányszövetség*, with author Menhert Lakatos as its head. Though it has never had any significant influence on Gypsy matters, it did, at least for Lakatos, move the Gypsy issue to a higher plateau of recognition, a fact he bemoaned in

1972 when he stated that "we have no schools of our own, no news-papers, and no organization. We hang onto a belief in our own existence—but perhaps even that is a hallucination."[31]

In 1979, the government decided that even though the Gypsies still did not warrant national minority status, they should have a more representative organization to help them develop along the lines of other minority groups. They appointed Jozsef Daroczi, a member of the Presidium of the International Romani Union, as head of the new *Országos Cigánytanács*. As a result of its activities and the successes of other government programs, the quality of Gypsy cultural life has improved substantially, so that by May 1986, when authorities created the *Ungro-themeske Romane Kulturake Ekipe* (Rom Cultural Association), with "800 million forints in initial funding," there were two hundred official Gypsy cultural groups and forty dance troupes nationwide.[32]

Unfortunately, serious problems still remain that plague efforts to assimilate Gypsies fully into Hungarian society, particularly prejudice. Over the past twenty years, Hungarian sociologists have conducted sophisticated public opinion surveys on the Gypsy question. One, conducted by Endre Hann for the Mass Communication Research Center in 1978, showed that there are still significant negative stereotypes nationwide. Of those polled, 28 percent alluded to immoral or illegal Gypsy behavior, while 21 percent felt that Gypsies abused the social welfare system, a perspective voiced by László Siklós in an earlier study of Hungarian Gypsies in 1970. In a story about relief aid sent to flood victims in the Szaboles-Szatmar region in May 1970, he noted that while non-Gypsies actively pitched in to help,

> most of the Gypsies however—several thousands of them lounged in the emergency quarters they were allotted, destroyed the furniture of cultural centers and schools, sold in the market places the canned food, quilts, and sheets given to them as flood victims, expressed contempt for the three meals they received daily, asking for more meat, and demanded that stone houses be built for them since the lot of the Gypsy people was an unfortunate one and life had dealt very hardly with them.[33]

The most pervasive anti-Gypsy sentiment is in the countryside, particularly in areas with heavy Gypsy concentrations, though there are exceptions. In the village of Tázár, a 1976 survey showed that public opinion toward two Gypsy families varied according to how steadily members of each family worked and how they took care of themselves and their homes. The author of the study concluded that prejudice toward Gypsies "is deep inside many Hungarians in the national context, despite consistent policies of the Government to improve the status and living conditions of Gypsies." Villagers felt that they were different because they had failed throughout Hungary "to benefit from what are seen as generous policies favoring them at the expense of the Hungarians." According to some of Tázár's residents, Gypsies "appear to reject every new possibility the State proposes for self-improvement" and seem unwilling to work.[34]

In a survey published in the Hungarian journal *Szociológia*, the author, Ferenc Pártos, concluded that while Hungarians in general were sympathetic to their plight, they became more intolerant when it came to issues involving schooling, homes, and interpersonal relations. Those who were most accepting were also the farthest removed from Gypsies in their everyday life, while those most critical of the Gypsies and government policies toward them were those with the most day-to-day contact with Gypsies, particularly in rural areas. He concluded

> that while Hungary's social policies have hardly changed the status of Gypsies, they have created tensions between certain Gypsy and non-Gypsy groups, moreover within the Gypsy population, and have generated some dissatisfaction with social policies in general.[35]

In a more recent analysis, János Kenedi compares the difference between traditional Hungarian anti-Semitism and contemporary Gypsy prejudice. He attributes the latter to "increasingly empty Hungarian ethnic consciousness" that "regains its self-awareness by differentiating itself from the Gypsies." Modern Hungarians, he notes, view "poverty . . . as a moral short-coming," and feel that those who are poor are not really Hungarians. He adds that these sentiments are tied to concern over the fate of Hungary and Hungarians in general, particularly to those outside the country. Fear that the number of Hungarians is too small leads to exaggerated concern that the number of Gypsies in Hungary is too large. The word "Gypsy," he observes, has become a "synonym for criminality" both in public use and in the "mass media," which he feels "goads opinion in an anti-Gypsy direction." As examples of current attitudes toward Gypsies, he points to a punk group that demands "a Gypsy-free zone" and wall slogans that say OMC (Oldmeg a cigányt! [KTG—"Kill the Gypsies"]). Anti-Gypsy prejudice, he argues, is "the folly of socialism."[36]

There is some merit in Kenedi's arguments, particularly in light of growing economic and political unrest in Hungary. One of the great concerns of the Hungarian government has been the country's declining population. In 1984, there were 10.7 million Hungarians, a figure that dropped to 10,624,000 three years later. This, in contrast to a Gypsy population whose birthrate is twice that of the non-Gypsy population, and doubles every twenty to thirty years, frightens officials. In a speech before the VIII Congress of the Patriotic People's Front on 13–15 December 1985, General Secretary Imre Pozsgay said, applauding Hungary's general minorities' policies, that it was important for the government to speed the "social integration of Gypsies" at the same time that it searched "for measures to halt the decline of Hungary's population."[37]

Other factors that affect anti-Gypsy feelings are concerns over monies spent to improve the quality of Gypsy life at the very time that some Hungarians still suffer from housing shortages, and general economic problems plague the nation.[38] A country that has linked its minorities policies to ties with other states faces a unique situation with the Gypsies, since they in no way affect Hungarians abroad. Consequently, the only recourse for officials in Budapest is to find ways to integrate the Gypsies into Hungarian society completely, or to grant them full minority status to accentuate their cultural and ethnic differences, a policy filled with problems in light of steady Hungarian antipathy for them and their rising numbers. Yet both paths have dangers since, according to Françoise Cozannet, one of the mistakes to avoid in dealing with Gypsies is to try directly to assimilate them into modern society, since it would destroy their unique culture. On the other hand, he observes, it would also be a mistake to try to pressure Gypsy culture along "an anachronistic and folkloristic course," because it would force it "to lose contact with reality."[39]

Unfortunately, according to Ferenc Pártos, the "changing of the condition of the whole Gypsy population does not seem possible in the near future."[40] With their growing numbers, which very much reflect the success of Hungarian policies toward them, Hungary faces a significant, difficult challenge on this issue.

Notes

1. László Siklós, "The Gypsies," p. 150; Miklos Tomka, "Die Zigeuner in der ungarischen Gesellschaft," p. 3; Józcef Vekerdi, "Earliest Arrival Evidence on Gypsies in Hungary," pp. 170–71. One of Hungary's most important historical figures, Sigismund, became Holy Roman Emperor in 1410 and King of Bohemia in 1420. See Denis Sinor, *History of Hungary*, pp. 60–103, passim; Rena C. Gropper mentions in her *Gypsies in the City: Culture Patterns and Survival*, pp. 7–8, that as a result of a rebellion among Gypsy slaves in Hungary in 1383 that "Sigismund of Hungary gave a group called the *Sincani* the right to choose their own leaders." Sigismund, however, did not become king until 1387, and was not in a position to grant such rights prior to this time.

2. Jean-Paul Clébert, *The Gypsies*, p. 71; Jean-Pierre Liégeois, *Gypsies and Travellers*, p. 99; Victor S. Mamatey, *Rise of the Hapsburg Empire, 1526–1815*, p. 118; Andrew Arjeh Marchbin, "A Critical History of the Origin and Migration of the Gypsies," notes the Magyar terms for "New Settlers" is *Ujlakosok* and for "New Hungarians" is *Ujmagyarok*; Siklós, "The Gypsies," p. 157; Konrad Bercovici, *The Story of the Gypsies*, pp. 91–93; Donald Kenrick and Grattan Puxon, *The Destiny of Europe's Gypsies*, pp. 50–51.

3. Bercovici, *The Story of the Gypsies*, pp. 92–93, says 220 Gypsies were executed, while Ian Hancock, in "Some Contemporary Aspects of Gypsies and Gypsy Nationalism," observes that "nearly 200 Gypsies were tortured, many beheaded, quartered and hung . . ."; Clébert, *The Gypsies*, p. 73, notes that only forty-five Gypsies were executed; Liégeois, *Gypsies and Travellers*, pp. 99–100; on the other hand, Joseph II "freed the Jews from most of the civil disabilities under which they suffered," and issued the Serfdom Patent in 1781 that emancipated Austrian serfs. Mamatey, *Rise of the Hapsburg Empire*, pp. 131–33; Tomka, "Die Zigeuner," p. 4.

4. Tomka, "Die Zigeuner," pp. 4–5; Siklós, "The Gypsies," p. 155, indicates that 49,000 of them did handicraft work (34,000 males and 15,000 women); Tamás Ervin and Y. Tamás Révész, *Búcsú a cigányteleptöl* [Farewell to the Gypsy Quarter], p. 11; József Vekerdi, Review of Balint Sarosi, *Cigányzene* [Gypsy Music], p. 50.

5. C.A. Macartney, *A History of Hungary: 1929–1945*, pp. 14–15, 69–70; G.C. Paikert, "Hungary's National Minority Policies, 1920–1945," pp. 202–7, 211; Andrew C. Janos, *The Politics of Backwardness in Hungary, 1825–1945*, pp. 205, 233, 253, 282.

6. Janos, *Politics*, p. 205; Paikert, "National Minority Policies," pp. 202, 208–10, 215, 217; László Kövágó, *Nemzétisegek a mai Magyarországon* [Nationalities in Today's Hungary], p. 9; Kenrick and Puxon, *Destiny*, p. 183.

7. Kenrick and Puxon, *Destiny*, pp. 124–25, 183; Kazimierz Smoleń, *Auschwitz, 1940–1945*, pp. 21–22. Bohdan Wytwycky, *The Other Holocaust: Many Circles of Hell*, pp. 36–38; Christian Bernadac, *L'Holocauste Oublié: Le Massacre des Tsiganes*, pp. 412–13.

8. Between 1946 and 1947, Hungary expelled 228,604 ethnic Germans, while a further 31,396 fled the country and, in 1946–1948, forced 73,373 Slovaks to leave in an exchange agreement with Czechoslovakia. Thomas Spira, "Worlds Apart: The Swabian Expulsion from Hungary after World War II," p. 197; Robert R. King,

Minorities under Communism: Nationalities as a Source of Tension among Balkan Communist States, pp. 52–53; Stalin criticized the concept of "Cultural Autonomy." He felt that though a minority group could have its own schools and languages, it would contradict the "spirit of Proletarian Internationalism" to allow them any more distinct cultural privileges than this. Steven Revay, "Hungarian Minorities under Communist Rule," pp. 42–47; Bertram D. Wolfe, *Three Who Made a Revolution*, p. 400.

9. *Constitution of the Hungarian People's Republic,* p. 31; Linda Degh, "Ethnology in Hungary," p. 297; Raphael Vago, "Nationality Policies in Contemporary Hungary," p. 45; Ivan Volgyes, "Legitimacy and Modernization: Nationality and Nationalism in Hungary and Transylvania," in George Kline and Milan F. Reban, eds., *The Politics of Ethnicity in Eastern Europe*, p. 135.

10. Paul S. Shoup, *The East European and Soviet Data Handbook: Political, Social, and Developmental Indicators, 1945–1975*, p. 137; Siklós, "The Gypsies," p. 151; Tomka, "Die Zigeuner," p. 8.

11. László Kosa, "Thirty Years of Ethnographic Research among the National Minority Groups Living in Hungary (1945–1974)," p. 232; "National Minorities in the Hungarian People's Republic," in Miklos Gardos, ed., *Hungary 1971,* pp. 135–36.

12. The creation of the *Cigányszövetség* was officially announced 20 October 1957 in *Népakarat,* Grattan Puxon, "Roma: Europe's Gypsies" (1973), p. 16; Shoup, *Handbook,* p. 137. Siklós, "The Gypsies," p. 151, says that the official figure was about "one-tenth the actual number."

13. Mihaly Hajdu, "Gypsies, 1980," pp. 32–33. Official justification for this change was that the Gypsies lacked one or more of Stalin's criteria for nationality status, which included common language, territory, economy, and culture. Consequently, they were nothing more "than . . . a social problem." In 1964, there was some disagreement among Gadže (non-Gypsy) specialists over this. One suggested, as with other minorities, the official recognition of Romani, the Gypsy language, and the creation of special schools for Gypsies; Puxon, "Roma" (1973), p. 16; Ervin and Tamás, *Búcsú a cigányteleptöl*, p. 16.

14. "The Gypsies," pp. 21, 23; "Discrimination," n.p.; "Minorities in Eastern Europe," p. 14.

15. Edit Fél and Tamás Hofer, *Proper Peasants: Traditional Life in a Hungarian Village*, pp. 247, 294–95, 346–47, 357, 378.

16. Hans-Georg Heinrich, *Hungary: Politics, Economics, and Society*, p. 139.

17. Hajdu, "Gypsies, 1980," p. 33; Siklós, "The Gypsies" pp. 153–54.

18. László Rózsa, "Gypsies and Public Opinion," p. 128; Rita Réger, "Bilingual Gypsy Children in Hungary: Explorations in Natural Sound-Language Acquisition at an Early Age," p. 80, n. 1, states that the Gypsies made up 3.2 percent of the Hungarian population; Siklós, "The Gypsies," p. 151, notes that there were over 3,200 villages and 70 towns in Hungary at that time; Hajdu, "Gypsies, 1980," p. 30, says that the figure of 320,000 was determined from a sociological survey done in Hungary in 1971; Tomka, "Die Zigeuner," p. 14.

19. Hajdu, "Gypsies, 1980," pp. 31–33; Karl Jokisch, "Zigeuner—Fremdgebliebene unter uns," p. 5; Siklós, "The Gypsies," p. 154. In Átány, the government program had enabled Gypsies to build five homes in the village proper. Unfortunate-

ly, they housed eleven families, and living conditions were not much different from the small crowded abodes "built in the Gypsy Way." Fél and Hofer, *Proper Peasants*, p. 247, n. 20; Grattan Puxon, "Tito and the Future of Roma," pp. 12–13, states that there were 65,000 Gypsies in Budapest by 1974.

20. Rózsa, "Gypsies and Public Opinion," p. 126; Puxon, "Roma" (1987), p. 10.

21. Puxon, "Roma" (1973), p. 16. This figure rose to 15,000 by the early 1970s. Puxon, "Roma" (1975), p. 13.

22. Andras Faludi, *Cigányok* . . . [Gypsies], p. 9; Puxon, "Roma" (1987), p. 13.

23. Rózsa, "Gypsies and Public Opinion," pp. 127–28, 130; Siklós, "The Gypsies," p. 156.

24. Siklós, "The Gypsies," p. 157.

25. Hajdu, "Gypsies, 1980," p. 30.

26. Rózsa, "Gypsies and Public Opinion," pp. 127–28; Siklós, "The Gypsies," p. 158. A government survey in 1971 estimated that 21.2 percent of Hungary's Gypsies were bilingual. Over half spoke "the Lovari dialect of the Romani language," with those speaking Lovari making up the Vlach (Wallachian) Gypsy group in Hungary. The country's second Gypsy group is the Romanian dialect Gypsies, who make up 7.2 percent of Hungary's Gypsies. The last group is "monolingual Gypsies," who speak Magyar, and are known as Romungros, Réger, "Bilingual Gypsy Children," p. 80.

27. In 1970–1971, Gypsy children made up 5.3 percent of the general student population in Hungarian schools, a figure that rose to 6.2 percent by 1978–1979, Rózsa, "Gypsies and Public Opinion," p. 128; in 1972, "three in every ten six-year-old children are of Gypsy origin." Réger, "Bilingual Gypsy Children," p. 80; Gypsy population estimates for this period were 320,000 (3.2 percent of population) in 1970 according to Rózsa, "Gypsies and Public Opinion," p. 128, and Réger, "Bilingual Gypsy Children," p. 80; Siklós, "The Gypsies," p. 151, and Hajdu, "Gypsies, 1980," p. 30, put this figure between 300,000 and 400,000. Puxon, "Roma,"(1973), says there were 480,000 Gypsies in Hungary in 1970. Over the next seven to eight years, official Gypsy population estimates were 350,000 in 1979, Rózsa, "Gypsies and Public Opinion," p. 128; Hajdu, "Gypsies, 1980," p. 30.

28. Réger, "Bilingual Gypsy Children," p. 60.

29. Puxon, "Roma" (1987), p. 10; Rózsa, "Gypsies and Public Opinion," p. 128.

30. Puxon, "Roma" (1987), p. 10; Siklós, "The Gypsies," p. 160.

31. Puxon, "Roma" (1975); Gratton Puxon, "Gypsies: Blacks of East Europe," p. 463.

32. Puxon, "Roma" (1987), p. 10.

33. Hajdu, "Gypsies, 1980," p. 34; Siklós, "The Gypsies," p. 162.

34. C.M. Hann, *Tázár: A Village in Hungary*, pp. 154–55.

35. Ferenc Pártos, "A cigány és nem cigány lakosság vélémenge a föbb társadalompolitikai célkitüzésekröl" [Gypsies and Non-Gypsies on the Main Goals of Social Policy], pp. 3, 14–16; Heinrich, *Hungary*, pp. 139–40.

36. János Kenedi, "Why Is the Gypsy the Scapegoat and Not the Jew?" pp. 11–14.

37. Hajdu, "Gypsies, 1980," p. 30; Richard F. Staar, *Yearbook on International Communist Affairs, 1987,* p. 301; Puxon, "Roma" (1987), p. 10, predicts that the

number of Gypsies will be 1.5 million by 2027; Staar, *Yearbook, 1987*, pp. 303–4.

38. Heinrich, *Hungary*, pp. 100, 121–24; for more details on the Hungarian housing problems, see Ivan Szelenyi, "Housing System and Social Structures," pp. 269–98, *passim*.

39. Françoise Cozannet, "Gypsies and the Problem of Acculturation," p. 69; Hajdu, "Gypsies, 1980," p. 34.

40. Hajdu, "Gypsies, 1980," p. 34.

9

The East European Roots of Romani Nationalism

IAN HANCOCK

The *Oxford English Dictionary* defines *nation* as "a distinct race or people, characterized by common descent, language or history, usually organized as a separate political state and occupying a definite territory." *Nationalism* in turn may be defined as a sense of identity as a people, and the efforts resulting to foster this and to obtain recognition as a distinct population, bound by common historical, cultural, linguistic, political, religious, or other ties in the eyes of the larger society.

While in the broadest sense the term *nation* may apply to a non-politically autonomous ethnic group consisting of only a few hundred individuals (cf. the West African or Native American use of the word as an equivalent to *tribe*), it is most often used synonymously with the notion of an actual country, the existence of an independent geographical homeland being an integral part of its interpretation. However, as the dictionary definition indicates, this is usually, and therefore by implication not invariably, a defining criterion. There have been nations of people lacking a homeland (or a homeland allowing them access or control) throughout history—the pre-1948 Jewish population, for example, or the Palestinians in the present day. Bloody wars have been fought because of the existence of nations of people lacking their own autonomous territory.

It is into this latter category that the Romani nation fits and, though the efforts to secure a geographical homeland were central to the nationalist movement, especially during the 1930s and 1940s, the price paid for not having one has been heavy.

Origins of the Roma

While bound by some of the criteria identified above, i.e., a common historical and linguistic heritage, the Roma or Gypsies appear to have been a composite people from the beginning. Although there has been no real doubt about an Indian origin for the Romani people for over two centuries, explanations for the time and circumstances of the exodus out of the subcontinent have been diverse, and often quite tenuous. *Nameh* is an example of this; not only is the connection of the people described in it with the contemporary Roma suppositional, but linguistic evidence cannot support a move out of India as early as the fifth century A.D.[1]

Evidence based on Romani language and history now points strongly to an origin in the Rajput population in northwestern India a millennium ago; the Rajputs themselves were composed of numbers of different non-Aryan (mainly Aryan-speaking Dravidian) peoples out of whom the state created a military society consisting of numbers of interrelated families. This new status moved them from the *śudra* (low) into the *kśattriya* (high) caste, and they were awarded certificates of descent from the sun and the moon,[2] symbolic associations that continue to exist among the Vlach Gypsies today.[3] These Rajput warriors, together with their camp followers (consisting of *Dom*, a class of people within the śudra caste who were primarily entertainers, porters, cooks, and so on) moved out of India at the time of the incursions against the Ghaznavids about the year 1000, and continued to move westward through Persia, Armenia, and the Byzantine Empire, reaching Europe by ca. A.D. 1250. The traditional Rajput ''facility for assimilating foreigners'' referred to by Watson has continued to be a characteristic of the Romani population, which has absorbed numbers of *gadžikané* (non-Gypsy) peoples during its migration west. Where this has happened, it has usually resulted in the accreted elements acquiring the Romani language, culture, and identity, and the children of such unions being regarded as Roma. While this can account for some of the factors which distinguish one group from another, it has not led to the dissolution of the Roma as a genetically related people. The Harvard medical study on American Gypsies undertaken in 1987 concluded that analysis of blood groups, haptoglobin phenotypes, and HLA types, establish the Gypsies as a distinct racial group with origins in the Punjab region of India. Also supporting this is the worldwide Gypsy language Romani, which is quite similar to Hindi.[4]

More recently, the Appeals Court in London, England, ruled that anti-Gypsyism in that country constituted racism, and that Gypsies

> were a distinct racial group [which . . .] had not lost their separate identity because, unlike Saxons and Danes, they had not merged wholly into the general population even though between a half and two thirds had abandoned a nomadic way of life.[5]

The Origins of Anti-Gypsyism

Despite the evidence that the Romani core of direct retention, genetically and historically, clearly demonstrates descent from India, the general public maintains an ambivalent attitude toward who and what Gypsies really are. The work of Mayall,[6] in particular, deals with the duality of this *gadžikanó* perception, which sees Gypsies either as a noble "Romany race" or else as "degenerate itinerants,"[7] i.e., as a racially pristine population aloof from mainstream society, with its own language and culture, or as an amorphous population of hobos and other vagrants open to anybody, intent on avoiding the responsibilities of established society. The reasons for this oddly disparate understanding of the Romani population go back to the last century, and have been accounted for by Mayall,[8] Brown,[9] and Hancock,[10] but they survive in the present day and are kept alive by writers of popular fiction and by the media.

There have been few untroubled periods during the seven or so centuries that Roma have been in Europe. Anti-Gypsyism became established from the very time of arrival, which coincided with, and was a result of, the Seljuk incursions into Europe. Mongols were encroaching upon Russia and Poland in the east, Tatars were threatening the Byzantine Empire in the south, and the Moors had occupied parts of western Europe. The Roma were themselves thought to be part of this threat to Christendom, as the various names applied to them indicate; such labels as *Heiden, Saracen, Tatar,* and *Egyptian* (hence *Gypsy*) are still current today. The other common name applied to the Roma, including variants such as *Zigeuner, Cigan,* and the like, is also the result of an ignorance of the Roma's true identity, and originate in the word Ατοίψψατῶολ, the name of a Manichaean sect in the Byzantine Empire with whom the Rom were confused.

In southern Europe, the gap in the work force, caused by the demand for men to fight in the Crusades, ensured that the skills of the newly arrived Gypsies were welcome. So welcome were they indeed that by the mid-1300s Gypsies were being held in the Balkans against their will to provide this labor, and were being treated as the property of their employers. With the passage of time, this became institutionalized slavery, a condition not abolished until the middle of the last century. Those Roma who were able to move on and up into northern and western Europe were charged either with being spies for the Turks, or plotters against the Christian establishment. Unfamiliar in every way, the Roma were not able to convince the white population otherwise, despite elaborate efforts to do so. As early as the 1400s, laws against Gypsies were in effect everywhere. These were either directed at deportation out of the country (following European settlement in the western hemisphere, the Portuguese, Spanish, French, Dutch, Germans, British, and Swedes all shipped Gypsies off to the American colonies), or made Gypsy presence a hanging offense.

Romani Reaction to Prejudice

Lacking a geographical homeland or any military presence, distinct in appearance, language, and cultural behavior from all those around them, the Roma were easy targets for persecution. Survival rested upon separating into small groups and living as unobtrusively as possible on the edges of *gadžikanó* society. Given the odds against survival under such conditions, the capacity not only to do so but to assimilate non-Gypsies into *řomanipé* must be seen as nothing less than remarkable.

In attempting to understand what it means to be a Gypsy, it is less productive to ask one what he *is* than to ask him what he is *not*. Circumstances have fragmented the original population to the extent that the differences that now exist oblige us to speak of different Gypsy groups rather than of one monolithic whole, although this is a point often ignored by fiction writers. Members of one group might deride members of another group as not being ''real'' Gypsies, and when pressed will say it is because ''they are not like us.'' But when asked whether they are Gypsies or *gadžé* they will say they are Gypsies. A parallel might be drawn with the Ashkenazic and the Sefardic populations, which differ appreciably in many respects. Nevertheless, both are ethnically Jewish.

The overriding factor of "gypsiness" is the firm acceptance of the fact that the world is divided into *Roma* and *gadžé,* and it is this, above all else, which has ensured the perpetuation of the Romani people. The division between the two worlds is kept intact by cultural behavior and by verbal reinforcement. Non-Gypsies and non-Gypsy cultures are seen as threatening to *řomanipé* ("Gypsiness") and to be avoided. Opportunities are taken to point out to the children unsanitary or disrespectful non-Gypsy behavior whenever examples occur, e.g., on television. The rudeness and hostility with which Gypsies have been treated by non-Gypsies over the centuries also reinforces the Gypsy's negative perception of the *gadžé.* Socializing between the two worlds is discouraged, and thus contact with *gadžikanipe* (non-Gypsy culture) is mainly through business and television. *Gicisori* (Vlach Gypsy fortune-tellers) in this country deal with the losers from non-Gypsy society, while soap operas and news broadcasts open an unattractive window on the outside world. Spending too long in non-Romani company is considered debilitating, and one's balance must be restored by being with other Roma. In the Romani language, the words for *man, boy, woman,* and *girl* differ depending upon whether they refer to a Gypsy or a non-Gypsy. Cuisine differs; many Roma will not eat food prepared by a non-Gypsy. For some groups, even illnesses and cures are categorized into Gypsy and non-Gypsy; *gadzikané nasvalimata* are non-Gypsy sicknesses and are contracted by being with non-Gypsies. They must be cured by a physician using non-Gypsy medication.

It is important to emphasize the aspects of Romani identity discussed here because in the absence of a political homeland, and with the population so widely spread around the globe, it is the sense of "us and them," and everything which rationalizes it, which has served as the principal cohesive factor; in a sense, *řomanipé* may be seen as the Gypsies' transportable homeland.

Non-Gypsy Attitudes to Romani Unity

Part of the process of devaluating a people entails eradicating or trivializing their history and aspirations. Efforts to direct this at the Romani people have included a denial of the legitimacy of their language, which, since it resembled nothing familiarly European, was said to be a "made up gibberish," and a denial of the physical distinctiveness of the Roma, who were said to have deliberately darkened their skin with dyes. The idea that Roma would want to organize themselves politically has also been resisted; it presumably gives lie to non-Gypsy perceptions of the Gypsy as a happy-go-lucky wanderer. If Gypsies have expressed such aspirations, they are charged with having been contaminated by the outside world, and with no longer being "proper" Gypsies.

During the Second World War, Himmler proposed that certain conservative Romani families be spared death under the "Law for the Protection of Historic Monuments" for anthropologists to study. While this proposal was overridden and never implemented, it illustrates the attitude that Gypsies belong in a "time capsule" very well. When non-Gypsies go from wagon to automobile, it is called progress; when Gypsies do the same thing, it is disappointment.

The late Dora Yates, who was honorary secretary of the Gypsy Lore Society for several decades, scorned the idea of Romani nationalism. "Except in a fairy tale," she asked, "could any hope ever have been more fantastic?"[11] Former subeditor of the society's *Journal*, Brian Vesey-Fitzgerald, echoed her sentiment some years later, deriding the notion as "romantic twaddle."[12] Other specialists in the field have expressed similar sentiments in the postwar period. In 1961 the Czech gypsiologist Jaroslav Sus wrote that

> It is an utterly mistaken opinion that Gypsies form a nationality or a nation, that they have their own national culture, their own national language. . . . It would be incorrect, and in the end reactionary, to act against the progressive decay of Gypsy ethnic unity. The way to achieve assimilation does not exclude force, which would tend to remove whatever differences exist.

Czechoslovak anti-Gypsy policy today includes the coercive sterilization of Romani women and the removal of Romani children from their families. Werner Cohn wrote that

> The Gypsies have no leaders, no executive committees, no nationalist movement. . . . I know of no authenticated case of genuine Gypsy allegiance to political or religious causes.[13]

Jiří Lípa wrote that "to make the Gypsies an ethnic minority in the conventional sense'' is for ''wishful thinkers,'' and would be ''artificially contrived.''[14]

And most recently, József Vekerdi has written that ''It is a grave mistake to suppose that either racial factors or the idea of ethnic identity unite the different Gypsy groups.''[15]

Romani Attempts at Reunification

Not only has the non-Gypsy establishment attempted to deny the notion of Romani political effort, but it has actively tried to suppress it where it has reared its head. In France, Czechoslovakia, Romania, and elsewhere, Gypsy political organizations have been made illegal.

There have, of course, been Romani spokesmen for their people from the beginning, who have interacted with the non-Gypsy establishment, and who have translated such Romani words as *Baró, Xuláj, Šeréngro,* etc., as *King, Earl, Duke,* and so on. ''Gypsy Kings and Queens'' still make good copy for pop journalists, although Romani society is not monarchical, and the equivalents of those words (*thagár, thagarní,* etc.) never occur as self-designations within *řomanipé.* However, the activities of single individuals, speaking for their group, must be seen differently from large-scale efforts to reunite Romani populations that have become distinct from each other. A sentiment common among Romani nationalists is that we were one people when we came into Europe, and that we must be one people again. It is felt that the fragmentation of the once cohesive population has been the result of hostile, external factors, not voluntary internal ones. After all, Gypsies made the journey from India to Europe intact.

There are probably many instances of Romani organizations having been formed, that have passed unrecorded into history. Some accounts, e.g., that of Bercovici,[16] which tells of a huge meeting of Roma from all over Europe in Switzerland at the end of the fifteenth century, require more documentation to substantiate them. We know that in 1722 a thousand armed Gypsies united unsuccessfully to fight for their freedom from oppression in the German states,[17] and a conference, again of German Gypsies, was reported from Darmstadt in the *London Times* (27 January 1872), though the details are scant. A slightly better documented pan-European Romani conference took place seven years later at Kisfalu, in Hungary.[18] On 1 June 1906, the *tsaribaši* of the Bulgarian Roma, Ramadan Ali, assembled Gypsy leaders from various parts of the country and drew up a petition demanding equal rights for his people, which he sent to the National Parliament. However, it was not acted upon. Stimulated by events in Europe,[19] an application was filed in Washington in the United States two years later by members of the Serbian Romani Adams family, for the establishment of the National Gypsy Association of America. Its principal aims were housing and education for American Roma. Two decades later the Russian American Rom, Steve Kaslov, founder of the Red Dress Gypsies' Association, approached President Roosevelt voicing the same concerns.[20]

The *Near East Magazine* for 12 June 1913 reported that "a vast concourse of Gypsies" had gathered at Piatră Neamţ in Romania to pay tribute at the unveiling of a statue of Mihail Kogălniceanu, a nineteenth century journalist whose writings were influential in bringing an end to Gypsy slavery in his country. The seeds of reunification, however, had been sown at the Kisfalu meeting some years before, and following the end of the First World War, Romani political activity flourished in Eastern Europe, particularly in Poland, Russia, Yugoslavia, and Romania.[21] In Russia, Romani activism was suppressed in 1929 by Joseph Stalin, although until that date, the Pan-Russian Romani Union, under the leadership of Aleksander Germanov, had been increasingly successful in coordinating some thirty Romani-run artisan cooperatives in Moscow, and fifty collective farms throughout the western Soviet Union. The largest of these, home to seventy families, was established in Krikunovo in Caucasia, and bred horses for the Red Army. In Romania, an Association of Roma was founded at Clabor in 1926, and between 1930 and 1934 published a journal called *Romani Family*. Another organization, the General Association of Roma, was created by a non-Gypsy called Lasurica. It was avowedly nationalistic in orientation, but survived only throughout 1933, managing to produce two widely distributed publications during that time, the *Romani Voice* and the *Rom*.

In October of the same year, the General Association of Gypsies of Romania organized and held an international conference under the title United Gypsies of Europe in Bucharest. Its leader was Gheorghe Nicolescu, an educated Rom whose inclinations were toward integration and education for his people. In the August 1935 issue of the *Romani Voice,* he spoke of the pain of the Romani experience as motivation for change, and of the necessity of alliance with those free of anti-Gypsy prejudice:

> As long as we travel the paths of justice, honor and duty, no one and nothing can detract us from our goal, for we have with us a steadfast and loyal ally—suffering. The way towards emancipation is clear: those who care about us will be cared for in return, and we shall march together forward, ever forward.

Among other things, the conference sought to erect a monument to the abolitionist Gregory Ghica and to make 23 December an annual Romani holiday commemorating emancipation from slavery. Proposals were also made for the establishment of a Romani library, hospital, and university, and—most important—to institute an international program of communication and cooperation among representative Romani groups everywhere, the specific aims being to strengthen the sense of ethnic solidarity, and to combat social inequality.[22] A national Romani flag, consisting of two horizontal bars, the lower green and the upper blue, was also adopted. The event was treated with some sarcasm in the press, however, and while Martin Block, writing in Nazi Germany in the mid-1930s, mentioned it in his influential book on Gypsies, he greatly minimized its significance. "Gypsies," he wrote, "offer no contribution to civilization, and do themselves in no way help to elucidate the problem of their survival."[23] Block's biased scholarship was used to justify Hitler's racial policies, and the eventual program to annihilate the Romani population.

In his chapter on Romani nationalism, Acton discusses the external stimuli which have affected its emergence:

> Gypsy nationalism has borrowed extensively from other nationalist traditions. Classical nineteenth-century nationalism, centered on the idea of a nation-state, presented to Gypsies above all the example of Zionism. . . . More recently, "third-world nationalism," Fanonism and the Black Power writings have given a new language in which to lay claim to self-determination and cultural autonomy *within someone else's* power structure. This latter ideological variant is the most radical . . . because it makes statements about the nature of the persecuting system.[24]

Tipler had already drawn attention to the model which Zionism provided for Romani nationalist sentiment, and indeed for the creation, later, of the international committee itself:

> The idea of an International Gypsy Committee has been inspired to a great extent by the success of Zionism, and the "philosophy of the

Gypsy nation'' as expounded by the Committee's president . . . is replete with references to [. . . the] apostles of Jewish nationhood. If his example is Zionism, his bible is the U.N. Charter of Human Rights.[25]

The closest approximation in adopting "someone else's power structure," as Acton has it, was in the emergence of a Gypsy royal line in Poland in the late 1920s, where it was particularly attractive to members of the Kwiek family, descendants of slaves liberated in Romania seventy years before. A number of Kwieks had been able to establish a dynasty and be recognized as "kings" by local police and government officials, who even endorsed their elections.[26] Michael Kwiek II, who succeeded his father King Gregory in 1930, held court regularly, and in 1932 announced a pan-European tour during which he was to be accompanied by "a bodyguard of secretaries and detectives."[27] Two years later, he announced his idea of creating a Romani state on the banks of the Ganges in India, the original homeland. This far-reaching plan was terminated when he was forced to abdicate and leave Poland by his successor, Mathias Kwiek. Mathias made a number of proposals to the Polish government for civil and social reform for the nation's population, but general anti-Gypsyism, and tensions within the Romani community over competition for the throne, resulted in little being accomplished. Among those contending were Joseph Kwiek, who had a plan for a Romani homeland in South Africa, and Basil Kwiek, who had helped to depose King Michael. It was not until 1937 that Janusz Kwiek successfully petitioned the Archbishop of Warsaw to recognize him as king of the Romani people in that country. As a consequence, invitations were sent to various European heads of state, and he was crowned Janos I before thousands of people in the National Army Stadium, with appropriate pomp and ceremony, on 4 July that year. At his coronation speech, in Romani, he made the following pledge:

> I shall send a delegate to Mussolini asking him to grant us a piece of land in Abyssinia where Roma can settle. Our people are weary of having to travel throughout the ages. The time has now come for us to cease living as nomads; if the Poles will only allow us to send our children to their schools to be educated, we shall soon have our own representatives in the League of Nations.[28]

According to a report in the *NS Landspost* for 19 March 1937, he kept his word and approached Mussolini's fascist government to ask that Gypsies be allowed to settle in an area between Somalia and Abyssinia. The following year, however, Rüdiger in Nazi Germany recommended that the Gypsy population be eliminated rather than simply removed from Europe,[29] and sterilization measures were stepped up. The establishment of a Romani colony in Africa never materialized, but Janusz Kwiek's dream of representation in the League of Nations—or, as it is today, the United Nations—has come true. With the Nazi invasion of Poland and the policy of extermination of the Gypsies, Romani unity was critically disrupted. Kwiek, as leader, was ordered to collaborate with death squads but refused and was executed.

Out of the chaos following war, Rudolf Kwiek proclaimed himself the new king, but there were few followers. With the Kwiek Dynasty no longer visible, he reappointed himself president of the World Council of Gypsies, but there was no actual council, and he died unheralded in 1964 at the age of 87. Meanwhile, some members of the Kwiek family had moved to France, where their talent for stimulating Romani political activity helped to establish a new organization, the World Romani Community.

The only other enduring organization to have come into being before the war was in Greece, where two Romani women, who were probably of Yugoslav nationality and then living near Athens, established the Panhellenic Cultural Association of Greek Gypsies. This is still very active today under the presidency of Yoannis Vrissakis.

During the years following the war, the Romani population in Europe was numb. Political activity was minimal, and Gypsies were reluctant even to identify their ethnicity publicly or draw attention to it through group effort. No reparations had been forthcoming for the Nazi atrocities committed against them, and no organized attempts had been made by any national or international agency to reorient the survivors, such as were being put into large-scale effect for survivors of other victimized groups. Instead, prewar anti-Gypsy legislation continued to operate against them. In Germany, until as late as 1947, those who had come out of the camps had to keep well hidden or risk being incarcerated once again—this time in labor camps—if they could not produce documentation proving German citizenship. Some of those laws remained in effect into the early 1950s, and it has come to light since then that Interpol continued to use, and may still be using, Gypsy-related files compiled by the Nazis in its own anti-Gypsy endeavors.

Things began to move again in 1959. In that year, another Romanian Gypsy, Ionel Rotaru, then living in France, emerged as a leader. Taking a title from the slave estates in old Wallachia, he renamed himself Vaida Voivod and attracted enough of a following among the Romani population in France to have himself acknowledged as "The Supreme Chief of the Romani People."[30] He used the non-Gypsy's stereotypes to his own advantage, creating a persona for himself which attracted media attention throughout France, and an increasing following among the Romani population. Rotaru, now Voivod, established two Gypsy organizations: the National Romani Organization, which was not particularly successful, and the World Romani Community, which was. The latter endeavor had input from the Kwieks, and gained support from as far afield as Poland and Canada. Rotaru drew up elaborate, nationalistic plans for the Roma, including the creation of an autonomous territory within France and a homeland in Somalia. He sought schooling, the repeal of anti-Gypsy laws, the development of Romani-language literature, and war crime reparations from the German government. He founded a Romani Cultural Center in Brussels and went so far as to have Romani passports printed.

His utopian ideals proved to be a threat to Charles DeGaulle's government, which was said to be embarrassed by Romani claims for war crimes reparations,[31] and which in 1965 banned the World Romani Community. Rotaru continued to fight, however, telling the press that "dissolution is not prohibition," and the notion of a geographical homeland, *Romanestan,* remained uppermost in his mind. It was important, he said, to have "a territory which would serve as a refuge in the event of persecution."[32] Although it still has some members today, in 1965 the World Romani Community suffered a serious setback with the creation of a breakaway organization called the International Gypsy Committee (the *Komitia Lumiaki Romani*). Its leader was the Hungarian Lovari Rom Vanko Rouda, whose more pragmatic approach concentrated on issues such as war crimes reparations rather than Gypsy passports. It established an official publication, *La Voix Mondiale Tsigane*, and stimulated the creation of affiliated bodies in other countries, such as the Gypsy Council in Britain and the Nordic Rom Council in Sweden. By 1972, twenty-three international organizations in twenty-two countries had been linked by the International Gypsy Committee. In Czechoslovakia, the Cultural Union of Roma of Slovakia, and the Union of Roma of the Czech Republic were declared illegal soon after their creation, but in the United States, Canada, Finland, Greece, Spain, Australia, and elsewhere, new Romani organizations were coming into being, not as independent entities, but as members of a worldwide Romani alliance.

The International Romani Union

In 1971 the International Gypsy Committee organized the first World Romani Congress. This took place in a location near London, announced at the last minute due to threats of disruption, between 8 and 12 April. The event was funded, in part, by the World Council of Churches and the Indian government; representatives from India and some twenty other countries were in attendance. At the congress, the green and blue flag from the 1933 conference, now embellished with the red, sixteen-spoked chakra, was reaffirmed as the national emblem of the Romani people, and the anthem, *Dželem dželem*, since sung at all congresses, was adopted. This was a traditional Romani song, with new words written for it by the late Jarko Jovanovich.

At this congress, the use of all ethnic labels for the Roma of non-Romani origins, such as *Gypsy, Zigeuner, Gitano,* and the like, was condemned; the organization itself was renamed the *International Rom Committee*. Vanko Rouda was reconfirmed as its president, and its aims were expressed by Chairman Slobodan Berberski:

> The goal of this congress is to unite Roma throughout the world, and move them to action; to bring about emancipation as we see it, and according to our own ideals; to advance at our own speed.[33]

The International Rom Committee became the permanent secretariat and executive authority presiding over the congress. Its first task was to create five standing commissions: Social Affairs, War Crimes, Language Standardization, Culture, and Education. From it, negotiations were successfully initiated with the Council of Europe (primarily in connection with the anti-Gypsy legislation and free passage), and with the government of West Germany (in connection with war crimes reparations). It was in the early 1970s that the Indian Institute of Romani Studies was established at Chandigarh, in the Punjab, under the directorship of Padmashri Weer R. Rishi, and the journal *Roma*, official organ of the Romani Union, commenced publication.

The second World Romani Congress took place in Geneva seven

years later from 8 to 11 April 1978. Sixty delegates and observers from twenty-six countries were in attendance. It was chaired by Dr. Jan Cibula, a Romano physician originally from Czechoslovakia now living in Switzerland, and a twelve-member presidium was appointed representing as many countries. This time, the Indian links were more heavily emphasized and better represented: the prime minister of the Punjab and his ministers of Foreign Affairs and of Education, as well as a number of other dignitaries from India, came and were instrumental in urging the congress to apply for nongovernmental status within the United Nations. Unlike the spirit of the first congress, this time factions differing ideologically were in evidence, a fact which attending journalists found confusing. Although no sense of a departure from the IRC was made evident, Vanko Rouda had opposed the organization of the second congress, and especially the existence of the working committee whose task it was to prepare for the next international meeting. This committee was called the *Romano Internacionalno Jekhethanibé* or International Romani Union, a designation which has gradually come to stand for the International Rom Committee itself.

At the Geneva congress, a petition was drawn up and, in November 1979, presented in person to the NGO bureau of the United Nations in New York. Making the formal request for consultative status was a delegation consisting of the honorary president of the Romani Union, the late Yul Brynner, Ronald Lee, John Tene, and the present writer. By early spring 1979, approval of the petition had been granted. An earlier petition seeking recognition of the Roma had been sent to the UN Commission on Human Rights by the International Gypsy Committee in 1968,[34] but was unsuccessful. Today, over seventy regional and national Romani organizations in some twenty-eight countries are linked under the umbrella of the International Romani Union.

The third World Romani Congress took place in Göttingen between 16 and 20 May 1981, with three hundred delegates from over twenty countries participating. This was organized by the German Sinti League, and partially supported by the Association for Threatened Peoples. The overriding theme of this meeting was the fate of Gypsies in the Third Reich, but while numbers of survivors of the Romani Holocaust (the *Poŕajmos*) testified, and the resolution was made that the issue of reparations be tackled head-on, the German governments still remain intractable in their position not to give full acknowledgment to Romani losses under the Nazis, now estimated to exceed one million.

The Third International Congress was important for its election of a new Union executive. Engineer Sait Balić (Yugoslavia) was appointed by ballot as president, Romani Rose (West Germany) as vice-president, and Dr. Rajko Djurić (Yugoslavia) as secretary. Former Chairman Cibula was appointed by ballot as head of the UN presidium, and is responsible for coordinating all Romani Union/United Nations activities.

The exclusion of Roma each year from participation in the annual Days of Remembrance by the U.S. Holocaust Memorial Council led to the organization of an all-Romani commemorative service in May 1989, at St. Adolphus' Church in Chicago.[35] This was planned by a subcommittee of the newly incorporated Sa-Roma, Inc. under the presidency of The Hon. William A. Duna who had been appointed in 1987 by President Reagan as the first Rom on the Holocaust Memorial Council. Sa-Roma had grown out of the earlier Minneapolis-based American Association of Gypsy Musicians, a mainly Bashaldo Romani organization. The ceremony was attended by over a hundred people and was covered by the media.

Among those present was Dr. Witold Lakatosz, a spokesman for the Polish Lovari Romani population in the United States. In discussion with the present writer it was agreed that Romani communities in the United States should be more closely allied with the International Romani Union, and that an international congress be held in this country. During the summer of the same year, Engineer Ioan Cioabă, Bulebaşa of the Romanian branch of the International Romani Union, came to the United States as the guest of this writer, and a series of meetings were held in Texas, California, Illinois, and New York, organized by Lakatosz, Hancock, and Cioabă. The aim of these meetings, each held in a hall rented for the purpose, was to invite local Romani leaders, to explain to them the union's function, and to elect regional representatives. A national conference of American Romani leaders was planned to be held in Chicago in late 1990.

Between 4 and 13 April 1990, the Fourth World Romani Congress took place at Serock on the outskirts of Warsaw, Poland, sponsored in part by UNESCO.[36] With nearly five hundred participants from twenty-seven countries, it was the best attended congress to date. Through a lengthy balloting process, Dr. Rajko Djurić (Yugoslavia) was elected as the new president, with Engineer Sait Balić (Yugoslavia), Stanislaw Stankiewicz (Poland), and Viktor Famulsen (Sweden) filling the three vice-presidential positions. Dr. Ian Hancock (United States) was voted to succeed Dr. Jan Cibula as head of the UN (ECOSOC/NGO) presidium. Replacing Dr. Djurić as general secretary is Dr. Emil Ṣçuka (Czechoslovakia). A twenty-eight member presidium of national representatives was also appointed, whose duty it is to coordinate in their respective countries the various national and regional organizations that have membership within the International Romani Union. A number of special-focus commissions were also created, and between six and ten members appointed to each. These included commissions on language standardization, cultural preservation and documentation, media interaction, the compilation of an exhaustive Romani encyclopedia, and war crimes reparations.

In 1986, application was made for the establishment of formal relationships with UNICEF, and was granted in record time. Application has now also been made for membership in UNESCO and the World Health Organization, and prospects for inclusion are encouraging. In just the past year, assurances have been received from the Vatican and the U.S. Department of Defense that they will include details of the Romani Holocaust in reports they are preparing. Because of such associations, humanitarian organizations such as the Pearl Buck Foundation, the Van Leer Foundation, and Helsinki Watch have approached the Romani Union for documentation on the current state of anti-Gypsyism. The U.S. Congressional Caucus on Human Rights intervened on behalf of the Romani Union in 1986 to protest against the sterilization program directed at Romani women in Czechoslovakia, and in August 1990 the Sub-Commission on Prevention of Discrimination and Protection of Minorities of the UN Commission on Human Rights included the Roma in its working group on slavery, at the union's request.

For those who insist that Gypsy political effort and the reunification movement are nonexistent, and that as a people we are unable to achieve such goals, or that such activity is ''un–Gypsy-like,'' the true situation clearly demonstrates otherwise. We must recognize that those who wilfully deny Romani self-determination perhaps have their own motives for doing so, and that, in the final analysis, such motives seek to keep Gypsies manageable and oppressed by the scholars and administrators of the non-Gypsy world. It is not merely coincidence that those who have paved the way have been those most directly descended from the freed slaves in Romania. From its roots in Eastern Europe a century ago, Romani nationalism has led to the creation of the International Romani Union, now vigorously planning its Fifth World Congress, and an emerging sense of *Jekhipe* (oneness), to resist and combat anti-Gypsyism and bring new opportunities for the next generation of Roma.

Notes

1. Ian Hancock, "The Development of Romani Linguistics."

2. Francis Watson, *A Concise History of India*, p. 88.

3. J. Chatard and M. Bernard, *Zanko: Chef Tribal*, pp. 93–94; Jean-Paul Clébert, *The Gypsies*, p. 127; Anne Sutherland, *Gypsies: The Hidden Americans*, p. 125.

4. James D. Thomas, et al., "Disease, Lifestyle and Consanguinity in Fifty-Eight American Gypsies," p. 379.

5. David Altheer, "Gypsies Are a Racial Group under Discrimination Act," p. 14; Terence Shaw, "Gipsies Win Race Relations Protection," p. 2.

6. David Mayall, "Lorist, Reformist and Romanticist: The Nineteenth Century Response to Gypsy Travellers," p. 53.

7. Ibid.

8. Ibid.

9. Marilyn Brown, *Gypsies and Other Bohemians*.

10. Ian F. Hancock, *The Pariah Syndrome: An Account of Gypsy Slavery and Persecution*.

11. Dora E. Yates, *My Gypsy Days*, p. 140.

12. Brian Vesey-Fitzgerald, "Gypsies," p. 2.

13. Werner Cohn, *The Gypsies*, p. 66.

14. Jiří Lípa, Untitled article on priorities in Romani studies.

15. József Vekerdi, "The Vend Gypsy Dialect in Hungary," p. 65.

16. Konrad Bercovici, *The Story of the Gypsies*, p. 153.

17. Elsie M. Hall, "Gentile Cruelty to Gypsies," p. 53.

18. This was also reported in the *London Times*, 29 September 1879.

19. According to a news item in the *Morning Leader* (New York), 7 March 1908.

20. Victor Weybright, "Who Can Tell the Gypsies' Fortune?"

21. Thomas A. Acton, *Gypsy Politics and Social Change*, p. 101.

22. William J. Haley, "The Gypsy Conference at Bucharest"; Donald Kenrick and Grattan Puxon, *The Destiny of Europe's Gypsies*, p. 205.

23. Martin Block, *Zigeuner: Ihre Leben und Ihre Seele*, p. 210.

24. Acton, *Gypsy Politics*, pp. 233–34.

25. Derek Tipler, "From Nomads to Nation," p. 61.

26. Jean-Pierre Liégeois, *Gypsies: An Illustrated History*, p. 144; Jean Perrigault, "Les compagnons de la Belle-Étoile," p. 1; Jerzy Ficowski, *The Gypsies in Poland*, pp. 29–37 (with photographs of Kwiek's coronation). See also the *Journal of the Gypsy Lore Society*, Third Series, vol. 9, 1930, pp. 147–48 and 150–51; and Gerhard Thimm, "Zigeunerbaron Mathias Kwiek, und das Schicksalsleben seiner Vasallen zwischen Rio, Peking und Warschau."

27. See the *Evening Standard* (London), 1 October 1932, p. 4.

28. Jerzy Ficowski, *Cyganie na Polskich Drogach*, p. 165.

29. K. Rüdiger, "Parasiten der Gemeinschaft," p. 88.

30. See *La Voix du Nord*, 9 September 1970.

31. Liégeois, *Illustrated History*, pp. 146–47; Kenrick and Puxon, *Destiny*, p. 207.

32. Liégeois, *Illustrated History*, p. 150.

33. Jean-Pierre Liégeois, *Mutation Tsigane*, p. 47.

34. Tipler, "Nomads to Nation," p. 61.

35. John Stebbins, "Gypsies Recall Their 'Forgotten Holocaust,' " p. 2.

36. Anon., "Citizens of Europe"; John Daniszewski, "Gypsies Gather to Celebrate Heritage, Urge End to Stereotypes."

10

Conclusion

DAVID CROWE

The rich collection of essays that make up this study detail the tragic story of a group that Professor Dennis Reinhartz has called the "forgotten people." From the time that they entered Eastern Europe in the Middle Ages, the Romani or Gypsies have suffered constantly from prejudice and mistreatment. Their entrance at a time of great political, social, and military upheaval there added to an existing prejudice toward dark-skinned nomads of mysterious origin, strange traditions, and culture. Ignorance of their roots caused them to be called Gypsies because some later suspected that they came from Egypt. This misnomer, however, represented more than geographic ignorance—it symbolized a deeper feeling of antagonism toward the Romani that has plagued them for seven centuries.

Their historical experience in modern Romania's nuclear kingdoms, Wallachia and Moldavia, perhaps represents the worst faced by the Romani until the *Pořajmos* or Gypsy Holocaust. This tragic relationship, in time, centered around their enslavement. Once enslaved, the social dehumanization that normally accompanies such practices began to take place. Stereotypes designed to justify one group's superiority over another evolved and increasingly depicted the Romani not as talented craftsmen and musicians, but as objects of derision and mistreatment. Laws designed to discourage a *gadžo* or male non-Gypsy for marrying or having intercourse with a Romani threatened him with enslavement or Gypsy-status. Such statutes helped define the dimensions of social and ethnic stereotypes that later were used by the Nazis to justify their genocidal policies against the Romani during the *Pořajmos*.

As Romani groups fled the unstable Balkans to other parts of Eastern Europe, bound even more closely to a nomadic life-style that enabled them to survive their constant, unwanted presence, they faced continued harassment and rejection. All across Eastern Europe and the Holy Roman Empire, laws arose to deal with their threatening presence. In almost every instance, the laws involved the harshest punishments, and in some instances encouraged rape, torture, and murder against them. What emerged was a mutual level of suspicion and hatred between the *gadže* and the Romani. For the former, it centered around a collection of stereotypes that saw the Gypsy as less than human and worthless, while for the Romani, it strengthened their resolve to reject everything from the *gadžo* world. *Gadžo* rejection of the Romani bred a determination among the latter totally to separate themselves from the former, which, though it became the principal motivating factor of Romani unity, also fortified *gadžo* stereotypes of the Gypsy.

By the second half of the eighteenth century, attempts were made by some of Europe's rulers to deal more creatively with the Romani. These efforts, which are remarkably similar to those used in other parts of Eastern Europe after World War II, centered around schemes designed to halt Gypsy nomadism and force them into an accepted life-style. To neutralize the Romani community and reeducate their youth, Empress Maria Theresa had almost 18,000 Gypsy children kidnapped and placed either in state schools or foster homes. Deprived of their families and cultural-linguistic nucleus, the children soon ran away and returned to their families. These policies were continued under the Empress's son, the "Enlightened Despot" Joseph II, who forced the Romani in his Empire to settle in villages, watched closely by officials. These efforts simply forced the Romani once again onto the road, and strengthened their ties to their nomadic life-style.

The Romani experience in nineteenth-century Eastern Europe varied from country to country. In Romania, the Gypsies were finally emancipated in 1864, though, in many instances, they simply traded one form of servitude for another. On the other hand, emancipation did stimulate the development of a sense of Romani ethnic identity, which paved the way for a very strong movement in that country between the two world wars. Similar activities took place in the Czech and Hungarian portions of the Austro-Hungarian Empire during this period, though the most significant development in both regions was the dramatic increase in the Romani population.

The breakup of the imperial empires at the end of World War I, and the creation of new nations based on idealistic concepts of equality to all minorities, seemed to promise a new era for Eastern Europe's Romani. In most countries, though, international idealism gave way to strong national sentiments that sought to romanianize or magyarize, for example, all within their borders. Regardless, the Romani were able to take advantage of this new atmosphere in the decade after the war, and organized the nucleus of movements that, if they had not succumbed to the growing fascist spirit of the 1930s, could have provided the basis for an entirely new era in Romani-*gadžo* relations.

The advent of the German Nazi regime of Adolph Hitler in early 1933 changed all of that, and introduced a period known for its unspeakable horror—the *Porajmos*, or Romani holocaust. Within months after taking power, Germany's Nazi rulers began to implement harsh racial laws against Gypsies, which deprived them of all basic civil rights and forced them into the regime's new concentration camps, where they were often sterilized. These policies, according to Huttenbach, paved the way for more extreme genocidal policies later.

The Gypsy experience during the wartime phase of the *Porajmos* varied from country to country. Those under direct German control suffered from hardened Nazi racial theories that placed Gypsies somewhere between the Slavs, who were considered subhumans, and the Jews, the ultimate anti-race, who were seen as antihumans. Seen as an alien people, the Romani were regarded, according to Huttenbach, as unclean and antisocial. Peculiarly enough, Heinrich Himmler's pseudo-scientific fascination with the Romani (particularly the "pure" German Sinti and the Lalleri, whose roots were the same as the Aryans—India) kept German officials in the pre-1938 Reich from deporting all of the Gypsies to the east until the end of 1942, when they were shipped to Auschwitz, Mauthausen, and other work or death camps.

Racially, wartime Croatia was the genocidal equal of Germany, and its Gypsy population, according to Reinhartz, suffered proportionally more losses than in Germany. As in Nazi Germany, the intensity of the Croatian reaction to its Romani population was directly tied to the special breed of Croatian Aryanism that was at the spiritual center of the *Ustaša* movement and its government under Ante Pavelić. In neighboring Serbia, proclaimed "Gypsy-free" by its German occupiers in 1942, Nazi officials began an in-country campaign of mass extermination a year earlier to avoid the costs of shipping the Romani to the General Gouvernement in Poland, which had become the dumping ground for all racial undesirables in German-occupied Europe, and the center for the mass killings of the Final Solution. Franz Böhme, Serbia's German military governor, rationalized the killings as an official reaction to partisan activities in the region.

In historic Czechoslovakia, the western portion of the country was transformed into the Reich protectorate of Bohemia and Moravia, which received the full force of Nazi occupation. The Gypsy population there was decimated, while the "independent" Nazi puppet state of Slovakia, which contained most of Czechoslovakia's Romani population, had a much higher rate of survival.

Fortunately, a greater percentge of Gypsies were able to survive in other parts of the Third Reich. In Albania, which, according to Kolsti, had become a haven for Gypsies from other parts of the crumbling Ottoman Empire in the nineteenth century, the Romani experience in the *Poṙajmos* was not quite so tragic. This was, in part, because most of wartime Greater Albania was run by Italian forces that had little stomach for significant pogroms against Gypsies or other minorities. In fact, for a time, there was some pro-German sentiment among the Romani, who saw them as an alternative to an even greater enemy—the Serbs. In the end, their high rate of survival in Albania centered around a number of historic, ethnic, cultural, and political factors, the most important being that the country was not occupied by the Germans until 1943, and then for less than a year. Kolsti correctly concludes that the level of Romani survival in the ex-Ottoman portions of southeastern Europe was much higher than in those parts of the region once under Austro-Hungarian control. In Romania, for example, most of those that died did so in Transnistria, a special province that was supposed to play the same role regionally that the General Gouvernement did to the north.

Gypsy losses in the *Poṙajmos* are difficult to determine, since scholars and demographers have trouble agreeing on the number of Romani in Europe prior to this tragedy, and even more so afterward. In Romania and Hungary, for example, particularly under their new communist regimes, Gypsies hesitated to declare Romani as their ethnic or linguistic status in the face of social, economic, and political pressures that discouraged close attachment to any minority identity. Consequently, both numerical totals and percentages range widely.

Regardless, Hancock feels that a greater percentage of Gypsies in relation to their population size died in German-occupied Europe than any other group. Complete figures will never be known until detailed, exhaustive research is made both of German records and local ones throughout Eastern Europe. Statistics, however, cannot alter the fact that the Romani suffered terrible losses at the hands of the Nazis and their collaborators.

At a distance, this unsettling tragedy, coupled with the political and social chaos that swept Eastern Europe after World War II, seemed to bode ill for the Gypsies. Historically, they suffered most during times of great upheaval. However, for a brief period in Romania from 1944 to 1947, the Gypsies joined the burgeoning communist movement and quickly acquired local and regional party jobs. At the end of this period, their status began to follow the course of their fellow Romani in Czechoslovakia and Hungary, who discovered that the new Stalinist-oriented governments only gave lip service to the concept of equal minority rights. Instead, what followed were policies that, according to Kalvoda, were designed, at least in Czechoslovakia, to destroy the traditional Gypsy life-style and force them to assimilate fully into the country's new, socialist society. The same held true for Hungary and Romania.

At this point, though, the stories begin to diverge, and tend to follow the individual strains of political and social development in each country. In Hungary, for example, the Romani ultimately gained from the evolution of mature ethnic policies for other minorities, as the government sought to develop programs designed as models for neighboring countries with large Hungarian populations. Unfortunately, despite these reforms, the Romani have not achieved full minority status, though they have, with significant government financial backing, been able to develop an array of cultural and social organizations topped by a national Gypsy Council and the Rom Cultural Association. This, blended with over twenty years of intensive efforts to house Gypsy families and educate Romani children, has, from the Hungarian point of view, at least begun to change the traditional status of the Gypsy in Hungarian society. What these policies have not done, however, is to alter the deep prejudice toward them. Furthermore, by completely failing to recognize the Romani's distinctiveness as an ethnic minority and grant them full, official minority status, the government has failed to create an atmosphere of respect for their historic and cultural traditions that are so important in combating the atmosphere of ignorance that has been the traditional breeding ground for much of the historic animosity toward this group.

In Czechoslovakia, the campaign forcibly to halt Gypsy nomadism, coupled with a program of forced assimilation, began in 1958, when the former practice was outlawed. Based on the idea that the Romani had no ethnic heritage, efforts to break up Gypsy caravans, force them into housing projects, and implement labor laws designed to stop the hiring of seasonal Romani workers, failed because of inadequate planning and implementation on the national and local level. Within a decade, government officials admitted their failure, and began to look to the Romani as collaborators in helping to plan their future in socialist Czechoslovakia. The atmosphere of openness and candor that swept that country in 1968 saw the creation of two branches of the Union of Gypsy-Romanies for the Czech lands and Slovakia. What followed, in the "Prague Spring," was a full blown discussion of Gypsy problems and prejudice toward them. Unfortunately, the Soviet invasion of Czechoslovakia gradually brought an end to these efforts, and in 1973 the Romani national associations were abolished, principally because of their demand for national minority status. Afterward, particularly in Slovakia, where most of the country's Gypsies lived, an official policy emerged that praised those who had successfully assimilated, and criticized those unwilling to follow this path. Kalvoda concludes that these policies of forced assimilation will fail, and only force the Gypsies to remain part of the country's indigent population, with all of the social and economic problems associated with such poverty.

The Gypsy situation in Romania is much the same. Romanian communist authorities were unwilling to grant them any official status until they had integrated more fully into the mainstream of Romanian society. At conflict here was a value system not unlike that of Hungary, where indolence and immoral behavior were seen as critical failings that ran counter to the norm of hard work and a settled lifestyle. Consequently, as in Hungary, but to an even greater degree as in Czechoslovakia, Romanian programs to settle and educate the Romani have met with mixed success. Prejudice, rooted in centuries of viewing the Gypsy or *Țigan* as a useless, lazy individual, remains one of the principal barriers to dealing with the role of the Gypsy in Romanian society.

Despite the dark picture painted of the Romani experience in Eastern Europe, there are hopeful signs, particularly on the international scene, that some positive changes are possible in the future. The most promising is the work of the International Romani Union, which over the past two decades has tried to make other international humanitarian and human rights organizations more aware of Romani losses in the *Pořajmos*, and of violations of Gypsy civil and human rights not only in Eastern Europe, but elsewhere in the world. Hopefully, this pressure, combined with the political and social transformations taking place in Eastern Europe, will lead to a change in governmental policies that will finally give the Romani full minority status, based on their unique cultural and linguistic heritage that has been so much a part of the history of that part of Europe.

Bibliography

Anonymous. "Citizens of Europe." *Economist* (London), 21 April 1990, pp. 55–58.

Anonymous. "Gypsy Punishment in 18th Century Germany." *Gypsy and Folklore Gazette* 1, 1 (1912), p. 45.

Acton, Thomas A. *Gypsy Politics and Social Change*. London: Routledge and Kegan Paul, 1974.

————. "The Social Construction and Consequences of Accusations of False Claims to Ethnicity and Cultural Rights." Paper presented at the Leiden Foundation Centennial Conference, 13–15 September 1990, at Leiden, Holland.

Adamovič, K., and P. Kurec, eds. *Problém výchovy a vzdelávania cigánskej mládeže* [Problem of Education and Upbringing of Gypsy Youth]. Bratislava: Psychodiagnostické a didaktické testy, 1976.

Altheer, David. "Gypsies Are a Racial Group under Discrimination Act." *Times* (London), Law Report, 29 July 1988, no. 14.

Amador, Antonio Martinez. "Technical Racism and Transformation in Spanish Gypsy Society." In *Romani Language and Culture*, pp. 139–42. Sarajevo: Institut za Proučavanje Nacionalnih Odnosa, 1989.

Arad, Yitzhak. *Belzec, Sobibor, Treblinka: The Operation Reinhard Death Camps*. Bloomington: Indiana University Press, 1987.

Bacon, Walter M., Jr. "Romania." In Teresa Rakowska-Harmstone, ed., *Communism in Eastern Europe*, 2d ed., pp. 162–85. Bloomington: Indiana University Press, 1979.

Bangu, Dezider, transl. *Pieseňnad vetrom. 41 cigánskych piesní v preklade Dezidera Bangu s drevorezbami Štefana Pruknera* [Song above Wind. 41 Gypsy Songs. Translated by Dezider Bangu with drawings by Štefan Prukner]. Bratislava: Slovenský spisovateľ, 1964.

Barth, Frederick H. *A Transylvanian Legacy: The Life of a Transylvanian*

Saxon. Salt Lake City: Transylvania, 1979.

Bauer, Yehuda. *A History of the Holocaust.* New York: Franklin Watts, 1982.

———. "Jews, Gypsies and Slavs: Policies of the Third Reich." In *UNESCO Yearbook on Peace and Conflict Studies*, pp. 73–100. New York and London: Greenwood, 1985.

———. "Continuing Ferment in Eastern Europe." *SICSA Report* 4:1–2. Vidal Sassoon International Center for the Study of Antisemitism, The Hebrew University of Jerusalem, n.d.

———. "Gypsies." In Israel Gutman, ed., pp. 634–38.

Beck, Sam. "The Emergence of the Peasant-Worker in a Transylvanian Mountain Community." *Dialectical Anthropology* 1 (September 1976), pp. 365–75.

———. "Ethnicity, Class, and Public Policy: Ţiganii/Gypsies in Socialist Romania." In Kot K. Shangriladze and Erica W. Townsend, eds., *Papers for the V. Congress of Southeast European Studies: Belgrade, September 1984*, pp. 19–38. Columbus: Slavica Publishers, 1984.

———. "The Romanian Gypsy Problem." In Joanne Grumet, ed., *Papers from the Fourth and Fifth Annual Meetings, Gypsy Lore Society, North American Chapter*. Publications No. 2, pp. 101–9. New York: Gypsy Lore Society, North American Chapter, 1985.

———. "Indigenous Anthropologists in Socialist Romania." *Dialectical Anthropology* 10 (April 1986), pp. 265–74.

———. "The Origins of Gypsy Slavery in Romania." *Dialectical Anthropology* 14 (1989), pp. 53–61.

Bednarz, W. *Obóz stracen w Chełmnie.* Warsaw: Państwowy Institut Wydawniczy, 1946.

Behrendt, Johannes. "Die Wahrheit über die Zigeuner." *NS Partei Korrespondenz* 10, 3 (1939).

Belfast. " 'Burn Gypsies' Belfast Councillor to Visit Glasgow." Bulletin issued by the Belfast City Hall, 5 February 1988.

Benedict, Ruth. "History As It Appears to Rumanians." In Margaret Mead and Rhoda Metraux, eds., *The Study of Culture at a Distance*, pp. 405–15. Chicago: University of Chicago Press, 1953.

Bercovici, Konrad. *The Story of the Gypsies.* London: Jonathan Cape, 1929.

Bernadac, Christian. *L'Holocauste Oublié: Le Massacre des Tsiganes.* Paris: Editions France-Empire, 1979.

Biester, Johann E. "Über die Zigeuner: besonders im Königreich Preussen." *Berlinische Monatschrift* 21 (1793), pp. 108–65.

Binding, Karl, and Alfred Hoche. *Die Freigabe der Vernichtung Lebensunwerten Lebens.* Leipzig: F. Meiner Verlag, 1920.

Binns, Dennis. "The Most Persecuted Minority." *The Manchester Paper*, May 1986, p. 4.

Blaga, Ion. *Romania's Population: A Demographic, Economic and Socio-Political Essay.* Bucharest: Meridiane Publishing House, 1972.

Block, Martin. *Zigeuner: Ihre Leben und Ihre Seele.* Leipzig: Bibliographisches Institut, 1936.

Bock, Gisela. "Racism and Sexism in Nazi Germany." *Signs* 8, 3 (1983), pp. 400–421.

The Book of Knowledge (The Children's Encyclopedia), "Who Are the People Called Gipsies?" Vol. 8, pp. 3014–15. New York: The Grolier Society, 1952.

Borovský, Štefan. *Cigánska otázka. Bibliografia* [The Gypsy Question. Bibliography]. Košice: Štátne vedecká knižnica, 1960.

Borrow, George. *Lavengro.* London: Murray, 1843.

———. *The Romany Rye.* London: Murray, 1857.

Brandis, Emil. *Ehegesetze von 1935 erläutet.* Berlin, 1936.

Broad, P. "Zigeuner in Auschwitz." *Auschwitz-Hefte* 9 (1959), pp. 41–42.

Brown, Marilyn. *Gypsies and Other Bohemians: The Myth of the Artist in 19th Century France.* Ann Arbor: UMI Research Press, 1985.

Browning, Christopher R. *Fateful Months: Essays on the Emergence of the Final Solution.* New York: Holmes and Meier, 1985.

Bubelini, Ján. "Skúsenosti z riešenia otázok cigánskych obyvatel"ov vo Východoslovenskom kraji" [Experiences with Solving Questions of Gypsy Inhabitants in the Region of Eastern Slovakia]. *Sociálna politika* 6 (1983), pp. 138–39.

———. "Potreba vedeckeho výskumu cigánskej problematiky" [The Need for Scholarly Research of the Gypsy Problem]. *Národné výbory,* 1988, pp. 24–25.

Buchheim, H. "Die Aktion 'Arbeitsche Reich.' " *Gutachten des Instituts für Zeitgeschichte, Munich II.* Stuttgart: Deutsche Verlags-Anstalt, 1966, pp. 185–97.

Bulíř, Michal. "Školní docházka cikánských dětí v létech 1980–1985" [School Attendance of the Gypsy Children during the Years 1980–1985]. *Demografie* 29, 1 (1987), pp. 86–89.

———. "Cikánské (romské) děti v mateřských školách" [Gypsy (Romani) Children in Kindergartens]. *Demografie* 29, 4 (1987).

Cargas, Harry James. "The Continuum of Gypsy Suffering." In idem, *Reflections of a Post-Auschwitz Christian,* pp. 75–90. Detroit: Wayne State University Press, 1989.

Castles, Stephen. *Here for Good: Western Europe's New Ethnic Minorities.* London: Pluto Press, 1984.

Chatard, J., and M. Bernard. *Zanko: Chef Tribal.* Paris: La Colombe, 1959.

"Cigáni" [Gypsies]. *Encyklopedia Slovenská.* Bratislava, 1977, p. 321.

Clark, Charles Upson. *United Roumania.* New York: Dodd, Mead, 1932.

Clark, Victoria. "Gypsies Caught in Spell of Hate." *The Observer* (London), 29 July 1990.

Claude, Patrick. "Gypsies Still Encounter Wide Discrimination." *Manchester Guardian*, 4 February 1990, p. 4.

Clébert, Jean-Paul. *The Gypsies*, translated by Charles Duff. New York: E.P. Dutton; London, Vista Books, 1963; reprinted by Penguin Books, 1967.

Cohn, Werner. *The Gypsies*. Reading: Addison-Wesley, 1973.

Conot, Robert E. *Justice at Nuremberg*. New York: Harper and Row, 1983.

Constitution of the Hungarian People's Republic. Budapest: 1959.

Correspondence of the Foreign Office. Great Britain: Public Records Office, FO371, R7914/1068/92, 4 May 1942; 7 and FO371, R5331/850/92, 17 February 1944, pp. 15–16.

Cozannet, Françoise. "Gypsies and the Problem of Acculturation." *Diogenes* 95 (Fall 1976), pp. 68–92.

Crane, Florence. *Gypsy Secret*. New York: Grossett and Dunlap, 1957.

Crowe, David. *World War I and Europe in Crisis (1914–1935)*. Piscataway, N.J.: Research and Education Association, 1990.

Czerniakow, Adam. *The Warsaw Diary of Adam Czerniakow*. Chelsea, Mich.: Scarborough House, 1978.

Daniszewski, John. "Gypsies Gather to Celebrate Heritage, Urge End to Stereotypes." *Chicago Tribune*, 13 April 1990, Sec. 1, 17.

David, Henriette. "Nouvelles de l'étranger: Allemagne." *Etudes Tsiganes* 19, 1/2 (1973), p. 75.

Davidová, Eva. "Lidové náboženství třebišovských Cikánů-Romů koncem padesátých let 20. století, před rozpadem jejich tradičnï komunity" [Popular Religion of Trebišov Gypsies-Romas toward the End of the 1950s, before the Break-up of Their Traditional Community]. *Slovenský národopis* (Bratislava), 1, 36 (1988).

Deak, Istvan. "The Revolution of 1848–49 in Transylvania and the Polarization of National Destinies." In John F. Cadzow, Andrew Ludanyi, and Louis J. Elteto, eds., *Transylvania: The Roots of Ethnic Conflict*, pp. 120–23. Kent: The Kent State University Press, 1983.

"Decree Regarding Race Membership." *Narodne novine*, 30 April 1941.

Dědič, M. *Výchova a vzdělání cikánských dětí a mládeže* [Upbringing and Education of Gypsy Children and Youth]. Prague: SPN, 1988.

Degh, Linda. "Ethnology in Hungary." *East European Quarterly* 4 (September 1970), pp. 293–307.

"Dělaji nám ostudu" [They Are Giving Us a Bad Name]. *Lidová Demokracie,* 3 May 1990, p. 6.

"Discrimination." *East Europe* 8 (December 1959), pp. 3–18.

Djilas, Milovan. *Wartime*. New York: Harcourt Brace Jovanovich, 1977.

Djordjević, Tihomir. *Naš narodni život* [Our People's Lives]. Vol. 2. Belgrade: Prosveta, 1984.

————. *Naš narodni život* [Our People's Lives]. Vol. 3. Belgrade: Prosveta, 1984.

Doerdelmann, B., ed. *Minderheiten in der Bundesrepublik*. Munich: Delp, 1969.

Döring, Hans-Joachim. *Die Zigeuner im Nationalsozialistischen Staat*. Hamburg: Kriminalistik Verlag, 1964.

Duirchová, Anna I. "Glimpses of the Rom: Excursions in Slovakia." *Journal of the Gypsy Lore Society* 50 (1970).

East, W.G. *The Union of Moldavia and Wallachia, 1859*. New York: Octagon Books, 1973.

Ervin, Tamás, and Y. Tamás Révész. *Búcsú a cigányteleptöl* [Farewell to the Gypsy Quarter]. Budapest: Kossuth Könyvykiadó, 1977.

Etnické procesy. Referáty z pracovní konference o cikánech [Ethnic Processes. Papers from a Working Conference on Gypsies]. Prague: Ustav pro etnografii a folkloristiku, 1978.

Evans, Ifor L. *The Agrarian Revolution in Romania*. Cambridge: Cambridge University Press, 1924.

Faber, Bernard Lewis, ed. *The Social Structure of Eastern Europe: Transition and Process in Czechoslovakia, Hungary, Poland, and Yugoslavia*. New York: Praeger, 1976.

Faludi, Andras. *Cigányok . . .* [Gypsies]. Budapest: Kossuth Konyvkiado, 1964.

Fatu, Mihai, and Mircea Musat, eds. *Hortheyist-Fascist Terror in Northwestern Romania September 1940–October 1944*. Bucharest: Meridiani, 1986.

Fein, Helen. *Accounting for Genocide: National Responses and Jewish Victimization during the Holocaust*. New York: The Free Press, 1979.

Fél, Edit, and Tamás Hofer. *Proper Peasants: Traditional Life in a Hungarian Village*. Chicago: Aldine, 1969.

Ferencz, Benjamin B. *Less Than Slaves: Jewish Forced Labor and the Quest for Compensation*. Cambridge: Harvard University Press, 1979.

Ficowski, Jerzy. *Cyganie na Polskich Drogach* [Gypsies along the Polish Way]. Cracow: Wydawnicwo Literackie, 1965.

————. "The Fate of Polish Gypsies." In *Genocide and Human Rights: A Global Anthology*, pp. 166–77. Washington, D.C.: University Press of America, 1982.

————."Condemned to Extinction." In idem, *Gypsies in Poland*, pp. 38–48. Warsaw: Interpress, 1989.

————. *The Gypsies in Poland*. Warsaw: Interpress, 1989.

Finková, Zuzanna. "Zištovanie plodnosti cigánskych žien" [Ascertaining Fertility of Gypsy Women]. *Demografie* 21, 4 (1981), p. 340.

Fischer, Mary Ellen."Nation and Nationality in Romania." In George W. Simmonds, ed., *Nationalism in the USSR and Eastern Europe*, pp. 504–21. Detroit: University of Detroit Press, 1977.

Fischer-Galati, Stephen. *The New Rumania: From People's Democracy to Socialist Republic*. Cambridge: MIT Press, 1967.

———. "Fascism, Communism, and the Jewish Question in Romania." In Bela Vago and George L. Mosse, eds., *Jews and Non-Jews in Eastern Europe, 1918, 1945*, pp. 157–75. New York: John Wiley and Sons, 1974.

———. "The Communist Takeover of Rumania: A Function of Soviet Power." In Thomas T. Hammond, ed., *The Anatomy of Communist Takeovers*, pp. 310–20. New Haven: Yale University Press, 1975.

———. "National Minorities in Romania, 1919–1980." In Stephen M. Horak, ed., *Eastern European National Minorities, 1919–1980: A Handbook*, pp. 190–215. Littleton: Libraries Unlimited, 1985.

Fischer, Julius S. "How Many Jews Died in Transnistria?" *Jewish Social Studies* 20 (April 1958), pp. 95–101.

———. *Transnistria: The Forgotten Cemetery*. New York: Thomas Yoseloff, 1969.

Fisk, Robert. "Fear of Nazis Reigns among Vienna Gypsies 50 Years On." *Times* (London), 14 March 1988, p. 2.

Foldes, Yolanda. *Golden Earrings*. New York: Dell Books, 1946.

Freiberg, Dov. "Testimony," Yad Vashem Archives, Microfiche A-361.

Friedman, Ina. "Bubili: A Young Gypsy's Fight for Survival." In idem, *The Other Victims*, pp. 7–24. New York: Houghton Mifflin, 1990.

Friedman, Philip. "How the Gypsies Were Persecuted." *Wiener Library Bulletin* 3–4, 1950.

———. "The Extermination of the Gypsies." In *Genocide and Human Rights: A Global Anthology*, pp. 151–57. Washington, D.C.: University Press of America, 1982.

Gaster, M. "Bill of Sale of Gypsy Slaves in Moldavia, 1851." *Journal of the Gypsy Lore Society*, Third Series 2 (1923), pp. 68–81.

———. "Rumanian Gypsies in 1560." *Journal of the Gypsy Lore Society*, Third Series 12 (1933), p. 59.

———. "Mixed Marriages." *Journal of the Gypsy Lore Society*, Third Series 13 (1934), p. 226.

Geiges, Anita, and Bernhard Wette. *Zigeuner Heute*. Bornheim: Lamuv-Verlag, 1979.

Gilberg, Trond. "Ethnic Minorities in Romania under Socialism." *East European Quarterly* 7 (January 1974), pp. 435–64.

———. *Modernization in Romania since World War II*. New York: Praeger, 1975.

———. "Rural Transformation in Romania." In Ivan Volyges, ed., *The Peasantry of Eastern Europe, 1: 20th Century Developments*, pp. 77–121. New York: Pergamon, 1978.

Gilbert, Martin. *The Holocaust*. New York: Holt, Rinehart, and Winston, 1985.

Gilliat-Smith, B. "Reviews." *Journal of the Gypsy Lore Society*, Third Series 18 (April–July 1939), pp. 137–40.

Gillie, Oliver. "The Gypsy King Tortured under Ceauşescu Returns to the Fold." *The Independent* (London), 17 February 1990, p. 12.

———. "Ceauşescu Is Dead, the Gypsy King Lives!" *The Independent* (London), 7 March 1990, p. 13.

Goodman, Fred. "The Conquering Kings." *Rolling Stone*, 5 April 1990, p. 23.

Graham-Yooll, Andrew. "In Search of Saint George." *The London Magazine*, August/September 1990, pp. 75–88.

Great Britain. *Foreign Office Weekly Political Intelligence Summaries*. New York: Kraus International, 1983: No. 83, 7 May 1941, p. 15; No. 87, 4 June 1941, p. 15; No. 96, 7 August 1941, pp. 15–16.

Grellmann, Heinrich. *Die Zigeuner*. Dessau and Leipzig: Auf Kosten der Verlags-Kasse und zu finden in der Buchhandlung der Gelehrten, 1783.

Gropper, Rena C. *Gypsies in the City: Cultural Patterns and Survival*. Princeton: The Darwin Press, 1975.

Grove, Lloyd. "Lament of the Gypsies: 40 Years after Auschwitz, Still Petitioning for a Place." *Washington Post*, 21 July 1984, C4.

Grulich, Tomáš, and Tomáš Haišman. "Instituciální zájem o cikánské obyvatelstvo v Československu v létech 1945–1958" [Institutional Interest in the Gypsy Population in Czechoslovakia in Years 1945–1958]. *Český lid* 73, 2 (1986), p. 74.

Günther, H. *Rassenkunde des Deutschen Volkes*. Munich: J.F. Lehmann, 1926.

Gutman, Israel, ed. *Encyclopedia of the Holocaust*. 4 vols. New York: Macmillan, 1989.

Guy, Willy. See Koudelka.

"The Gypsies." *East Europe* 14 (October 1965), pp. 20–25.

"Gypsies Hear Pledge of Aid on Holocaust." *New York Times*, 7 September 1986.

Hajdu, Mihaly. "Gypsies, 1980." *Hungarian Digest* 6 (1980), pp. 28–34.

Haley, William J. "The Gypsy Conference at Bucharest." *Journal of the Gypsy Lore Society*, Third Series 13, 4 (1934), pp. 182–90.

Hall, Elsie M. "Gentile Cruelty to Gypsies." *Journal of the Gypsy Lore Society*, Third Series 11, 2 (1932), pp. 49–56.

Halliday, W.R. "Roumanian Gypsies." *Journal of the Gypsy Lore Society*, Third Series 3 (1924), p. 143.

Hana, Jiří. "Vybrané problémy cikánské etnické skupiny v okrese Cheb" [Selected Problems of the Gypsy Ethnic Group in the Cheb District].

Demografie 29, 2 (1987), pp. 167–71.

Hancock, Ian. "Some Contemporary Aspects of Gypsies and Gypsy Nationalism." *Roma* 1 (1975), pp. 46–56.

———. "Gypsies, Jews and the Holocaust." *Shmate: A Journal of Progressive Jewish Thought* 17 (1987), pp. 6–15; 18 (1987), pp. 14–17.

———. *The Pariah Syndrome: An Account of Gypsy Slavery and Persecution.* Ann Arbor: Karoma, 2d ed., 1988.

———. "Uniqueness of the Victims: Gypsies, Jews and the Holocaust." *Without Prejudice: The EAFORD International Review of Racial Discrimination* 1, 2 (1988), pp. 45–67.

———. "The Development of Romani Linguistics." In Jazyery and Winter, eds., *Languages and Cultures,* pp. 183–223.

———. "Gypsy History in Germany and Neighboring Lands: A Chronology Leading to the Holocaust." *Nationalities Papers* (forthcoming).

Hann, C.M. *Tázár: A Village in Hungary.* Cambridge: Cambridge University Press, 1980.

Hausner, Gideon. *Justice in Jerusalem.* New York: Harper and Row, 1966.

Hefer, Stejpan. *Croatian Struggle for Freedom and Statehood.* U.S.A. and Buenos Aires: Croatian Liberation Movement, 1979.

Heinrich, Hans-Georg. *Hungary: Politics, Economics, and Society.* Boulder: Lynne Rienner, 1986.

Hilberg, Raul. *The Destruction of the European Jews.* Chicago: Quadrangle Books, 1961; New York: Harper and Row, 1979; (student edition) New York: Holmes and Meier, 1981.

Hilberg, Raul, et al., eds. *The Warsaw Diary of Adam Czerniakow: Prelude to Doom,* translated by Stanislaw Staron and the staff of Yad Vashem. New York: Stein and Day, 1978.

Hirschbiel, Henry H. "Kiselev, Pavel Dmitrievich (1788–1872)." In Joseph L. Wieczynski, ed., *The Modern Encyclopedia of Russian and Soviet History,* vol. 17, pp. 41–44. Gulf Breeze, Fla.: Academic International Press, 1980.

Hitler's Ten Year War against the Jews. New York: Institute of Jewish Affairs of the American Jewish Congress/World Jewish Congress, 1943.

Hohmann, J.S. *Zigeuner und Zigeunerwissenschaft.* Marburg: Guttandin und Hoppe, 1980.

———. *Geschichte der Zigeunerverfolgung in Deutschland.* Frankfurt: Campus Verlag, 1981.

Holmes, Colin. "The German-Gypsy Question in Britain, 1904–1906." In Lunn, ed., *Hosts, Immigrants and Minorities,* pp. 134–59.

Holomek, Miroslav. "Současné problémy Cikánů v ČSSR a jejich řešení" [The Current Problems of Gypsies in Czechoslovakia and Their Solution]. *Demografie* 11, 3 (1969), p. 205.

Hondros, John L. *Occupation and Resistance: The Greek Agony 1941–1944.*

New York: Pella, 1983.

Hoppe, E.O. *In Gypsy Camp and Royal Palace: Wanderings in Rumania.* New York: Charles Scribner's Sons, 1924.

Höss, Rudolf Franz. *Kommandant in Auschwitz.* Stuttgart: Deutscher Verlag, 1958.

————. *Commandant of Auschwitz.* New York: Popular Library, 1959.

Hrvatski Narod [Croatian Nation], 19 July 1941, p. 7.

Hübschmannová, Milena. "Co je tak zvaná cikánská otázka" [What Is the So-called Gypsy Question]. *Sociologický* časopis 6, 2 (1970), pp. 105–20.

Human Rights in Czechoslovakia: The Documents of Charter 77, 1977–1982. Compiled by the Commission on Security and Cooperation in Europe. Washington, D.C.: Congress of the United States, 1982.

Illyes, Elemer. *National Minorities in Romania: Change in Transylvania.* Boulder: East European Monographs, distributed by Columbia University Press, 1982.

Inalcik, H. "Servile Labor in the Ottoman Empire." In Abraham Ascher, Tibor Halasi-Kun, and Bela K. Kiraly, eds., *The Mutual Effects of the Islamic and Judeo-Christian Worlds: The East European Pattern*, pp. 25–52. New York: Brooklyn College Press, distributed by Columbia University Press, 1979.

Infield, Glenn. *Secrets of the SS.* New York: Stein and Day, 1952.

International Military Tribunal. Nuremberg Documents.

Janos, Andrew C. *The Politics of Backwardness in Hungary, 1825–1945.* Princeton: Princeton University Press, 1982.

Jazyery, Ali, and Werner Winter, eds. *Languages and Cultures: Studies in Honor of Edgar C. Polomé.* The Hague: Mouton, 1988.

Jelavich, Charles and Barbara. *The Establishment of the Balkan National States, 1804–1920.* Seattle and London: Washington University Press, 1977.

Jochimsen, J. "Zigeuner hirzulande." In Doerdelmann, ed., *Minderheiten in der Bundesrepublik,* pp. 21, 34.

Johansen, John O. *Sigøyneres Holocaust.* Oslo: Cappelen, 1989.

Jokisch, Karl. "Zigeuner—Fremdgebliebene unter uns." *Aus Politik und Zeitgeschichte* 12 (21 March 1981), pp. 3–17.

Justin, Eva. "Lebensschicksale artfremd erzogener Zigeunerkinder und ihre Nachkommen." *Veröffentlichungen aus dem Gebiet des Volksgesundheitsdienstes* 57, part 4, 1944.

Kalvoda, Josef. "National Minorities in Czechoslovakia, 1919–1980" In Stephan Horak, ed., *Eastern European National Minorities: 1919–1980, A Handbook.* Littleton, Colo.: Libraries Unlimited, 1985.

Keller, Larry. "Witness Ties Artuković, Killing . . ." *Press Telegram* (Long Beach, California), 23 April 1986, p. 6.

Kellogg, Frederick. "The Structure of Romanian Nationalism." *Canadian Review of Studies in Nationalism* 11 (1984), pp. 21–50.

Kenedi, János. "Why Is the Gypsy the Scapegoat and Not the Jew?" *The East European Reporter* 2, 1 (1986), pp. 11–14.

Kenrick, Donald, and Grattan Puxon. *The Destiny of Europe's Gypsies*. New York: Basic Books, Chatto-Heinemann; Sussex: Sussex University Press, 1972.

Kephart, William. *Extraordinary Groups*. New York: St. Martin's Press, 1982.

Kerswell, W.F. "Gipsy Sites." *The North Shropshire Echo*, 18 June 1979, p. 6.

Kideckel, David A. "Economic Images and Social Change in the Romanian Socialist Transformation." *Dialectical Anthropology* 12 (1987), pp. 399–411.

Kifner, John. "A Country Is Haunted." *New York Times*, 20 February 1990, A6.

King, Robert R. *Minorities under Communism: Nationalities as a Source of Tension among Balkan Communist States*. Cambridge: Harvard University Press, 1973.

Klee, Ernst. *Euthenasie im NS-Staat: die Vernichtung Lebensunwerten Lebens*. Frankfurt: S. Fischer, 1983.

Kosa, László. "Thirty Years of Ethnographic Research among the National Minority Groups Living in Hungary (1945–1974)." *Acta Ethnographica Academiae Scientiarum Hungaricae* 24 (1975), pp. 231–46.

Kosovo Kosovo. Belgrade: Kultura, 1973.

Kostelancik, David J. "The Gypsies of Czechoslovakia." Unpublished thesis. University of Michigan, 1988.

Koudelka, Josef. *Gypsies*. Prague: Aperture Books, 1975.

Kövágó, László. *Nemzétisegek a mai Magyarországon* [Nationalities in Today's Hungary]. Budapest: Kossuth, 1981.

Kramer, Kathryn. *Under Gypsy Skies*. New York: Dell, 1987.

Krautz, see Münster.

Kulturno-výchovná práca medzi cigánskymi obyvateľmi. Zborník . . . [Cultural-Educational Work among Gypsy Population. Symposium . . .]. Bratislava: Osvetový ústav, 1978.

Kulturno-výchovná práca s cigánskymi obyvateľmi. Zborník . . . [Cultural-Educational Work with Gypsy Population. Symposium . . .]. Bratislava: Osvetový ústav, 1983.

Kueppers, H. "Die Beschäftigung von Zigeunern." *Reichsarbeitsblatt V*, 25 March 1942.

Lacková, Elena. L'udové liečenie olašských Rómov východného Slovenska v minulosti" [Popular Medical Treatments of Olsš's Romas in Eastern Slovakia in the Past]. *Slovenský narodopis* (Bratislava), 1, 36 (1988).

Lawrence, D.H. *The Virgin and the Gypsy.* New York: Random House, 1930.

Leeds. "Gipsies Face Apartheid Policy." *Leeds Other Paper* 377 (17 May 1985), pp. 6–7.

Lehrer, Milton G. *Transylvania: History and Reality.* Silver Spring: Bartleby Press, 1986.

Lewis, William Dodge, ed. *The American International Encyclopedia.* Vol. 7. New York: J.J. Little and Ives, 1953.

Liégeois, Jean-Pierre. *Mutation Tsigane.* Brussels: Editions Complexe, 1976.

————. *Gypsies: An Illustrated History.* London: Al-Saqi Books, 1986.

————. *La Scolarisation des Enfants Tziganes et Voyageurs.* Luxembourg: Commission des Communantés Européennes, 1986.

————. *Gypsies and Travellers.* Strasbourg: Council for Cultural Cooperation, 1987.

————. *School Provision for Gypsy and Traveller Children.* Manchester: Commission of the European Communities Traveller Education Service, 1988.

Lifton, Robert J. *The Nazi Doctors: Medical Killing and the Psychology of Genocide.* New York: Basic Books, 1986.

Lincoln, W. Bruce. *Nicholas I: Emperor and Autocrat of All the Russias.* Bloomington: Indiana University Press, 1980.

Lípa, Jiří. Untitled article on priorities in Romani studies. *Newsletter,* North American Chapter of the Gypsy Lore Society 6, 1 (1983), pp. 3–4.

Littell, Franklin H. "Early Warning." *Remembering for the Future: The Impact of the Holocaust on the Contemporary World.* Oxford: Pergamon, 1988, pp. 2125–33.

Lockwood, William G. "Balkan Gypsies: An Introduction." In Joanne Grumet, ed., *Papers from the Fourth and Fifth Annual Meetings, Gypsy Lore Society, North American Chapter*, pp. 91–99. New York: Gypsy Lore Society, North American Chapter, 1985.

Logoreci, Anton. *The Albanians: Europe's Forgotten Survivors.* Boulder, Colo.: Westview, 1978.

Lunn, Kenneth, ed. *Hosts, Immigrants and Minorities.* London: Dawson Books, 1980.

Macartney, C.A. *A History of Hungary: 1929–1945.* New York: Frederick A. Praeger, 1956.

Macartney, C.A., and A.W. Palmer. *Independent Eastern Europe.* London: Macmillan, 1972.

McCartney, Robert J. "East Berlin Said to Agree to Holocaust Payments." *Washington Post,* 19 October 1988, A25–26.

McClure, Erica F., and Malcolm M. McClure. "Factors Influencing Language Variation in a Multilingual Transylvanian Village." *Rumanian Studies* 3 (1973–1975), pp. 207–20.

McGrory, Mary. "Romania Feeling Free to Hate Again." *Shreveport Times,* 21 March 1990, 8A.

Mamatey, Victor S. *Rise of the Hapsburg Empire, 1526–1815.* New York: Holt, Rinehart, and Winston, 1971.

The Manchester Guardian, 15 March 1969.

Mann, Arne B. "Obyčaje pri umrtí Cigánov-Rómov v troch spišskych obciách" [Customs during the Death of Gypsies-Romas in Three Spiš Communities]. *Slovenský narodopis* (Bratislava), 1, 36 (1988).

Marchbin, Andrew Arjeh. "A Critical History of the Origin and Migration of the Gypsies." Ph.D. dissertation, University of Pittsburgh, 1939.

Marmullaku, Ramadan. *Albania and the Albanians.* London: C. Hurst and Company, 1975.

Matley, Ian M. *Romania: A Profile.* New York: Praeger, 1970.

Maur, Wolf in der. *Die Zigeuner: Wanderer zwischen den Welten.* Vienna, Munich, Zurich: Molden, 1969.

Mayall, David. "Lorist, Reformist and Romanticist: The Nineteenth Century Response to Gypsy Travellers." *Immigrants and Minorities* 4, 3 (1985), pp. 53–67.

———. *Gypsy Travellers in Nineteenth Century Society.* Cambridge: Cambridge University Press, 1988.

Meagher, Anthony E. "Gypsies in Germany Make a Stand." *Christian Century,* 11 April 1990, pp. 370–72.

Mesko, Jaroslav. *Pravda* (Bratislava), January 28, 1983, p. 4.

Michalewicz, Bogumila. "Another Sour Note from Poland." *Newsletter,* North American Chapter of the Gypsy Lore Society 5, 3 (1982), p. 7.

Miller, Jim. "Mačwaya Gypsy Marime." Master's thesis, University of Washington, 1968.

———. "A War to Remember." *Newsweek,* 4 September 1989, pp. 64–66.

Miller, Marshall L. *Bulgaria during the Second World War.* Stanford: Stanford University Press, 1975.

Miletić, Antun. *Koncentracioni Logor Jasenovac 1941–1945* [The Jasenovac Concentration Camp 1941–1945]. Belgrade: Narodna Kniga, 1986.

"Minorities in Eastern Europe." *East Europe* 8, 3 (March 1959), p. 14.

Mitrany, David. *The Land and the Peasant in Rumania: The War and the Agrarian Reform (1917–1921).* London: Humphrey Milford, 1930.

Mode, H., and S. Wolffling. *Zigeuner: Der Weg eines Volkes in Deutschland.* Leipzig: Koehler and Amelang, 1968.

Müller-Hill, Benno. *Murderous Science: Elimination by Scientific Selection of Jews, Gypsies and Others, Germany 1933–1945,* translated by George R. Fraser. Oxford: Oxford University Press, 1988.

Münster, Sebastian. *Cosmographiae Universalis.* Basel: Heinrich Peters Verlag, 1550.

Nachtwey, James. "Romania's Lost Children." *New York Times Magazine*, 24 June 1990, pp. 27–33.

"National Minorities in the Hungarian People's Republic." In Miklos Gardos, ed., *Hungary 1971*, pp. 133–46. Budapest: Zrinyi, 1971.

Nečas, Ctibor. *Nad osudem českých a slovenských cikánů v létech 1939–1945* [On the Fate of Czech and Slovak Gypsies during the Years 1939–1945]. Brno: Universita J.E. Purkyně, 1981.

Noakes, Jeremy. "Life in the Third Reich." *History Today* 33 (1985), pp. 15–19.

———. "Social Outcasts in Nazi Germany." *History Today* 18 (1985); and *New York Times*, 17 September 1986.

Novitch, Miriam. *Le génocide des Tziganes sous le régime nazi*. Paris: AMIF Publication No. 164 (La Comité pour l'Erection du Monument des Tziganes Assassinés a Auschwitz), 1968. All quotations from English translation, Romani Union Publication, Buda, 1987.

Oberdorfer, Don. "East Germany Agrees on Reparations for Nazis' Jewish Victims." *Washington Post*, 26 January 1988.

Oțetea, Andrei, ed. *A Concise History of Romania*. English edition edited by Andrew Mackenzie. London: Robert Hale, 1985.

Paikert, G.C. "Hungary's National Minority Policies, 1920–1945." *The American Slavic and East European Review* 12 (1953), pp. 201–18.

Palmer, Alan. *Alexander I: Tsar of War and Peace*. New York: Harper and Row, 1974.

Panaitescu, P.N. "The Gypsies in Wallachia and Moldavia: A Chapter of Economic History." Translated by Doris Hardman. *Journal of the Gypsy Lore Society* Third Series 20 (April 1941), pp. 58–72.

———. "The Gypsy Flower-Sellers of Bucharest." *Journal of the Gypsy Lore Society*, Third Series 27 (January–April 1948), pp. 76–77.

Paris, Edmond. *Genocide in Satellite Croatia, 1941–1945: A Record of Racial and Religious Persecutions and Massacres*. Chicago: The American Institute for Balkan Affairs, 1961.

Pártos, Ferenc. "A cigány és nem cigány lakosság vélémenge a föbb társadalompolitikai célkitüzésekröl" [Gypsies and Non-Gypsies on the Main Goals of Social Policy]. *Szociológia* 1 (1980), pp. 1–16.

Pearson, Raymond. *National Minorities in Eastern Europe, 1848–1945*. London: Macmillan, 1983.

Pelesky, Vladimir. "Die Zigeunerfrage in den Ost- und Südosteuropäischen Staaten." *Osteuropa* 20 (September 1970), p. 618.

Perrigault, Jean. "Les compagnons de la Belle-Étoile." *Le Matin* 17 (July 1932), p. 1.

Petyt, K.M. "Romania: A Multilingual Nation." *International Journal of the Sociology of Language* 4 (1975), pp. 75–101.

Plant, Richard. *The Pink Triangle: The Nazi War against the Homosexuals.* New York: Holt and Company, 1986.

Plasari, Ndreçi, and Shyqri Ballova. "Politique et Stratégie dans la Lutte Antifasciste de Libération Nationale du Peuple Albanais (1939–1944)." *Studia Albanica* 2 (1975).

Plotkin, Diane. "Historiographic Analysis of a Survivor's Narrative: The Story of Leo Laufer." Ph.D. dissertation, The University of Texas at Arlington, 1990.

Polo, Stefanaq, Alex Buda, et al., eds. *Historia e popullit Shqiptar.* Vol. 2, Prishtinë. (Originally published in Tiranë by the University of Tiranë, 1965.)

Pond, Elizabeth. "Romanies: Hitler's Other Victims." *Christian Science Monitor*, 7 March 1980, p. 17.

Portschy, Tobias. "Kein Schulbesuch für Zigeuner." *Grenzmark-Zeitung*, 4 September 1938, p. 1.

Prodan, David. "The Origins of Serfdom in Transylvania." Translated by Katherine Verdery. *Slavic Review* 49 (Spring 1990), pp. 1–18.

Proester, F. "Vraždění čs. Cikánů v Buchenwaldu" [The Murder of Czechoslovak Gypsies in Buchenwald]. Document No. ÚV ČSPB-K-135 of the Archives of the Museum of the Fighters against Fascism, Prague, 1940.

Puxon, Grattan. "Gypsies: Blacks of East Europe." *The Nation* 222 (17 April 1976), pp. 460–64.

———. "The Forgotten Victims." *Patterns of Prejudice* 11, 2 (1977), pp. 23–28.

———. "Tito and the Future of Roma." *Roma* 5 (July 1980).

———. *Gypsies: The Holocaust's Forgotten Victims.* Los Angeles: Publication of the U.S. Romani Council, 1984.

———. "Roma: Europe's Gypsies." Minority Rights Report no. 14. London: Minority Rights Group, 1973, 1975, 1983, 1987.

Puxon, Grattan, and Donald Kenrick. *Bibahtale Berša.* London: Romanestan Publications, 1990. (Romani translation of Kenrick and Puxon, revised and updated.)

Rakelmann, G.A., ed. *Loseblattsammlung für Unterricht und Bildungsarbeit.* Freiburg im Breisgau, 1979.

Ramet, Pedro. "From Strossmayer to Stepinac: Croatian National Ideology and Catholicism." *Canadian Review of Studies in Nationalism* 12 (Spring 1985), pp. 123–39.

Réger, Rita. "Bilingual Gypsy Children in Hungary: Explorations in Natural Sound-Language Acquisition at an Early Age." *International Journal of the Sociology of Language* 19 (1979), pp. 59–82.

Reichsgesetzbuch 1934/1, No. 531.

Reinhartz, Dennis. "Holokaust kao poslanje" [An Extreme of the

Holocaust]. *Danas*, 15 April 1986, pp. 27–28.

———. "Aryanism and the Independent State of Croatia, 1941–1945." *The South Slav Journal* 9 (Autumn–Winter 1986), pp. 19–25.

Reitlinger, Gerald. *The Final Solution: The Attempt to Exterminate the Jews of Europe, 1939–1945*. New York: The Beechurst Press; London: Vallentine, Mitchell, 1953.

Revay, Steven. "Hungarian Minorities under Communist Rule." *The Hungarian Quarterly* 1 (October 1961), pp. 42–47.

Riker, T.W. *The Making of Romania: A Study of an International Problem, 1856–1866*. London: Oxford University Press, 1931.

Ritter, Robert. *Die Bestandsaufnahme der Zigeuner*. Berlin: Offizielle Gesundheitsdienst Publication, 1941.

Rosenblum, Mort. "The Gypsy Problem Grows: East Europeans Can't Control Gypsies." *San Antonio Express*, 25 March 1984, C1.

Roucek, Joseph S. *Contemporary Romania and Her Problems*. Stanford: Stanford University Press, 1932.

"Roznodně proti násilí" [Resolutely against Violence]. *Svobodné Slove*, 11 May 1990, p. 4.

Rózsa, László. "Gypsies and Public Opinion." *The Hungarian Quarterly* 20 (Spring 1979), pp. 126–30.

Ruches, Pyrrhus J. *Albania's Captives*. Chicago: Argonaut Publishers, 1965.

Rüdiger, K. "Parasiten der Gemeinschaft." *Volk und Rasse* 13 (1938), pp. 87–89.

Rullmann, Hans P. "Child Slave-Trade in Yugoslavia: Gypsies' (Romas) Oppression." *That's Yugoslavia* 5 (1986), pp. 5–8.

"Rumania." *Encyclopedia Judaica*. Vol. 14. Jerusalem: Encyclopedia Judaica, 1971, pp. 386–416.

Russell, Alex. "Classification and Numbers of Wallachian Gypsies in 1837." *Journal of the Gypsy Lore Society*, New Series 6 (1912–13), p. 150.

———. "Roumanian Gypsies." *Journal of the Gypsy Lore Society*, New Series 6 (1912–13), pp. 153–55.

Scharfenberg, J. "Omstreiferondet." *Arbeiderbladet*, 31 October, 11, 19, 24, and 25 November 1930.

Schechtman, Joseph B. "The Transnistria Reservation." *YIVO Annual of Jewish Social Science* 8 (1953), pp. 178–96.

———. "The Gypsy Problem." *Midstream* (November 1966), pp. 52–60.

Schmemann, Serge. "Millions of Jewish Fund's Marks Missing." *The Oregonian*, 19 May 1988, A8.

———. "Case of the Missing Millions." *New York Times*, 26 May 1988, A5.

Schöpflin, George. *The Hungarians of Rumania*. London: Minority Rights Group, 1978.

Schuckenak, J. *Sie sind auch umgekommen: Polen, Homosexuellen, Juden, Zeugen Jehovahs und andere nich-Zigeunerische Opfern Hitlers Gewaltherrschaft.* Tübingen: Klaffende Tür, 1988.

Serboianu, C.J. Popp. *Les Tsiganes.* Paris: Payot, 1930.

Sereni, Gitta. *Into the Darkness.* London: Deutsch, 1974.

Seton-Watson, Hugh. *Eastern Europe between the Wars, 1918–1941.* Boulder, Colo.: Westview, 1986.

Seton-Watson, R.W. *A History of the Roumanians.* Cambridge: Cambridge University Press, 1934.

Shaw, Stanford. *History of the Ottoman Empire and Modern Turkey,* Vol. I: *Empire of the Gazis: The Rise and Decline of the Ottoman Empire, 1280–1808.* Cambridge: Cambridge University Press, 1976.

Shaw, Stanford, and Ezel Kural Shaw. *History of the Ottoman Empire and Modern Turkey,* Vol. II: *Reform, Revolution, and Republic: The Rise of Modern Turkey, 1808–1975.* Cambridge: Cambridge University Press, 1977.

Shaw, Terence. "Gipsies Win Race Relations Protection." *Daily Telegraph* (London), 28 July 1988, p. 2.

Shoemaker, Henry W. "Banishment to Polynesia." *Journal of the Gypsy Lore Society,* Third Series 12, 3 (1933), pp. 158–60.

Shoup, Paul S. *The East European and Soviet Data Handbook: Political, Social, and Development Indicators, 1945–1975.* New York: Columbia University Press, 1981.

Sibley, David. *Outsiders in Urban Society.* Oxford: Blackwell, 1981.

Siklós, László. "The Gypsies." *The New Hungarian Quarterly* 11 (1970), pp. 150–62.

Simson, James. *A History of the Gipsies, with Specimens of the Gipsy Language.* London: Sampson Low, Son and Marston, 1871.

Singhal, Damodar P. *Gypsies: Indians in Exile.* Meerut, India: Archana Publications, 1922.

Singleton, Fred. *A Short History of the Yugoslav Peoples.* Cambridge: Cambridge University Press, 1989.

Sinor, Denis. *History of Hungary.* Westport, Conn.: Greenwood Press, 1976.

Slovenský národopis [Slovak Ethnography]. Bratislava: Vydavatelstvo slovenskej akademie vied 1, 1988.

Smedley, Scott, and Christopher Stephen. "Gypsies in Fear as Democracy Unleashes Hate." *Times* (London), 15 April 1990, A23.

Smoleń, Kazimierz. *Auschwitz, 1940–1945.* Auschwitz: Państwowe Muzeum Oświecimiu, 1969.

Soest, Georg von. *Aspekte zur Sozialarbeit.* N. p., n. d.

Somers, Suzanne. *Romany Curse.* New York: Belmont Books, 1971.

Spira, Thomas. "Worlds Apart: The Swabian Expulsion from Hungary after World War II." *Nationalities Papers* 13 (Fall 1985), pp. 188–97.

Srb, Vladimír. "Cikánské obyvatelstvo v roce 1967" [The Gypsy Population in 1967]. *Demografie* 10, 3 (1968), p. 270.

――――. "Ustavující sjezd svazu Cikánů-Romů v ČSR v Brně" [The Founding Congress of the Alliance of Gypsy-Romani in Czechoslovakia in Brno]. *Demografie* 11, 4 (1969), the whole issue.

――――. "Některé demografické a kulturní charakteristiky cikánského obyvatelstva v ČSSR 1980" [Some Demographic and Cultural Characteristics of the Gypsy Population in the Czechoslovak Republic in 1980]. *Demografie* 26, 2 (1984), pp. 161–78.

――――. "Změny v reprodukci Československých Romů 1970–1980" [Changes in the Reproduction of the Czechoslovak Romas, 1970–1980]. *Demografie* 30, 7 (1988), pp. 305–8.

Starr, Joshua. "Jewish Citizenship in Rumania (1878–1940)." *Jewish Social Studies* 3 (1941), pp. 57–80.

Staar, Richard F. *Yearbook on International Communist Affairs, 1987*. Stanford: Hoover Institution Press, 1987.

――――. *Communist Regimes in Eastern Europe*, 5th edition. Stanford: Hoover Institution Press, 1988.

Stebbins, John. "Gypsies Recall Their 'Forgotten Holocaust.' " *Chicago Sun-Times*, 29 April 1989, p. 2.

Streck, see Rakelmann.

Stroheim, Erich von. *Paprika, the Gypsy Trollop*. New York: Universal Publishing, 1935.

Strom, Margot, and William Parson. *Facing History and Ourselves*. Brookline, Mass.: Facing History and Ourselves Foundation, 1978.

Sugar, Peter. *Southeastern Europe under Ottoman Rule, 1354–1804*. Seattle and London: University of Washington Press, 1977.

Sus, Jaroslav. *Cikánská otázka v ČSSR*. Prague, 1961.

Sutherland, Anne. *Gypsies: The Hidden Americans*. London and New York: Free Press/Macmillan, 1975.

Švarbalík, Jozef. "Ako dălej v skultúrnení cigánskych obyvatelóv" [How to Proceed with Acculturation of the Gypsy Population]. *Osvetová práca* 7 (1986), pp. 28–29.

Swire, Joseph. *King Zog's Albania*. New York: Liverright, 1937.

Sylvain, Nicolas. "Rumania." In Peter Meyer et al., eds., *The Jews in Soviet Satellites*, pp. 493–556. Syracuse: Syracuse University Press, 1953.

Szász, Zsombor de. *The Minorities in Romanian Transylvania*. London: The Richards Press, 1927.

Szelenyi, Ivan. "Housing System and Social Structures." *The Sociological Review*, Paul Halmos, ed., Monograph 17: *Sociological Studies*, pp. 269–98. Keele: University of Keele, 1972.

Tenenbaum, J. *Race and Reich*. New York: Twayne Publishers, 1956.

Thesleff, A. "Report on the Gypsy Situation." *Journal of the Gypsy Lore*

Society, New Series 2, part 5, 1900.

Thimm, Gerhard. "Zigeunerbaron Mathias Kwiek, und das Schicksalsleben seiner Vasallen zwischen Rio, Peking und Warschau." *Welttag*, 23 May 1936, p. 2.

Thomas, James D., et al. "Disease, Lifestyle and Consanguinity in Fifty-Eight American Gypsies." *The Lancet*, 15 August 1987, pp. 376–79.

Thompson, T.W. "Gypsies in the Mezoseg of Transylvania." *Journal of the Gypsy Lore Society*, New Series 8 (1914–1915), pp. 194–95.

———. "Gypsy Prisoners at Szamos Ujvar, Transylvania." *Journal of the Gypsy Lore Society*, New Series (1914–1915), pp. 195–96.

Thurner, Erika. *Kurzgeschichte des nationalsozialistischen Zigeunerlagers in Lackenbach, 1940–1945*. Eisenstadt, 1984.

Tillon, Germaine. *Ravensbrück*. New York: Anchor Press, 1975.

Tipler, Derek. "From Nomads to Nation." *Midstream*, August/September 1968, pp. 61–70.

Tomašević, Nebojša Bato, and Rajko Djurić. *Gypsies of the World: A Journey into the Hidden World of Gypsy Life and Culture*. New York: Henry Holt and Company, 1988.

Tomforde, Anna. "Holocaust Victims Seek Payments: Denial of Further Compensation by West Germany Revives Debate." *Boston Globe*, 9 January 1988.

Tomka, Miklos. "Die Zigeuner in der ungarischen Gesellschaft." *East European Quarterly*, vol. 4, March 1970, pp. 2–24.

Trumpener, Katie. "Peoples without History and the Narratives of Nationalism." Ph.D. dissertation, University of Chicago, 1990.

Twigg, Bob. "East Germany to Aid Holocaust Victims." *USA Today*, 9 February 1990, 4A.

"Two Rumanian Documents Concerning Gypsies," translated by M. Gaster. *Journal of the Gypsy Lore Society*, Third Series 9 (1930), pp. 179–82.

Tyrnauer, Gabrielle. "Germany and Gypsies." *Genocide and Human Rights: A Global Anthology*. Washington, D.C.: University Press of America, 1982, pp. 178–92.

———. *The Fate of the Gypsies during the Holocaust*. Washington: Special Report to the U.S. Holocaust Memorial Council, 1985, 114 pp.

Vago, Raphael. "Nationality Policies in Contemporary Hungary." *Hungarian Studies Review* 11 (Spring 1984), pp. 43–60.

Van Kappen, O. *Geschiedenis der Zigeuners in Nederland*. Assen, 1965.

Vaux de Foletier, François de. *Mille ans d'histoire des Tsiganes*. Paris: Fayard, 1970.

Vekerdi, József. Review of Balint Sarosi, *Cigányzene* [Gypsy Music]. *Journal of the Gypsy Lore Society*, Third Series 1 (1972), pp. 49–53.

———. "Earliest Arrival Evidence on Gypsies in Hungary." *Journal of the Gypsy Lore Society*, Third Series 1 (1976), pp. 170–72.

_____. "The Vend Gypsy Dialect in Hungary." *Acta Linguistica Scientiarum Hungaricae* 34, 1/2 (1984), pp. 65–86.

Vesey-Fitzgerald, Brian. "Gypsies." *Birmingham Post*, 14 July 1973, p. 2.

Volgyes, Ivan. "Legitimacy and Modernization: Nationality and Nationalism in Hungary and Transylvania." In George Kline and Milan F. Reban, eds., *The Politics of Ethnicity in Eastern Europe*, pp. 127–46. Boulder, Colo.: East European Monographs, distributed by Columbia University Press, 1981.

Vossen, Rüdiger. *Zigeuner: Roma, Sinti, Gitanos, Gypsies, zwischen Verfolgung und Romatisierung*. Frankfurt: Ullstein Fachbuch, 1983.

Vrissakis, Yoannis. "Nazis and the Greek Roma: A Personal Testimonial." *Roma* 30 (1988), pp. 15–17.

Watson, Francis. *A Concise History of India*. London: Thames and Hudson, 1981.

Weber, Bruce. "A Hard Lesson." *New York Times Magazine,* 23 March 1988.

Weissenbruch, Johann Benjamin. *Ausführliche Relation von der famosen Zigeuner- Diebs- Mord- und Räuberbände*. Frankfurt and Leipzig, 1727.

Weybright, Victor. "Who Can Tell the Gypsies' Fortune?" *The Survey* 27 (1938), pp. 142–46.

Weyrauch, Walter O. "Gestapo Informants: Facts and Theory of Undercover Operations." *Columbia Journal of Transnational Law* 24, 3 (1986), pp. 553–96.

Weyrich, Becky Lee. *Gypsy Moon*. New York: Fawcett Gold Medal Publications, 1986.

Wiernick, Jakob. *A Year in Treblinka*. New York: American Representation of the General Jewish Workers' Union of Poland, 1944.

Wiesenthal, Simon. "Tragedy of the Gypsies." *Bulletin of Information* 26 (1986), p. 6. Vienna: Dokumentationszentrum des Bundes Jüdische Verfolgter des Naziregimes.

————. "Juifs et Tsiganes." In idem, *Justice n'est pas vengeance: Une autobiographie*, pp. 234–38. Paris: Editions Robert Laffont, 1989.

Wilkinson, William. *An Account of the Principalities of Wallachia and Moldavia*. London: Longman, Hurst, Rees, Orme, and Brown, 1820; reprinted by Arno Press, 1971.

Williams, Frances. "Swiss Shame over Stolen Children." *Times* (London), 8 June 1986, p. 10.

Winnifrith, T.J. *The Vlachs: The History of a Balkan People*. New York: St. Martin's Press, 1987.

Wolfe, Bertram D. *Three Who Made a Revolution*. New York: Dell, 1964.

Wytwycky, Bohdan. *The Other Holocaust: Many Circles of Hell*. Washington: The Nowak Report, 1980.

Yates, Dora E. *My Gypsy Days*. London: Phoenix House, 1953.

————. "Hitler and the Gypsies." In *Genocide and Human Rights: A Global Anthology*. Washington, D.C.: University Press of America, 1982, pp. 158–65.

Yoors, Jan. *The Gypsies*. London: George Allen and Unwin, 1967.

————. *Crossing*. New York: Simon and Schuster, 1971.

"Zásady poskytovania knižničných služieb cigánskym obyvateľom v lúdových knižniciach" [Rules for Book Services for the Gypsy Population in Public Libraries]. *Čitateľ* 5 (1987), Annex, 1–2.

Zinovieff, Maurice, and François Thual. *Le Paysage Linguistique de la Roumanie*. Paris: Societé d'edition "Les Belles Lettres," 1980.

Zucotti, Susan. *The Italians and the Holocaust: Persecution, Rescue, and Survival*. New York: Basic Books, 1987.

Zulch, Tilman. *In Auschwitz Vergast, Bis Heute Verfolgt: Zur Situation der Roma (Zigeuner) in Deutschland und Europa* [Gassed in Auschwitz, Pursued to the Present: About the Situation of the Roma (Gypsies) in Germany and Europe]. Hamburg: Rowohlt Taschenbuch Verlag, 1979.

Index

Contributors

David Crowe is a Professor of History at Elon College (North Carolina) and Chairperson of the Department of History. He serves on the Education Committee of the U. S. Holocaust Commission, is a Vice-Chairman for the Association for the Study of Nationalities (USSR and Eastern Europe), is General Editor of its Series in Issues Studies, and is on the Editorial Board of *Nationalities Papers*. He has contributed to numerous books and published over one hundred scholarly articles on topics ranging from the Holocaust to Chinese-American relations. He recently published *World War I and Europe in Crisis, 1914–1935* (1990).

Ian Hancock is a Professor of Linguistics at The University of Texas at Austin. A renowned Romani scholar and activist, his *The Pariah Syndrome* (1987) is considered one of the most important studies on the Romani historical experience worldwide. In addition to numerous other articles on Romani linguistics, culture, and history, Professor Hancock currently serves as President of the UN Presidium of the International Romani Union and Chairman of the IRU's Committee for the Compilation of the *Great Romani Encyclopedia*.

Henry R. Huttenbach is a Professor of History at the City College of New York and the editor of *Nationalities Papers*. A specialist on Jewish affairs in Central and Eastern Europe, as well as minority questions in Russia and the Soviet Union, he recently edited *Nationalities Policies in the USSR* (1990).

Josef Kalvoda is a Professor of History and Political Science at Saint Joseph College (Connecticut). A specialist on Czechoslovakia, his publications include *Titoism* (1958), *Czechoslovakia's Role in Soviet Strategy* (1978), and his recently acclaimed *The Genesis of Czechoslovakia* (1986). He has also published several hundred articles on different facets of East European and American politics, history, foreign policy, and other topics in numerous journals in Europe and the United States.

John Kolsti is an Associate Professor of Slavic Languages and Literature at the University of Texas at Austin. A specialist on South Slavic languages, he has recently published *The Bilingual Singer: A Study in Albanian and Serbo-Croatian Oral Epic Trandition* (1990), and also articles on Albanian politics, women, music, and literature. He has served as the President of the Rocky Mountain Association of Slavic Studies, and is currently completing work for a study that deals with the influence of the British and Foreign Bible Society on Orthodox communities in nineteenth-century Turkey.

Dennis Reinhartz is an Associate Professor of History at the University of Texas at Arlington. His numerous publications include *Milovan Djilas: A Revolutionary as a Writer* (1981), and he is coeditor of *The Mapping of the American Southwest* (1987) and *Essays on the History of North American Discovery and Exploration.* He has also contributed to studies on European revolutionary history and human rights in Yugoslavia.